PENGUIN BOOKS

ENGLAND IN THE TWENTIETH CENTURY
⟨1914 79⟩

David Thomson, M.A., Ph.D., late Master of Sidney Sussex College, Cambridge, was born in 1912. He was a scholar of the college from 1931 to 1934, and took first class honours in both parts of the historical tripos. He then became in turn a Research Fellow, Fellow and Senior Tutor, and was Master of the College from 1957 until his death in 1970. He was also a University Reader in History. He was twice Visiting Professor of Public Law and Government at Columbia University, and he lectured in the United States and in South Africa.

His other writings include *Democracy in France since 1870* (1946), and *Europe Since Napoleon* (1957). The latter is available in Pelicans. His earlier volume in the 'Pelican History of England', *England in the Nineteenth Century*, first published in 1950, has been reprinted many times. Among the works he edited was that volume of the new *Cambridge Modern History* which deals with the twentieth century.

David Thomson also undertook a fair amount of journalism and broadcasting on contemporary political affairs and educational issues. He once said: 'I enjoy lecturing, teaching and writing; find a don's life a very busy and happy one; and believe the study of history to be the best liberal education a student can have in the modern world.'

Geoffrey Warner, M.A., F.R.Hist.S., was born in 1937. He was educated at Sidney Sussex College, Cambridge (where David Thomson was one of his teachers) and at the Fondation Nationale des Sciences Politiques in Paris. After posts at the University of Reading and the Australian National University in Canberra, he successively held chairs at Hull, Leicester and the Open University, and was a visiting professor at the Bologna Center of the Johns Hopkins University. Increasingly exasperated by the Conservative government's policy towards the universities, he took early retirement at the end of 1989 and now writes and lectures on a freelance basis. His other writings include *Pierre Laval and the Eclipse of France* (1968).

THE PELICAN HISTORY OF ENGLAND

edited by J. E. Morpurgo

DAVID THOMSON

ENGLAND IN THE TWENTIETH CENTURY

⟨1914–79⟩

with additional material by
Geoffrey Warner

PENGUIN BOOKS

PENGUIN BOOKS

Published by the Penguin Group
Penguin Books Ltd, 27 Wrights Lane, London W8 5TZ, England
Penguin Books USA Inc., 375 Hudson Street, New York, New York 10014, USA
Penguin Books Australia Ltd, Ringwood, Victoria, Australia
Penguin Books Canada Ltd, 10 Alcorn Avenue, Toronto, Ontario, Canada M4V 3B2
Penguin Books (NZ) Ltd, 182–190 Wairau Road, Auckland 10, New Zealand

Penguin Books Ltd, Registered Offices: Harmondsworth, Middlesex, England

First published in Pelican Books 1965
Reprinted, with minor revisions and
new Chapters 11 and 12 by Geoffrey Warner, 1981
Reprinted in Penguin Books 1991
3 5 7 9 10 8 6 4

Printed in England by Clays Ltd, St Ives plc
Set in Monotype Baskerville

To

MY SISTER WITH LOVE

CONTENTS

*

PART IV
FROM AFFLUENCE TO UNCERTAINTY (1964–79)

Preface

THIS book differs from earlier volumes of the series in at least two respects. It spans a much shorter period of time – only half a century; and it comprises the lifetime of the author and that of most of his readers. The first makes it possible to give appropriate attention to that wider context of world history and to Britain's changing participation in it, without which the evolution of twentieth-century England would be unintelligible. The second makes it unusually difficult to see the whole sequence of events and their effects in due perspective and proportions, though it may also lend an immediacy of interest and atmosphere to supplement the historian's efforts to interpret the past.

The main divisions of the half-century seem inevitable. It is irresistible to regard the beginning of the Great War in 1914, the Great Depression of 1929–32, and the end of the Second World War in 1945 as the decisive punctuation marks: the more so as they happen to cut the period into three roughly equal spans of convenient length. That these are important dates in world history, not only in British, serves to emphasize how inseparable are the two stories. They will here be kept in close correlation.

Even in our age of greatly accelerated change history, like human life itself, is a continuum in which all events (save perhaps birth and death) have only a relative significance. Accordingly, it will be emphasized throughout that even such cataclysmic events as world slumps and world wars do not totally divert or disperse the strongest currents of historical change. Continuities will be revealed as much as contrasts. It is to both that the writer of contemporary history must turn for clues to help him uncover the most meaningful long-term trends of his times. The progress of science and technology, the development of the Welfare State, and the transformation of colonial empire into free commonwealth were processes going on, at varying speeds and with temporary halts, throughout the whole half-century.

The fabric of history is woven of such threads of continuity. The bomb at Hiroshima in 1945 was a direct consequence of Lord Rutherford's work on radio-activity before 1919; the social legislation passed by the Labour Government after 1945 built directly on foundations laid by Lloyd George before 1914 and extended by Neville Chamberlain between the wars; the independence of India and Pakistan as Dominions in 1947 had continuous connexions with the announcement in 1917 that Britain's aim in India was 'responsible government ... as an integral part of the British Empire'. On a more sombre note, the black areas for unemployment in 1963 were not only the 'distressed areas' of the inter-war years but also the main locations of the classic nineteenth-century industries – coal, iron, and ship-building.

Such connexions and consequences are seldom simple or direct. They are made by the hazards and the tortuosities of events; only rarely are consequences the precise outcome of a deliberate intention to produce them. The bedrock, then, of any history of England in the twentieth century must be an unravelling of the events and their consequences which accumulatively turned the England of Asquith into the England of Macmillan. That, in the end, is what this book is about.

To the protest that this is not 'history' at all, since many of us can remember it all happening, there are two replies. One is that political decisions, economic judgements, and even philosophical reflections are every day made on the basis of certain generalizations about the recent past: so it is not unimportant to see how far such generalizations can survive historical analysis. The other is that, however much later historical perspective may amend our views about the earlier twentieth century, it can hardly obliterate a few important conclusions. It was in these decades that Britain became more fully a democracy, in social structure no less than political system; that it led the world in implementing the ideals of the Welfare State and in establishing a free multi-racial Commonwealth; that it persistently withstood tyranny, if need be alone, and seldom without good effect. To record these indisputable things now may lend encouragement to their further pursuit.

D.T.

Sidney Sussex College, Cambridge
1964

As a former student, and one who owed him much, I was honoured to be asked to revise one of David Thomson's most successful books. At the same time, the invitation placed me in something of a dilemma. Should I attempt to go through the entire book, rewriting a paragraph here or modifying a sentence there in the light of what I considered to be the most significant contributions of recent scholarship, or should I simply confine myself to adding a final section which would bring the book up to date from a chronological point of view? In the end, I decided to adopt the latter course in the belief that much of the value of the author's original text might be lost if altered by another hand. My sole contribution to the present edition, therefore, is the new Part IV on the period 1964–79, together with some fresh linking material at the end of Part III and a brief addendum to the bibliography. Only users of the book can judge whether this approach has been a success, but I shall be well satisfied if it gives a fresh lease of life to a brilliant study by someone who was not only a distinguished historian, but also an unfailingly kind and considerate person.

I should perhaps add that, with the exception of one or two brief passages, my contribution to this book was completed in the autumn of 1979. Apart from the occasional reference, therefore, it contains no discussion of the policies of the new Conservative Government elected in that year and takes no account of work published more recently.

G.W.

University of Leicester
1980

PART I

FROM GREAT WAR TO GREAT DEPRESSION

(1914–29)

CHAPTER ONE

Britain and the British Empire in 1914

OPTICAL ILLUSION

IN 1919, looking back across the chasm of the Great War at the England of pre-war days, men tended to see it as a golden age of stability and prosperity, a civilization to be as far as possible recaptured and restored save for those few fatal flaws which, they believed, had led to the disaster of general war. Chief of such flaws was the so-called 'international anarchy', the lack of any appropriate machinery for resolving disputes and for keeping the peace between States. With it went certain bad habits, such as 'secret diplomacy', the negotiation of secret alliances between the Powers. Another blemish of the pre-war order, as seen retrospectively in 1919, was the existence of old-fashioned dynastic empires whose very survival depended on denying to their subject peoples rights of national self-determination. But that, happily, had been largely removed with the collapse of these empires in 1918, and their replacement by a number of smaller national States speedily adopting democratic constitutions. Yet a third defect in the pre-war order had been the defectiveness of democracy itself, but that, too, was now being fast remedied by extension of the franchise in the United Kingdom and elsewhere, and by the vogue, everywhere in Europe west of Russia, for democratic institutions and ideals.

With these maladies of the old order soon to be put right, there was a great yearning to return to the halcyon days, made more alluring in retrospect by the contrasting horror

of the intervening years. The favourite prefix of the twenties, in English politics as in international affairs, was 're-'.
People wanted recovery and restoration, a 'return to
normalcy', just as from the peace with Germany they
wanted reparations and retribution for war-crimes. In
British eyes the period of 'the Great Peace' between 1815
and 1914 still had its charms, which even 'the Great War'
had not despoiled or dispelled. Perhaps that brighter world
could be recaptured, or at any rate rebuilt, without its
disadvantages. Hopes for the future were cast very much
in the mould of the past. Only in the course of the later
twenties was the focus shifted forward to the unfamiliar
features of a 'Brave New World', hardly less terrifying in
aspect than the recent horrors of war.

Looking back now to the Britain of 1914, after experience
of a Second World War which we know to have been an
emanation from the First, we see it in a very different light.
We know that the British Foreign Secretary, Sir Edward
Grey, came near to the truth that August evening in 1914
when Britain declared war on Germany. Grey, gazing
wistfully from the windows of the Foreign Office, uttered
the plaintive prophecy that has echoed down the years:
'The lamps are going out all over Europe; we shall not see
them lit again in our lifetime.'

We can see that the lights never had been quite so bright
as men remembered them in 1919. There were already
present in Britain of the pre-war decade many of the seeds
of later troubles which were attributed, wrongly, to the
war. 'The War' had been so unexpectedly shattering, so
long and abominable, that it could be advanced as explanation of everything that went wrong after it: until men became disillusioned with 'the Peace' and its terms, and its
makers came to be blamed instead, equally exaggeratedly,
for whatever in the post-war, post-peace world seemed most
objectionable. We can now ask, more detachedly and dis-

passionately, 'Was the pre-war British economy as healthy as it looked, for extensive unemployment was already not unknown?' 'Was British society harmoniously united – when suffragettes and syndicalists were so militant, big strikes not uncommon?' 'Was the British Empire firmly founded – with civil war about to break out in Ireland in 1914?'

Moreover, if these defects in the dream were real, could it not also be that the Great War had important causes other than the 'international anarchy' and 'secret diplomacy': collisions of economic interests, perhaps, or a wave of popular mass hysteria, or some deep, mysterious volcanic upheaval in the national groupings and gropings that made up Eastern Europe? The student of history learns to suspect the view that events as massive and violent as great wars have simple self-evident causes. He comes to see them, rather, as manifestations of complex conditions prevalent in our civilization, as impersonal eruptions more than personal performances. He learns to look to internal changes or forces within States for explanation of international events such as wars, just as he finds in international events trends that help to explain national developments. Conventional distinctions between internal and international affairs, between British and European history, for instance, which still seemed so firm and sharp in the twenties, now blur and leave us with a starker image. It is an image not of our tight little island and its sea-girt shores, but of a fragment of Europe pointing westwards to the Americas and beyond, exposed to all the gusts of change and the blizzards of world crisis. Certainly Britain before 1914 could not be self-contained and self-sufficient, and her lively interest in overseas connexions showed she had little wish to be. From 1914 onwards she became ever less self-contained, but remained reluctant to confront the full consequences of this fact.

A further result of this new perspective on Britain in the

twentieth century is the tendency to regard the whole period of British history since the beginning of the century as indeed one unity. It appears as one long, complex development of the British people from being the industrial and commercial heart of a world-wide overseas empire into an economically very vulnerable member of a Commonwealth of free States. Within this Commonwealth, in all save traditional prestige and sentiment, the British Isles have become less of a heartland and more of an outpost; while in relation to Europe they have become less of a peripheral oceanic power and more of a central strategic link between the Western European systems of defence and trade, and the transatlantic Powers. There has occurred a revolution in the political and economic geography of the British Isles.

Domestically, too, the United Kingdom has undergone transformation from the most powerful and successful example of a liberal capitalist economy, which she was before 1914, into a prototype of the social-democratic Welfare State. This can be traced not only in the growth of social legislation and the expansion of social services but also in replacement of the Liberal Party by the Labour Party as one of the two major political parties in the country, and in the changing character of Conservatism in modern Britain. These developments, too, are continuous throughout the half-century; they give coherence and unity to its story.

It is continuities and contrasts, trends and transformations of this kind, that the students of contemporary history must examine, clarify, and assess in their inter-relationships. It is by these means and routes that the England of Mr Asquith became the England of Mr Macmillan. What the student of his own times is unable to do, since he knows no more than anyone else about what the future holds, is to determine whether these trends are good or bad, whether they point to progress or to retrogression. A Britain of relatively less military might in the world is not self-evidently a worse country than before; nor is the more affluent society of the sixties necessarily better, spiritually or culturally, than the Britain of 1914, which certainly knew more social injustice. Size, power, and wealth are not the only criteria of progress, though they are the most easily measureable attributes of any society. Recognizing these limitations and provisos of the task, it may be useful to begin by taking the dimensions of size, power, and wealth of Britain before 1914.

THE SINEWS OF POWER

The essential basis of power in any society – man-power – was increasing in pre-war Britain. Despite considerable emigration the population was growing, especially in England and Wales; but it was growing much more slowly than in the nineteenth century. During the half-century before 1901 the total net increase in England and Wales had been 81 per cent. During the half-century after 1901 it was only 34 per cent. The round figures to be reached during the period are as follows:[1]

POPULATION (*Thousands*)

	United Kingdom Total	England and Wales	Scotland	N. Ireland
1911	42,082	36,070	4,761	1,251
1921	44,027	37,887	4,882	1,258 (est.)
1931	46,038	39,952	4,842	1,243 (est.)
1941	No census [48,216 est.]			
1951	50,225	43,758	5,096	1,371
1961	52,673	46,072	5,178	1,423
1971	55,347	48,750	5,229	1,368

1. In all such figures confusion must be avoided by keeping distinct figures for England and Wales computed alone, for Great Britain (these plus Scotland), and for the United Kingdom (Great Britain plus Northern Ireland). Whenever possible in this volume figures will be given for the United Kingdom as a whole.

The growth was mainly due to natural increase (excess of births over deaths), which in turn was mainly due to the fall in infant death-rates. The number of babies who died before the age of one year in the United Kingdom was 110 per thousand live births in 1910–12. It declined fairly steadily between the wars, and sharply after 1945, until it was only 24·4 in 1956. The decrease in infant death-rates after 1945 was accompanied by a sharp rise in birth-rate which did not, however, reach pre-1914 level.

One result of the changes before 1914 was a higher proportion of the population within the working age groups: two-thirds, by 1911, were between the ages of fifteen and sixty-four. The effect on the social structure of the British people has been described like this:

There were proportionately more people at the peak of their mental and physical powers; individual skill and training and experience were yielding their fruits for a longer period: the task of providing more thorough education and training was made less daunting as the proportion of children declined and, indeed, the disappearance of the superabundance of children made them seem a more precious asset, to be preserved and made the most of by public action as well as private care.[1]

By 1914 these changes were providing plentiful labour for an expanding economy. Much of this new labour found an outlet in emigration, which increased again after 1900. In the last three years of peace it reached a record average of 464,000 a year. But this emigration affected the Irish, Scots, and Welsh more than the English, who experienced an internal immigration from Scotland and Wales, as well as a foreign influx from Europe. Nor was the increase in labour supply used only to provide more labour: children stayed longer at school, and in many occupations working hours were reduced, providing more education and more

1. William Ashworth: *An Economic History of England, 1870–1939* (1960), p. 42.

leisure rather than more output. Here was a tendency, later to be much accelerated, to rate social services and amenities for the populace as a whole more highly than they had been valued during the nineteenth century.

As in many other respects, however, such tendencies were detectable rather than prevalent before 1914. The age to which education was compulsory had been raised to twelve in 1899. After 1900, local authorities had power to raise it to fourteen. Only half of them made new by-laws, and even these allowed so many exemptions between the ages of twelve and fourteen that two out of every five children still left school before reaching the age of fourteen. Yet this proportion, which now seems so high and which is often quoted as showing the backwardness of English schooling, was a great advance on previous generations. The striking fact is that more and more children were staying longer at school, one in eight receiving some form of education after fourteen. A new tendency, firmly there, was unlikely to be stemmed and could not be reversed.

The economy of the country was in a comparably formative phase. During the fifteen years before 1914 world trade as a whole was expanding rapidly, and a high proportion of it was British trade. The total value of United Kingdom exports and imports in 1913 (some £5,186 million) still substantially exceeded Germany's or France's, and was 80 per cent more than it had been twenty years before. Britain possessed the largest merchant fleet in the world, as well as the strongest navy, though in both she was increasingly challenged by Germany. Her agriculture had by 1914 largely recovered from the long 'depression' and was again strong. Although more than four-fifths of Britain's wheat was now imported, adaptations to pasture, market gardening, and more scientific methods lifted farming out of its earlier crisis.

World trade, on which Britain's security and prosperity

now depended, was changing in pattern. There was a tendency for Europe and North America to become relatively less important, and for Asia, Africa, and Australasia to become more important in British overseas trade-relations than during the later nineteenth century. In the 1890s rather more than 50 per cent of the exports from the United Kingdom had gone to Europe or North America: by 1913 only some 46 per cent went to those areas. Whereas in the 1890s the United Kingdom took nearly 72 per cent of its imports from these two areas, by 1913 it took only 62 per cent. The shift of emphasis away from Europe and North America, and towards the less highly developed areas of the world, reflected the economic growth of Germany and the United States. These two powers, now growing fast in productivity and trade, imported less from Britain and broke into neighbouring markets as competitors with Britain. On the other hand, since these were diminishing proportions of an increasing total bulk of trade, the economies of the three countries were closely interdependent. Maynard Keynes noted in 1919, 'we sent more exports to Germany than to any other country in the world except India, and we bought more from her than from any other country in the world except the United States'.

In general, the world economy was becoming more fully multilateral, with trade a three-cornered or four-cornered operation and with less direct matching between export and import markets. British exports now went relatively more to Australasia, Asia, and Africa, which did not develop comparably as providers of imports for Britain. This more intricate trade network, resting less on direct exchanges of goods and services and more on a delicate system of multilateral exchanges and of credit managed by the City of London, would suffer more than the old from the violent dislocations of war.

Trade within the British Empire as a whole, especially

between the United Kingdom and India, bulked large in the total picture. Some 37 per cent of United Kingdom exports went to countries of the Empire, 13 per cent of them to India, which took nearly two-thirds of her total imports from the United Kingdom. Within the world economy the British Empire loomed large. It covered roughly one-quarter of the land surface of the globe and included a quarter of mankind. Its population was unevenly distributed, being mainly concentrated in the two densely populated areas of India and the British Isles. The rest was very widely scattered over the face of the globe, in Africa, Australasia, Canada, and many small outposts and islands. Naval power, like the merchant fleet, was a vital element in its cohesion and its security. The sinews of power, apparently overwhelmingly strong still, lay exposed to competition, in armaments as in commerce; and this peril, at least, was fully appreciated.

There were some signs even before 1914 that Britain had become excessively dependent on dealings with the outside world and paid too little attention to the use of home resources. Competition from Germany and the United States challenged her old easy supremacy, and she was dilatory in adapting herself to new conditions. More than half her whole exports was textiles, and too large a part of her foreign earnings came from the vulnerable market for cotton textiles, increasingly likely to be threatened by competition from new producers. While this exposed sector was actually extended and attracted heavier investment, the other great mid-Victorian industry, coal-mining, was developed in spite of the introduction of new fuels which boded ill for its future. The range of commodities exported remained narrow. A willingness to go on thinking in old ways and rely on old recipes for prosperity, and a disinclination to keep pace in pioneering enterprise, were omens of troubles ahead. Such over-confidence and lack of foresight were, no doubt, the penalties of earlier prosperity in unusually favourable conditions. The economy was still so strong that it could afford these faults in time of peace. They could prove much more costly defects in a dislocated post-war world in which the old organic unity had been for ever destroyed, and with it Britain's easy-going mastery of trade, capital, and credit.

The economic power of the United Kingdom in the world was derived not only from industrial production, trade, and shipping but also from its immense investments overseas and its services of banking, credit, and insurance. These sources of so-called 'invisible exports' had developed immensely in the previous half-century. Britain's capital assets abroad amounted to about £4,000 million by 1913, and during the years 1911–13 additions to foreign investment had been more than 20 per cent of the income earned abroad. British willingness to go on exporting capital, even in the international tensions of the years before 1914, was one sign of her strength and her self-confidence. By 1914 nearly half Britain's overseas investments were within the Empire. Other countries, moreover, transacted many of their international transactions in sterling, and the London money market was the chief factor in the financial equilibrium of the world. Through this channel the Bank of England manipulated credit policy and exerted a powerful influence for stability and confidence throughout the world. Britain's financial power, like her commercial power, was intricately linked to her imperial and international relations. It infused these relations with a spirit of confidence and a sense of stable order: in return, it came to depend for its own continued vigour on the maintenance of an established and peaceful system of international relations. No country enjoyed 'the Great Peace' more than Britain: none was liable to suffer more deadly damage from 'the Great War'.

The material wealth of the country may be gauged in

two ways: by figures of national wealth, or in terms of national income. A broadly similar picture is given by either means. If national wealth be defined as 'the sum total of the exchangeable and transferable possessions of the country, whether individually or corporately held', that of the United Kingdom in 1914 was estimated to be £14,319 million. Statisticians differ about precisely how this capital wealth was distributed, but none dispute that it was distributed very unevenly. It is likely that three-quarters of the people over twenty-five had to share little more than 5 per cent, while less than 1 per cent of the population owned two-thirds of the capital wealth. But the important fact historically is that trends existed – soon to be accelerated by war – towards some lessening of the widest disparities. Graduated estate duties, payable on both personal and real property at death, had existed since 1894, and had been steepened in 1907.

The national income of the United Kingdom (excluding the area of the Irish Free State) in 1911 was estimated at £1,988 million.[1] Of this wages took 39·5 per cent, salaries 15·6 per cent, profits 33·8 per cent, and rent 11·1 per cent. Income, like capital wealth, was very unevenly distributed, but again modifying factors were at work to diminish the greatest extremes. The British economy passed, at the turn of the century, from its late Victorian speed of growth to a much slower rate of growth. Average real incomes went up during the last ten years of peace, but they went up more slowly than people had become accustomed to expect: probably a mere 7 per cent above the average of the preceding decade. This slowing down in the pace of growth caused relative hardships and gave an impression of greater poverty. Some trades and occupations suffered positive deterioration, and advance was irregular.

1. i.e. 'the total of goods and services becoming available after deducting what is required to maintain real capital intact'.

...ut jerky changes in the economy were ...out various shifts in the fortunes of classes and ...People on the average enjoyed a somewhat higher ...andard of living than before because of the rise in real wages and the growth of social services. But some – the very poor – were possibly even worse off than before, because people who had to spend almost all their income on basic necessities were hit by a rise in urban rents, dearer coal, less nourishing cheap foodstuffs, and risks of unemployment. Yet the very poor now were a smaller proportion of the whole of society. Poverty, as a social evil measured, investigated, publicly discussed, and considered remediable, was viewed as something unnecessary in so rich a society. Perhaps the greatest of all social changes was in the attitude to poverty. No longer evidence of thriftlessness or lack of industry, nor regarded as a natural and inevitable calamity like earthquakes, poverty was treated increasingly as a social disorder and an economic lapse. Closer study and understanding could find redress for it. It became a matter for political action. Here, surely, was one of the seeds of the Welfare State. Seebohm Rowntree, investigating poverty in York in 1899, found its commonest cause to be inadequate wages. There was sound basis for the view that one remedy, at least, would be a better spread of the national income to wages rather than profits or rents, as the new Socialists were urging.

But if low wages were probably the chief reason for poverty, the cause which was to predominate between the two wars – unemployment and widespread underemployment – was not unknown. In 1909 William Beveridge published his study of *Unemployment, a Problem of Industry*. Labour Exchanges were set up, which by 1914 were filling over a million vacant jobs each year. The National Insurance Act of 1911 introduced, in only seven industries at first, compulsory insurance against unemployment. By

1914 some 2,326,000 workers were thus insured. But before the war the phenomenon of mass unemployment was an occasional, not an enduring one. It was not 'structural unemployment'. It happened in years of trade depressions, such as 1904 and 1909, but with a revival of trade the numbers of unemployed usually shrank back to those of the casually employed.[1] It was the rumblings of a future problem, not the problem itself, that confronted economists before 1914. In this it was of a piece with most other economic and social problems of the pre-war scene. In 1914 Beatrice Webb noted in her diary: 'The landslide in England towards Social Democracy proceeds steadily, but it is the whole nation that is sliding, not the one class of manual workers.'

THE SOURCES OF INFLUENCE

Neither in the advancement of popular education, nor in the provision of social security against the misfortunes of industrial society, was Britain ahead of such advanced European nations as Germany and the countries of Scandinavia. In the provision for better secondary education inaugurated by the Education Act of 1902, and the scheme for National Insurance introduced by David Lloyd George in 1911, Britain had made efforts to catch up on the more advanced systems of Europe. The first decade of the new century brought a remarkable expansion of universities, based on a combination of civic pride in the larger industrial towns and a hunger for higher education stimulated by the growth of secondary education. New universities were founded at Birmingham (1900), Liverpool (1903), Leeds (1904),

1. According to Sir William Beveridge (*Full Employment in a Free Society* (1944), p. 73), the thirty years before 1914 probably had a mean unemployment rate of about 6 per cent in contrast with the 14·2 per cent for the years 1921–38, i.e. post-war 'structural unemployment' was probably some two-and-a-half times more severe.

Sheffield (1905), and Bristol (1909), while the University of Wales was formed in 1893. As yet no university students received aid from the central government, and very few from local authorities. Scientific studies, again in the wake of Germany, were increasingly introduced into the universities. Serious scientific research was mostly done within the universities; but even there, education in science still did not rank as high in the social and intellectual scale as education in the traditional disciplines of mathematics, theology, classics, medicine, or law. In scientific, technical, and even philosophical education Germany ranked first in the whole world.

In one field, especially, British science made new discoveries: in nuclear physics. J. J. Thomson began to reveal the structure of the atom, and in 1911 Ernest Rutherford, by his researches into radio-activity, brought about 'the greatest change in our idea of matter since the time of Democritus'. But it was 1919 before Rutherford achieved the first 'transmutation' of elements. The practical applications of these new concepts of matter lay far in the future, but the remarkable group of men in the Cavendish Laboratory in Cambridge had already laid the foundations of modern nuclear physics.

The application of science and technology to practical invention had produced several potentially momentous results, none of which, as yet, was fully developed or appreciated. The internal-combustion engine had made possible the motor-car and the aeroplane, but the extent of their use was still limited, and, in developing both, the United States and France were more adventurous than Britain. The same was true of the cinematograph and wireless telegraphy. These four contributions of twentieth-century science and industry to the history of mankind were in their infancy before 1914, and in all of them the United States had greater natural advantages than Britain. Similarly, in the chemical and electrical industries Germany was advancing farther and faster than Britain. The future lay more with these new industries than with the older ones, cotton and coal, upon which Britain still heavily relied, and in which her methods were the most old-fashioned.

In at least two fields of culture, however, British thought already led a vigorous reaction against Germanic influences. In philosophy the prevalence of Hegelianism and of Utilitarianism was challenged by G. E. Moore and Bertrand Russell from 1903 onwards. In that year had appeared Russell's *Principles of Mathematics* and Moore's *Principia Ethica*. It is notable that their influence radiated from Cambridge, where Rutherford and Keynes were also to revolutionize human thinking – the latter under their direct influence through the famous 'Bloomsbury Circle'. In historiography, too, their contemporary at Cambridge, George Macaulay Trevelyan, struck doughty blows against the prevalence of Germanic 'scientific history' which incurred the danger, in his eyes, of destroying the enjoyment of writing and reading history as a literary pursuit. By his learned yet exciting histories of the Italian *Risorgimento* and the role in it of the romantic Garibaldi, Trevelyan asserted the traditions of a literary culture with permanent effect on the study of history in England. In C. R. Mackintosh and C. F. A. Voysey British architecture found two pioneers who were to exert considerable influence on European design, later to return to England in much more dynamic form in the work of Walter Gropius and the functional interpretation of the 'Bauhaus'.[1]

Britain's most original and outstanding achievement in the realm of the arts was on the stage. With the full flourishing of George Bernard Shaw, John Galsworthy, and a host of lesser dramatists, the theatre enjoyed a renaissance that gave it the leadership of Europe and America. Shaw owed

1. See below, p. 185.

much to Ibsen; but the drama of ideas and argument attained new heights and popularity in Britain. Harley Granville-Barker's productions of Shaw, and his presentations of Shakespeare on modern lines, abandoned the clumsy realism of earlier fashion. They brought a new era in the theatre. The Abbey Theatre in Dublin made its own unique contribution to the 'Celtic Renaissance' in drama and poetry. The novels of H. G. Wells, Arnold Bennett, George Moore, and Joseph Conrad rivalled in popularity and influence the drama of Shaw and Galsworthy. Apart from the poetry of the elderly Thomas Hardy and the young John Masefield, English poetry did not share in the vigour of these other literary revivals. Nor, apart from theatre and novel, did English culture fully hold its own in comparisons with France or with the United States.

Britain won pre-eminence, however, in the drama and novel of ideas – of social problems such as the emancipation of women and human equality, ethical problems of family and industrial relationships, political problems of labour unions and socialism. It was one indication of what Britain most firmly stood for in the world: the continuance and extension of the great nineteenth-century experiment in democracy, in which Britain and the overseas settled Dominions were conspicuously successful. Their special achievement was to comprise within a constitutional framework of representative parliamentary institutions a form of government which denied all arbitrary power, preserved the rule of law and an impartial code of justice, and kept government strong yet accountable to public opinion. In public administration, too, the British had devised a civil service which was honest, efficient, public-spirited, yet not excessively bureaucratic in outlook or despotic in authority. The Indian Civil Service administered, through a tiny corps of men, a vast land that owed its coherence to their rule, and peace to the public order and security kept by the Indian Army. By the development of responsible government a new style of imperial relationship, too, had arisen within the *Pax Britannica*. Canada, Australia, New Zealand, and most recently the Union of South Africa (1910), not only adopted parliamentary systems modelled closely on that of the United Kingdom but also enjoyed within the Empire rights of independent self-government. Contrasted with a continent wherein dynastic empires and autocratic monarchies still predominated, the British constitutional monarchy and the Empire of which it was the heart remained a beacon of freedom and a defiance of despotism for the whole world. Europeans still looked westwards for their hope of freedom, whether individual or national.

The 'Mother of Parliaments' at Westminster had shown herself able to keep pace with fast-moving change, and to bring within her moderating influence the fierce forces of organized trade unionism, proletarian socialism, and the violent surges of raw public opinion. Since the formation of the Labour Party in 1906, with its twenty-nine representatives in the House of Commons, there had existed a steady pull towards constitutional action through elections and parliamentary alliances, rather than through the 'direct action' favoured by the more extremist kinds of trade unionism and socialism. The solid basis of the Labour Party was the growing trade-union movement. The T.U.C., by its support of Labour candidates, channelled new forces into parliamentary life. The conservative forces most stubbornly opposed to liberal and socialist reforms had been sharply defeated in 1911, after the long and bitter controversy about the claim of the House of Lords, with its entrenched Conservative majority, to block legislation. The Parliament Act of 1911 reduced the veto of the Lords to a mere delaying power, and removed even that control over finance bills. In the same year the Commons began the practice of paying Members of Parliament a stipend – a prerequisite of real working-class representation in Parliament. The democratic reorganization of local government at the end of the previous century, and the creation of local education committees under the Education Act of 1902, bore fruit in a rapid extension of public services before 1914. The material environment of urban life was greatly improved by the facilities now provided by active local authorities, whether in cleaner and better-lit streets, better water-supply and sanitation, or recreation-grounds, free libraries, and schools. In visible, concrete terms democracy worked: it improved the lot of working-class people, and it gave them greater say in the running of the country.

Yet here, more than in any other sphere of national life, there was ground for apprehension. Liberalism, at the very moment of its greatest triumphs after 1906, was disintegrating. The stubborn refusal of Liberals and Conservatives alike to contemplate yielding to the demands of the suffragettes for women's right to vote in parliamentary elections (it already existed in local elections) drove the women to violence and excess. The question of Home Rule for Ireland, a live issue for the past generation, drove both major parties into postures of violent intransigence. By 1914 the Liberals were ready to coerce Ulster into submission in order to grant the Irish Home Rule; the Unionists were equally ready to provoke mutiny in the British Army rather than let Ulster go. The intrusion of so much explosive 'direct action' in central politics was accompanied by a revival of it among trade unionists. The years 1911–12 saw a great movement of unrest involving big strikes among seamen, dock and transport workers, and a general railway strike. Encouraged by rising prices and stationary wages, these strikes also had links with ideas of revolutionary syndicalism borrowed from France. The strike-fever ended with the miserable surrender of the London Dock strikers in July 1912. These many evidences, at all social levels, that violence smouldered beneath the apparently orderly life of twentieth-century Britain, were the most ominous of all signs that troubled times would lie ahead. Was this the class war, the portent of proletarian revolution, of which the Marxists and Syndicalists spoke? Could it, together with the violence of the suffragettes and the passions aroused by the Irish Question, destroy even British constitutional habits?

Moods of intense public excitement and surges of passion had for long been encouraged, too, by war-scares and anxieties about the challenge of German naval armaments. The popular image of the German, not long since regarded as an admirably hard-working, stolid, family-loving man, began to be that of a goose-stepping, militaristic dullard, who permitted a hysterical and histrionic emperor to dispose without question of his immense capacities for work and discipline. The French, formerly Britain's traditional enemies, became sympathetic friends, anxious to remain on good terms despite colonial frictions and certain incompatibilities of temperament. In the days of the new, popular, sensational Press such mass-images became important: especially when they chimed neatly with the nation's real fears of German competition in trade and sea-power, and greater reliance upon France for the defence of Britain's position in the Channel and the Mediterranean.

For all these reasons British national life in 1914 was subject to many schisms and tensions, and even the future of constitutional government seemed in jeopardy. Mr Herbert Henry Asquith, leader of the Liberal Party, had been Prime Minister since April 1908. He had shown re-remarkable pertinacity in staying in power through all these upheavals. King George V had been on the throne since 1910, and had revealed a rich store of tact and good sense in his handling of the constitutional crisis about the House of Lords, already erupting when he ascended the throne. One thing, and perhaps only one thing, could have united the British people in concerted support for a single policy: a flagrant threat to Britain's national security. She had, indeed, entered into understandings and agreements with both tsarist Russia and republican France, and since 1902 she had a treaty of alliance with Japan. But her most menacing enemy, the German Empire, was allied with the Habsburg Dual Monarchy of Austria-Hungary and with Italy. When, in July 1914, Austria-Hungary went to war with Serbia, Russia mobilized on Serbia's side, and Germany mobilized against Russia, it was inevitable that France should prepare to support her ally, Russia. Even now there were many who hoped that the conflict might be localized or limited, and that Britain could keep at least a free hand. Her pledge to support France in such circumstances was neither formal nor categorical. But all doubts were removed by Germany when she invaded Belgium, whose neutrality Germany and other western Powers had undertaken to respect.

Britain declared war on Germany on 4 August 1914. She did so formally because Germany had violated a joint treaty obligation to respect the neutrality of Belgium. She did so substantially for several other reasons as well: because it was her traditional defence strategy to make sure that the Low Countries were not dominated by a hostile Power, because the naval agreements of 1912 with France made it morally necessary to stand by France in case of general war, because deep-rooted fear of German naval power impelled her to avoid isolation in a world of international fears and tensions.

In these circumstances most of the disruptive forces subsided almost immediately; though until the last two days even the Cabinet was deeply divided about entry into the war. Whilst the Conservative Press wanted war the Liberal Press demanded neutrality. It was the cynicism of Germany's invasion of Belgium that rallied to the side of the ministers not only their own neutralist minority but also the support of public opinion and, from the Irish benches, the voice of John Redmond. The opposition of Ramsay MacDonald, leader of the Labour Party, did not represent the views of his whole party. The suffragettes dropped their militant tactics and turned their animosities against Germany instead of Mr Asquith. The Irish troubles temporarily subsided. The Syndicalists, for the most part, fell silent. Some fourteen months later Nurse Edith Cavell, facing a German firing-squad, was to proclaim that 'Patriotism is not enough'. For the moment, it seemed quite enough.

The nation stood firm. So, too, did the Empire. It was astonishing that a declaration of war, over which the United Kingdom itself was so hesitant and divided until the last moment, should evoke support from all the Dominions and from India. The fully self-governing parts of the Empire contributed richly in men and materials to the allied war-effort; though the strains told there, as in Britain and Europe. Canada was torn between British and French on the question of compulsory military service, Australian labour was divided, South Africa hesitated and suffered a revolt, as did India and Ireland, both to feature as problem areas of the Commonwealth between the two wars. In the end the Dominions were willing to share in the efforts and sacrifices of Britain's war because they already shared the benefits of her institutions and the hopes and values of her ideals. But, like the United Kingdom itself, the Empire (as people still called it) would not escape the transformations and the strains brought about by such efforts and sacrifices. The British Government's decision to go to war carried with it momentous implications for the future of peoples all over the world.

CHAPTER TWO

Britain at War, 1914–18

THE WAR EFFORT

WHEN war began Britain had some 250,000 men 'with the colours'. Since at least half of them were overseas, little more than 100,000 men could be spared for the first battles on the western front. These constituted a very highly trained and efficient force. The 'British Expeditionary Force' under Sir John French, which crossed to France in August 1914, reached Mons in time to take the blow of General von Kluck's First Army and did much to thwart the Schlieffen Plan for a vast wheeling hammer-blow down through France to envelop Paris. In September it attacked on the Marne, helping to force the German armies back across the Aisne. Reinforced by troops brought from garrisons overseas and by two Indian Divisions, in October it took part in the first battle of Ypres which checked the German push to the Channel ports. In these early battles the B.E.F., like the Belgians and the French, lost heavily. They did not succeed in driving the German invaders off French soil. But their gains, hardly apparent at the time, may eventually have been decisive.

The Schlieffen Plan had been the German blueprint for speedy victory in the west – an aim necessitated by Germany's traditional nightmare of a long war on two fronts. With Russia France's ally, this nightmare had to be dispelled at all costs; and the Germans had pinned everything on the total success of the Schlieffen Plan. They had no other and were prepared to incur the cost of invading Belgium rather than abandon the Plan. Speed and decisiveness were the essence of success, but the early battles robbed the Germans of both. By December major operations were suspended on the western front. Both sides dug in while they sought fresh reserves and munitions to replenish their exhausted resources. A war of attrition and exhaustion, with the main trial of strength with Russia yet to come, was the one situation Germany most dreaded. The failure of the master-plan was complete.

On the other hand, Germany had begun the war very well prepared. It could muster some 5 million trained men against France's 4 million. Its fine system of railways and supplies, its military organization and strategic advantages, were fully geared to war. Britain's resources, though potentially immense, were not immediately available for war, and she lacked even the organization for developing and utilizing them. She needed time, which was now given her. Lord Kitchener, who became Secretary of State for War, set about the long-term labour of making an army of millions and at the same time improvising the organization and supplies needed to equip it. It was decided to rely upon voluntary enlistment. This provided all the men who could be trained with the limited facilities, and produced a fighting force of excellent morale and valour. When these new armies, in turn, suffered decimation in the holocausts of 1915 and 1916 it was found that Britain had sacrificed an undue proportion of her best-trained and most courageous manhood. Compulsory military service, first introduced early in 1916, could with advantage have come sooner. Although between two and three million men were recruited first by voluntary enlistment, the initial smallness of the British land forces placed an excessive burden on the French. They had long known conscription in peace-time and regarded Britain's war effort as inadequate until it was introduced.

At sea, where Britain was very well prepared in 1914,

there was little activity during the first twenty months. Anglo-French naval superiority kept the German merchant marine off the oceans. The B.E.F. was successfully landed in France and kept supplied there. No German landing on British shores was attempted. These were great silent achievements. The big ships of each side kept at respectful distances from one another until May 1916.

The immense losses of life and expenditure of munitions during 1915 brought home to people and government alike that this was an entirely new kind of war, in which the liabilities were unlimited, the commitment indefinite, the whole nation involved. The concept of total warfare, in which professional fighting men were but the spearhead and the framework for an all-out national effort in a life-or-death struggle, was too new and too horrible to be easily accepted by Englishmen. They had not even had the French experience of the shattering blows of 1870–1. At first Britain, like most other belligerents, had expected the war to be over in six months. Since Bismarck's localized *Blitzkriegs* of the 1860s Europe had come to think of wars between major Powers as inevitably short and decisive. This was general war, with remarkably evenly matched forces arrayed on either side: a struggle in which the will to fight and to win grew greater after initial reverses and losses, and capacity to continue the struggle expanded as the whole national man-power of each participant was organized in war-factories, transport systems, and armed forces. Deadlock, once created, could last for a long time. War of this kind had not happened before.

Because of reluctance to believe that war had assumed this entirely new character, and because improvisation is always easier than fundamental rethinking, the battles of 1915 and 1916 were usually fought on principles which took insufficient account of the deadliness of artillery and machine-gun fire. Immensely heavy artillery barrages, pounding enemy positions before an attack, could at great cost force the enemy out of one line of trenches. They might then be occupied without incurring too heavy losses from machine-gun fire; but these, once occupied, could again be pounded by enemy artillery and recaptured. Thus were millions of lives lost, and vast quantities of shells expended, taking and retaking the same small area of mud. The Generals on both sides remained perplexed by this dilemma; and even when the best available answer – the tank – was invented, it was adopted slowly and without confidence. Machine-guns and barbed-wire entanglements had made obsolete the old-fashioned cavalry charges and infantry advances. The command on each side went on using them and incurred casualty figures which still stun the imagination.[1] During 1915 the British Army in France suffered 300,000 casualties, 60,000 of them at Loos alone. In 1916, in a single day's battle which on 1 July opened the allied offensive on the Somme, it endured another 60,000 casualties, of whom one-third were killed. This offensive lasted five months and cost the British more than 400,000 casualties, the French 200,000, and the Germans nearly 500,000. At Passchendaele in 1917 the British advanced five miles at a cost of 400,000 men. Nor do the cold, round figures give any idea of the immense human suffering, the heart-break anxieties, and the grief-stricken homes, the fate of millions maimed with shrapnel and bullets or the legacy of 'shell-shock' among even the unwounded. Before long all nations taking part learned to look upon the war as a vast and almost impersonal calamity, insatiable in its exaction of human sacrifice yet profitless in its consequences. The most remarkable fact of all was that peoples endured so much for so long.

The heaviest cost of the war-effort to the British Empire was the death of almost 1 million men and the maiming of probably three times that number. Of those killed, 744,000

1. Casualty figures here include killed, wounded, prisoners, and those missing.

came from the United Kingdom. The French calculated that in the years before February 1917, when their armies bore the brunt of the heavy fighting in the west, one Frenchman was killed, on average, every minute.

Efforts to replace such losses had to be tempered by the need to keep an adequate labour force in the munitions factories, for the expenditure of munitions vastly exceeded expectations. By the end of the war Britain had 8 million men and nearly 1 million women serving either in the fighting services or in munitions factories. Even before the end of 1914 the consumption of shells and other munitions absurdly exceeded reserves and supply, and in 1915 all belligerents experienced a crisis of supply. Asquith had to reconstruct his government in May 1915. He put David Lloyd George in charge of a newly created Ministry of Munitions. Special legislation gave Lloyd George almost dictatorial control over industry, in order to direct all its energies to the urgent manufacture of munitions of all kinds. The civilian population learned to endure more discipline and centralized direction than it had ever known in peace-time, and the State evolved a great new apparatus of control and of planning.

From direct attack, except from the few sporadic raids by zeppelins over the east coast, the civilian population was kept immune by the shield of the Royal Navy. But the war at sea, especially from February 1915 onwards, caused increasing hardship on the home front. Britain, as has been shown, relied on imports for a high proportion of her food and for many essential raw materials. In February 1915 the Germans declared the western approaches to the British Isles to be a zone of war, into which neutral vessels entered at the risk of being sunk by German mines or submarines. In April that year a German submarine torpedoed the British liner *Lusitania* off the Irish coast and, of the 1,200 people drowned, 118 were United States citizens. President

Woodrow Wilson warned Germany that any repetition of
such an act would be treated by the United States as
'deliberately unfriendly'. His warning deterred Germany
for the next two years from unrestricted submarine warfare.
It left the naval forces of Britain and Germany engaged in
the constant tussle of blockade and counter-blockade.

Anglo-French naval power enforced the blockade against
Germany by stopping the shipping of all goods destined for
Germany or her allies, and by requiring even neutral ships
to submit to examination. Neutral countries (such as
Holland and the Scandinavian countries) had to restrict
their own imports of goods which might find their way from
these countries into Germany. Such measures were naturally
resented, especially by the United States, but resentment
against Germany's counter-blockade, by submarine war,
proved greater. This resentment reached its climax in
January 1917, when Germany again proclaimed unrestricted submarine warfare. She hoped to sink enough British or
allied shipping within six months to bring Britain to her
knees by starvation and shortages. She avowed the intention
of sinking at sight, regardless of loss of life, all merchant
ships within a zone of water around the British Isles and
around France and Italy in the Mediterranean. President
Wilson retaliated by breaking off diplomatic relations and
ordering that American ships be armed.

The ruthlessness of U-boat sinkings which now took place
made the entry of the United States into the war virtually
inevitable. Sinkings totalled nearly 540,000 tons of shipping
in February, 600,000 tons in March, and another 870,000
tons in April. The German High Command took a calculated risk – that it could by this means starve out Britain
before American patience would be exhausted and American
supplies could reach her. At the end of April Britain had
stores of food to last only six weeks. By adopting rationing
of essentials, and by real deprivation, this proved just

enough. Meanwhile improved weapons against the U-
boats had been devised and adopted: other submarines,
depth charges and mines, hydrophone and aeroplane spot-
ting, and above all the armed escort to protect whole
convoys of merchant ships. This last was a bone of political
contention between two schools of thought. It was eventually adopted, with great success, under pressure from
Lloyd George. It had become imperative to diminish sinkings, for ships were being sunk faster than shipyards could
build new ones. As soon as submarine losses became heavy,
and trained crews for them more difficult to replace, the
menace receded. The entry of the United States into the
war, in April 1917, transformed the whole situation. United
States shipping resources were vast and its shipbuilding
capacity far exceeded losses. Nevertheless, by the end of
hostilities, Britain had lost over 6 million tons of shipping.
At home she was enduring severe rationing and shortages.

The one battle between capital ships, at Jutland on 31
May 1916, remained for long controversial because its
result seemed inconclusive. It was the only major action
between the British Grand Fleet and the German High
Seas Fleet, and ships of all types except submarines took
part in it. It was provoked by Admiral Scheer, under pressure of the tightening blockade, in an effort to destroy at
least part of the Grand Fleet. He sent out Admiral Hipper
with a decoy force. The British Admiralty since war began
had enjoyed the advantage of knowing the German signal
code. It ordered the Grand Fleet to sea in good time. On
the afternoon of 31 May Hipper's force of battle and light
cruisers made contact with Admiral Beatty's force of comparable strength. Beatty lost two ships, but the engagement
brought the two great fleets, under Scheer and Jellicoe,
rushing to the scene. After several hours of cautious
manoeuvres and occasional contacts, night fell and the main
action was broken off. The Germans had inflicted heavier

losses than they had suffered – the British losses in men were
more than twice the German. Six cruisers and eight des-
troyers were sunk. But under cover of darkness the Germans
retreated behind mine fields, and at dawn on 1 June the
Grand Fleet sailed an empty sea. Scheer made another
attempt, in August, to lure the British into an ambush of
submarines. He failed. What had appeared to be a minor
German success proved, in the end, to be a major British
victory, for the High Seas Fleet did not leave harbour again
until it bloodlessly surrendered two-and-a-half years later.
Most of it was scuttled by its own crews at Scapa Flow to
forestall humiliation. It was a strange anticlimax to a
quarter-century of bitter Anglo-German rivalry for supremacy on the high seas, and to the heated controversies about
capital ships in the pre-war years.

Thrusts were made elsewhere in the world to harass
Germany or her allies or to aid and encourage Britain's
allies. After Turkey entered the war on Germany's side in
November 1914, Britain planned an attack on the Dardanelles which might relieve Turkish pressure on the
Caucasus and reopen the supply-route to Russia through
the Straits. It was especially urged by Winston Churchill,
First Lord of the Admiralty, against the opposition of the
French who deplored any diversion of effort away from the
western front. The Anglo-French naval expedition sent to
the Dardanelles in March 1915, and the allied landing on
the Gallipoli peninsula in April, failed in their purpose and
cost heavy losses of men and materials. By the end of the
year, despite the belated arrival of reinforcements, the
peninsula had to be evacuated. Churchill, ironically, was
largely responsible for Britain's greatest failure of the war.

At the same time, in the ill-fated campaign in Mesopo-
tamia (modern Iraq), General Townshend advanced on
Baghdad, only to suffer great losses and get besieged in
Kut-al-Amara until it surrendered in April 1916. The losses

and failures in the Dardanelles, Gallipoli, and Mesopotamia precipitated a crisis in Britain which overthrew the Asquith Government, as will be considered in the next section. It was March 1917 before British forces under General Maude entered Baghdad, and December before Allenby entered Jerusalem. By then Russia was in military collapse and the throes of revolution. In March 1918 the new Bolshevik Government led by Lenin and Trotsky, which had seized power the previous November, made separate peace with Germany at Brest-Litovsk. The Near Eastern campaign, however, had touched off the Arab revolt, with far-reaching future results: and the Oxford archaeologist, T. E. Lawrence, became one of the world's greatest 'resistance leaders'.

Such diversions, despite the strategic arguments of the 'easterners' as against the 'westerners' and despite eventual victories against the Turks, were not the decisive events. The result of the war against Germany was determined in the only place where it could be, on the western front. There the severe losses she had incurred in the east, no less than in repeated offensives in the west, as at Verdun in 1916 (330,000 casualties), put her at decisive disadvantage now that United States troops were pouring into Europe. Now, too, the allied armies were abundantly equipped with good supplies of food and munitions, with large numbers of tanks and the newly developed arm of the Royal Flying Corps. The last mighty battles of the western front in 1918, on the Somme, at Ypres, and on the Aisne, again brought at first German advances and allied retreats. By June the Germans once more stood on the Marne. The very place-names, made grimly familiar in 1914, came back into the news in 1918. Then the tide turned abruptly. The concerted offensives of Marshal Foch, Haig, and Pershing during the summer broke the nerve and will of the German High Command. By the end of September the German commanders were urging negotiations for peace, and on 5 October the German Government asked President Wilson to arrange for an armistice. The Kaiser abdicated on 9 November, and two days later an armistice was signed by the leaders of the new German Republic. The imperial militarist leaders and the bulk of the conservative nationalist *Junker* class slipped away. They shed their responsibilities, to return and fight another day. Allied armies had not yet advanced into German territory when the armistice was signed.

WAR-TIME POLITICS

The prolonged national effort imposed strains on the machinery and personnel of government and administration, no less than on the economy and the population as a whole. Because 1914 had been preceded by a century of near-peace, and because the character of warfare was so novel, neither civil nor military organization was readily adaptable to the needs of war. Some materials already existed, however, from which a suitable organization could be built.

The Committee of Imperial Defence had been set up by Balfour in 1904. It consisted of the Prime Minister, the Secretary of State for War, the First Lord of the Admiralty, the Secretary of State for India, and the Chancellor of the Exchequer. To it could be coopted such persons, including the Dominion Prime Ministers, as the Prime Minister chose to summon. It was there to advise rather than to decide, but it considered every aspect of defence and it had a secretariat such as the Cabinet had not yet evolved for itself. A Committee of this C.I.D., set up in 1911, produced for every department a scheme of action in the event of war.

When war began these prudent preparations proved valuable, but the central conduct of the war fell to a committee of the Cabinet, consisting of those ministers responsible for the day-to-day operations, in consultation with the established C.I.D. and with the rest of the Cabinet. The arrangement was too loose to work well. Lord Hankey, who was associated with the C.I.D. from 1908 until 1938, declared in 1945:

My own idea was that the Committee of Imperial Defence should be reorganized ánd tuned up to the pitch of actual war and should take over the control. That is what eventually happened, but it took longer than was expected, and nearly two and a half years of trial and error elapsed before a really satisfactory system was evolved. ... The Cabinet was too large to meet day in and day out, and too cumbrous to be called together rapidly at short notice. It did not work to an Agenda Paper and had no Secretary and no records. Ministers sometimes misapprehended the decisions, and the Staffs of the Admiralty and War Office and the Civil Service Chiefs were often in the dark as to what had been decided and what action they had to take.[1]

The Government lived on well-laid pre-war plans throughout the autumn of 1914; but when new plans were needed, with the prospect of prolonged deadlock in the west and war with Turkey in the east, the arrangement became more clearly unwise. By November 1914 the exigencies of a war which, quite clearly, was not going to be 'over by Christmas', dictated the creation of a special Cabinet committee, the War Council. This body absorbed the C.I.D. and took over its permanent secretariat. Even so, political responsibility remained with the whole Cabinet, to which important decisions had to be reported and which could assert an overriding authority.

A one-party Cabinet soon proved unworkable in war-time. Asquith was a skilled parliamentarian, adept at accumulating support for such measures as he deemed practicable. But he was unfitted, by temperament and experience, to conduct a war. It was not that he lacked political courage or powers of positive decision. In May he was

1. Lord Hankey, *Government Control in War* (1945), pp. 32–3.

compelled to accept the principle of a national coalition, and Winston Churchill described the event:

When Lord Fisher resigned in May and the Opposition threatened controversial debate, Asquith did not hesitate to break his Cabinet up, demand the resignations of all Ministers, end the political lives of half his colleagues, throw Haldane to the wolves, leave me to bear the burden of the Dardanelles, and sail on victoriously at the head of a Coalition Government. . . . These were the convulsive struggles of a man of action and of ambition at death-grips with events.[1]

The new Coalition Government was at first an unwieldy body of twenty-two, including along with a dozen Liberals eight Conservatives, Arthur Henderson of the Labour Party and Lord Kitchener as Secretary of State for War. In June the inner War Cabinet was replaced by the larger and looser Dardanelles Committee, in which efficiency of action was sacrificed to breadth of political representation. The War Committee that succeeded it was better, but soon became too cumbersome for the tasks confronting it.

At the end of 1916 Asquith was ousted from power by a complex intrigue, conducted by Lloyd George with ruthless skill. Asquith chose not to defend himself by seeking support from the House of Commons in a secret session. The change was justified, historically, by the proven need to reorganize the central machinery of government in a more drastic way than Asquith could be expected to attempt. Since the normal procedure of appealing to the electorate was ruled out in war-time, less regular ways of changing a government came into use: what Churchill dubbed 'secret, obscure, internal processes of which the public only now know the main story'.[2] Lloyd George, in effect, detached the Unionists

1. W. S. Churchill, *Great Contemporaries* (1947), p. 114.
2. The story has been told by Lord Beaverbrook, *Politicians and the War, 1914–1916* (2 vols. 1928–) and by Robert Blake in *The Unknown Prime Minister: The Life and Times of Andrew Bonar Law, 1858–1923* (1955), chapters XIX–XXI.

under Bonar Law from Asquith and compelled them to support himself. His conception of how to run a coalition government was very different from Asquith's.

With Lloyd George's coming to power on 7 December 1916 the government of Britain in war-time entered into a new phase. He established a small War Cabinet of five, consisting of himself, Bonar Law, Lord Milner, Lord Curzon, and Arthur Henderson – a compact corporate leadership, representing the main political forces of the country. It was mostly free from heavy administrative burdens and as regards all major decisions of policy was under his own vigorous personal guidance. Other Ministers or the Chiefs of Staff came when required, and with the attendance of representatives of the Dominions and India this 'War Cabinet' became the 'Imperial War Cabinet'. In May 1917 General Smuts of South Africa was made a member; during that year it met more than 300 times. Standing Committees were appointed for such special problems as Home Affairs, Eastern Affairs, and War Priorities, and these enabled other ministers, too, to meet regularly. The Secretariat was adapted to the new organization. The new structure made possible a more highly concerted conduct of the war-effort of the nation, and a more intelligent and consistent policy. There remained the elusive problem of how national policy and military strategy could be as closely interrelated as, in modern total warfare, they clearly needed to be if victory were to be won without over-costly delays.

On what terms, in short, were the politicians and the soldiers to work together in this new type of war? At the end of 1915 Sir William Robertson became Chief of the Imperial General Staff. He made himself the one authority through whom advice on actual military operations should reach the War Council, which consisted of civilian ministers and was the supreme directing authority. Lloyd George later accused Robertson of keeping from the Imperial Cabinet essential facts which told against policies he himself wanted them to adopt. But the arrangement was at least an improvement on what had gone before, when Kitchener had served simultaneously as Secretary of State for War and as chief military adviser to the Government: an amalgam of political and technical military functions which merely confused strategy with politics.

The same problem was projected on to the larger screen of inter-allied cooperation. Lloyd George reflected later that 'instead of one great war with a united front there were at least six separate and distinct wars with a separate, distinct, and independent strategy for each'. It was November 1917 before experience of repeated disasters brought into being the Allied Supreme War Council, which even then was partly hamstrung by mutual suspicions between British and French. But it led to the appointment of Marshal Ferdinand Foch as Generalissimo commanding all the allied forces in France. Foch was able to concert that series of sustained blows which forced the German Command to insist on an armistice.

Upon the whole development of central government and all the machinery of governmental control in Britain rests the stamp of a single personality – David Lloyd George. Not only did his initiative shape it in all its essentials, but the pattern he made survived. It was to become the accepted system of control during the Second World War, a quarter of a century later.

Thus, in the hour of our desperate need for war material in 1915, taking his political life in his hands, he founds the Ministry of Munitions. To the shattering submarine campaign in 1917 he finds an antidote in the convoy system. Amid the chaos of Cabinet crisis in December 1916 he creates the War Cabinet system, which has ever since remained the central feature of Government Control in peace and war. By calling the Dominions and India to our counsels he paves the way for Empire and Commonwealth developments that have staggered the world. He seizes on the Italian disaster at Caporetto as the occasion to secure acceptance of the Supreme War Council, which prepares the way for the unified command within six months and victory within a year. . . . I wish to place on record my conviction that the man who won the war was David Lloyd George.[1]

Attention has been given first to the central control of the war because there resided the decisive authority in all government. But the other parts of the British Constitution – the monarch, Parliament, and public opinion – likewise assumed roles in war that were different from their roles in peace. King George V not only became the symbolic father-figure of the nation at war, reflecting its moods of grief and courage; he made himself, by hard work and good sense, a source of stability and equilibrium in the country. His detailed knowledge of what went on was as remarkable as was his memory. His official biographer has endorsed the impressions of others:

During the whole course of the war the King was kept very fully informed of events and problems on the home and battle fronts. Not only did he receive the regular minutes of the Cabinet and War Councils, not only was he in constant touch with Ministers, but the Commanders and their subordinates in the field would provide him with frequent personal information, and in addition there were the confidential reports addressed to him by the Viceroy, the Governors General overseas and the Ambassadors and Ministers at foreign capitals. His naval friends would write him long private letters, in which they described their experiences and not infrequently voiced their anxieties or complaints.[2]

The King firmly resisted tendencies to popular hysteria or brutality, and opposed pressure for harsh treatment of conscientious objectors or for retaliation on prisoners of war. In deference to those who murmured against his family having

1. Lord Hankey, *Government Control in War*, pp. 49–50.
2. Sir Harold Nicolson, *King George V: His Life and Reign* (1952), p. 254.

German names, in July 1917 he adopted the House and Family name of Windsor. He strove to alleviate the distrusts between Lloyd George and the Commander-in-Chief, Sir Douglas Haig, whom the King much admired. He resisted party demands if he thought they might harm the country or hinder the war-effort, as when he refused Bonar Law's proposals for a dissolution of Parliament in December 1916. He visited industrial areas showing signs of unrest, and regularly used his considerable personal influence in favour of humanity and moderation. His popularity, as Sir Harold Nicolson remarked, 'grew from the fact that he never courted it; that he never allowed himself to be deflected by the transient gusts of public agitation from what, in his unsophisticated fashion, he felt to be just or unjust, right or wrong'.

Parliament inevitably surrendered wide powers to the Government, and suffered from the impossibility of renewing its popular basis by elections. Under the Defence of the Realm Acts (D.O.R.A.), passed when war began, any Government acquired wide powers to issue regulations affecting armed forces and civilians alike, including even the right to intern individuals without trial. Virtually all powers, other than that of taxation, were concentrated in the executive, and the Government knew that even extravagant demands for money would not be refused by Parliament. Under a coalition the forces of parliamentary opposition were too weak to assert stringent control.

One basic cause of dissension was the artificial distinction, too long preserved in principle, between home front and battle front, worker and fighter. It was August 1917 before man-power was treated as one whole source of effort, to be recruited for either factories or forces under a single Ministry of National Service. Until then skilled workers became soldiers when they would soon be needed desperately to produce munitions, or industries competed for a dwindling number of skilled men, or trade unions resisted controls and demanded higher wages in the name of that very 'freedom' for which some of their members were dying in the trenches. It took most of the war and much wastage before this consequence of total warfare was fully accepted by the Government or by public opinion.

The necessary control was reached piecemeal, through the creation of a Man-Power Board, the Munitions of War Act (July 1915), and the Ministry of Labour (1916). Wartime control of economic life was evolved almost entirely under the pressure of exigencies, hardly at all as the result of deliberate policy or consistent principle. Thus the crisis in the supply of munitions led first to the building of national factories and the requisitioning of nearly all iron and steel, and eventually to a distortion of the equipment of many industries. Its political by-product was the rise to eminence and power of Lloyd George. Improvisation and empirical development had great merits: they shelved basic principles which might have divided the country politically. But they involved heavy cost in wastage, slowness, and temporary inefficiency, and the unseen costs accumulated. The costs had to be counted in the post-war years, after exaltation of spirit had been dissipated with the coming of peace: counted in terms of war-profiteers and a sharp deterioration in the quality of parliamentary life and public affairs. As with many other consequences of the Great War, the reckoning could be deferred, even for many years, but it had to be paid in the end. The character of the House of Commons elected in December 1918 was an ill omen for the fortunes of parliamentary democracy during the next decade.

The House of Commons elected in December 1910 had prolonged its life for eight years. By the end of 1918 the split in the Liberal Party, which Lloyd George had caused by becoming Premier in 1916, prompted the idea of forming a new Coalition Government after the war. Since his Conservative allies, led by Andrew Bonar Law, were prepared to fight the election under his lead and could provide the electoral machinery which he lacked, it was in his interests to perpetuate the split. Sitting members who supported the Coalition, whether they were Conservatives or Liberals, were endorsed as candidates. Most new candidates were Conservatives. Endorsement (in the form of a letter signed by both Lloyd George and Bonar Law, which Asquith contemptuously christened 'the Coupon') was denied to all Liberals who supported Asquith against Lloyd George. The test of party loyalty was taken to be the votes cast in the famous 'Maurice debate' of 9 May 1918, which thus marked the permanent disintegration of the Liberal Party.

The dispute arose directly out of the severe losses of the spring of 1918 on the western front. Lloyd George was accused of dangerously weakening the forces of Sir Douglas Haig and of withholding reinforcements. Lloyd George retorted that the British armies in France were stronger at the beginning of 1918 than they had been a year before. This was flatly contradicted, in a letter to *The Times*, by the recent Director of Military Operations, Major-General Sir Frederick Maurice. In the House Asquith pressed for a Select Committee of Inquiry. Lloyd George treated the motion as one of censure. The 106 Liberals who voted for Asquith against Lloyd George, on this motion, were ostracized by the new Coalition in the 'Coupon Election'. In this way the inner schism of the Liberal Party, already apparent in 1914 and deepened in 1916, was renewed and widened in 1918. At the same time the Labour Party withdrew from the Coalition and fought the election on its own – a decision of considerable importance for the future, for it made the new Government predominantly Conservative and kept the Opposition divided between Labour and Asquith Liberals.

The major conflict of strategy between 'easterners' and 'westerners' at times coincided with the contest between civilians and soldiers, at other times with tensions between Britain and her allies. A week after the battle of Jutland Lord Kitchener, on his way to Russia in the cruiser *Hampshire*, was killed when it struck a mine off the Orkneys. Lloyd George, who took over the War Office from him, had to argue for his own 'eastern' propensities against two soldiers who were convinced 'westerners', Sir Douglas Haig and Sir William Robertson. Against the cautious conservatism of Haig and Robertson, and backed by such extraneous forces as the Press of Northcliffe and Beaverbrook, Lloyd George pressed his conviction that the war could be ended in the east. The imaginative attractiveness of using British naval power to more decisive effect, to aid Russia or demolish Turkey, appealed strongly to Lloyd George and Winston Churchill. The French inevitably resisted any diminution of all-out concentration on the western front. The inherent danger was enough diversion and dissipation of effort to lose in both theatres, and indeed the initial campaigns in both resulted in severe losses and reverses. Yet given German concentration on the west the allies had little choice: they had to fight back in Flanders and France and, until the United States brought its weight to bear, expeditions elsewhere could be safely attempted only with forces not immediately needed in the west. What the allies most lacked in the west was an adequate strategy for the offensive.

About such matters of national policy public opinion at large (greatly influenced by the inflammable popular Press) set the pace. Parliamentary opinion tended to reflect, often in milder form, the differences of opinion in the country, and it would be wrong to underrate the virulence and disruptiveness of these differences. As Sir Harold Nicolson remarks, 'credulity and inequity of the civilians during the first war were in excess of any similar emotions provoked by the even greater and more immediate perils of 1940'. Germanophobia, too, was more raw and raucous than it was to be in 1940. There were, moreover, moments when the pre-war spectre of insurrection walked again. On Easter Monday 1916 the Irish Volunteers staged a rebellion in Dublin and proclaimed the Irish Republic. Sir Roger Casement, whom a German submarine had landed at Kerry, was arrested and a German ship with a consignment of rifles was intercepted off the Irish coast. The rebellion was crushed; Casement was convicted of treason and executed. The British Government made contradictory statements of policy which left the Irish nationalists resentful and still more distrustful. In July 1917 a scheme (which Mr L. S. Amery claimed to have initiated) was made to hold an Irish National Convention to seek agreement in preference to partition. It met until April 1918, but found no solution to which both Ulster and the Sinn Fein extremists would agree. So was laid the basis of post-war strife in Ireland.[1]

THE PRICE OF VICTORY

The cost of war, for reasons already described, proved greater than any had expected in 1914. But to that heavy cost which, though payment might be deferred, had to be met in the end, must be added the further price – more calculable and avoidable – of victory. This price was paid partly in promissory notes, some of which were dishonoured; partly in money and wealth, in the form of loans which were not fully repaid; partly in a debasement of public life.

Most of the promissory notes, given in secret treaties to win or retain allies, need never have been given at all. The diplomacy of war-time, caught between the immediate exigencies of military operations and the passions of popular opinion, was cast in a mould of secrecy and lack of scruple unusual by pre-war standards (though not by post-war

1. See Chapter 3, below.

standards). Two examples from among many illustrate the point: allied relations with Italy, and with the Near East.

Italy remained neutral in 1914, taking her stand with literal correctness on the terms of the Triple Alliance treaty of 1882. By the secret Treaty of London of 26 April 1915 she undertook to declare war on her former allies, Germany and Austria-Hungary, in return for certain promises. France and Britain, feeling no hesitation about arranging for the disposal of Austrian territories, promised Italy eventual accessions of territory which would give her domination of the Adriatic and 'adequate' colonial compensations. Any suspicions that such hopes would doubtless conflict with the aspirations of other peoples, or that Italy need not be paid too generously once the war had been won, were smothered beneath the overriding desire to win. Italy's support might well have been gained without such bribes, and her alliance proved to be of dubious military value. Her failure to satisfy her expectations played no small part in breeding that mood of national exasperation and intransigence which produced Fascism: so heavy costs were paid in the end.

Similarly, in the Middle East, France and Britain encouraged expectations on the part of both Arabs and Jews that were incompatible. The two allies were highly suspicious of one another, though in the Sykes–Picot agreement of March 1916 Britain acknowledged the claims of France in the Levant. But in 1915 Britain had already agreed to support an Arab movement for independence, and by the Balfour Declaration of November 1917 she advocated 'the establishment in Palestine of a national home for the Jewish people'. On 7 November 1918, after the campaigns of Allenby led to the conquest of Palestine and Syria, a joint Anglo-French statement was issued simultaneously in Palestine, Syria, and Iraq, envisaging 'the complete and final liberation of the peoples who have for so long been op-

pressed by the Turks, and the setting up of national governments and administrations . . .'. To the Arab peoples this
meant support for Arab predominance in Palestine. It is not
certain that such inducements were needed to gain Arab
support for the allies, nor (despite the heroic exploits of
T. E. Lawrence) was their support decisive in the campaigns.

To complicate matters even further, the Sykes–Picot
agreement was made without the knowledge or participation of the Italians, though they had by then joined the
allies. The subsequent agreement of April 1917, by which
Italy tried to secure Anglo-French support for her own
claims, was subject to Russia's endorsement and that – because of the Bolshevik revolution – was never forthcoming:
so it lapsed. The main link between all these agreements was
Great Britain. Her relations with all Powers in the Near East
were henceforth to be haunted by distrusts and resentments.
As Balfour later philosophically remarked, the necessities of
war sometimes induce one to undertake commitments that
one would otherwise prefer not to have made. It was surprising how often these 'necessities' proved, in the end, not
to have been so urgent after all. The price of victory was
artificially inflated.

The material and financial cost of the war for Britain was
immense. As was shown above (in Chapter 1) Britain's live-
lihood was closely bound up with the working of the international economy, and the world's financial equilibrium
was largely controlled by the City of London. Even before
hostilities began in 1914 a financial crisis set in, and it was
not resolved until the end of the year. The war brought disruption of international trade and investment, but until the
pinch was really felt in 1916 the attitude most commonly
adopted and encouraged was Mr Churchill's 'Business as
usual'. To raise its revenue the Government resorted only
mildly to higher taxation, and relied mainly on borrowing.

Throughout the war years taxes met rather less than 30 per cent of the Government's expenditure. Loans were raised on unnecessarily expensive terms. Until the last eighteen months of the war financial policy was highly inflationary in its effects: and when war ended purchasing power was roughly one-third of what it had been in 1914.

Because of her rich accumulation of private and public investments oversea, Britain suffered only slight and temporary foreign-exchange problems. Private owners of dollar securities were invited, at the end of 1915, to sell or lend them to the Treasury, and by the beginning of 1917 the Government took power to requisition some types of security. Of £623 million of securities requisitioned, £332 million were ultimately returned to their owners. The accumulated savings of nineteenth-century Britain went a good way to meet the costs of the war.

War loans, to the Dominions and to the European allies, were a heavier burden and left Britain, in turn, in debt to the United States. These involved depleting the permanent financial assets of the country, and by the end of 1919 such loans by the British Government to other governments totalled some £1,825 million and its borrowings amounted to £1,340 million. To the net loss of 10 per cent of the country's long-term foreign assets must be added another 4 or 5 per cent of her total foreign investment, lost by confiscation in enemy countries or in Russia. Her loss of capital equipment at home (mines, factories, plant) was small as compared with the losses of Belgium or France which became battlefields: a dubious economic advantage in the long run, since the Belgian steel industry, re-equipped with more up-to-date plant at low cost to its owners, was to become a fierce competitor of Britain. The sinking of about 40 per cent of the merchant fleet was her largest single loss of capital equipment; but that was more than replaced during and soon after the war.

To the price paid by such losses must be added the financial burden of pensions and benefits to war-widows and war-veterans, the internal burden of national debt imposed by interest due on war-time borrowings, and the long-term indebtedness to the United States. The price of victory, clearly, would continue to be paid in many instalments during the post-war years: in heavy taxes, economic tensions and crises, and international frictions, no less than in hard cash.

More intangible, yet real, was the price paid in a debasement of values and a sense of moral bankruptcy. The exalting of victory as an end that justified virtually any means was bound to debase moral standards. To devote so much energy to training and equipping men to kill other men, to subject the whole population to the hate-propaganda of war-time and to the slogans of patriotic exhortation coined by the sensational Press, was to contract the horizons of education and of thought. Poison gas was first used by the Germans in April 1915 at Ypres, as an auxiliary to artillery fire in preparation for an attack. It was used contrary to conventions and proved indecisive, but thereafter each side used gas intermittently for the rest of the war. Perhaps hate-propaganda should be regarded as a parallel to poison gas. None dared neglect a weapon which might contribute to victory, however much it violated promises or humanity. National morale was sustained by a flow of tendentious publicity and propaganda that seems shoddy in retrospect, but which was felt to have great virtue at the time. Pacifists and conscientious objectors were treated less gently than in the Second World War. The mood to encourage 'For Victory' was one of militant intransigence – a spirit of ruthlessness and herd-conformity, intolerant of individuality and insensitive to whispers of reason or conscientious scruple. Yet it was, men said, a war to make the world safe for democracy, even a 'war to end war'.

CHAPTER THREE

Into the Waste Land, 1919–23

AFTERMATH GOVERNMENT

PARLIAMENT was dissolved a fortnight after the signing of the armistice, and the result of the 'Coupon Election' was known before the end of the year. Only twenty-six Asquithian Liberals survived the landslide. The Labour Party, with fifty-nine seats representing 2,375,000 voters, became the official Opposition. Otherwise Lloyd George, at the head of the 'coupon' coalition, swept the country. There was so little opposition that there was little active enthusiasm. The few notoriously bloodthirsty remarks of Lloyd George and Sir Eric Geddes, about hanging the Kaiser and squeezing Germany until the pips squeaked, have attracted exaggerated importance by dint of frequent repetition. Yet the mood of the country, if quiet, was not such as would favour any policy of leniency or compromise. Mr L. S. Amery, a successful Conservative Unionist candidate in the election, remarks:

Milner who, in an interview, had deprecated 'gratifying our own feelings of anger or indignation against Germany, however justified,' so long as Prussian militarism was effectively crushed, had been furiously attacked as a pro-German. And in the then state of the public mind Lloyd George was running no risk of incurring that charge. Even my own later campaign speeches, I fear, lapsed somewhat from their opening level.[1]

The elections were unprecedented for other reasons besides the Coalition's tactics and triumph. They were held on the basis of the Representation of the People Act, passed in

[1]. L. S. Amery, *My Political Life*, vol. II (1953), p. 175.

1918, which greatly extended the electorate. Complete manhood suffrage for all men over twenty-one (except peers, lunatics, and felons) was at last established. Women aged thirty or more gained the vote, provided that the woman or her husband was qualified on the local government franchise by owning or occupying land or premises of an annual value of at least £5. These measures added to the electoral registers some 2 million men and 8½ million women, and more than doubled the electorate. Constituency boundaries were changed so as to produce roughly uniform single-member constituencies. Soldiers could vote, though only about a quarter of them did, so rushed were the arrangements for the polls. There were thus many unpredictable factors in the new electorate, which perhaps induced anxious party-leaders to vie with one another in making promises. Of the 478 seats held by the Coalition, no less than 335 were held by Conservatives. The election inaugurated nearly twenty years of Conservative hegemony in British politics. The age of Mr Baldwin was heralded by the victory of Mr Lloyd George.

The uneasy spirit of the new Coalition Government is also well illustrated by Mr Amery, who became Under-Secretary of State for Colonies under Lord Milner as Secretary of State. Milner consented to remain in that office with great reluctance and only on the understanding that Amery would be appointed as his Under-Secretary. 'At the very last moment he discovered that, in spite of Lloyd George's and Bonar Law's promises, I had been dropped out to make way for some more troublesome candidate for office.' Milner's reaction was that 'he not only gave Lloyd George an ultimatum, but held back his own acceptance of office till he knew for certain that my formal invitation from the Prime Minister had reached me'. The ministry was made in this atmosphere of unedifying distrust.

The new Cabinet was, indeed, little different from the old

Coalition Government. It was impressive at the top. It was led by the 'Welsh wizard', then at the climax of his prestige, and his influence on British history was to be prolonged thereby for another few crucial years. Winston Churchill's verdict is indisputable, even when Lloyd George's many faults are weighed in the balance: 'When the English history of the first quarter of the twentieth century is written, it will be seen that the greater part of our fortunes in peace and in war were shaped by this one man.' His chief colleague, leader of the Conservatives and of the House of Commons, was Andrew Bonar Law: a Canadian Scot whose cautious moderation and melancholy scepticism made him a sharp contrast, if also a natural complement, to the ebullient and self-confident Welshman. Their colleagues included several brilliant men who, if they did not constitute a real 'team', were a remarkable coterie of talent. There was Lord Birkenhead who, as 'Galloper' (F. E.) Smith, had risen rapidly in fame and esteem since his entry into Parliament in 1906. He became Lord Chancellor. There was the former Premier Arthur James Balfour, urbane and charming as ever now that he ranked (at seventy) as a veteran statesman: he went, as befitted the nephew of Lord Salisbury, to the Foreign Office. The Chancellor of the Exchequer, a key post in these years of financial upheaval, was the able Austen Chamberlain, son of Joseph. And there was Winston Churchill, at forty-five already a minister of great experience and versatility, who became Secretary of State for War and the most influential Liberal in the Cabinet next to the Prime Minister.

This assemblage of powerful men – and others such as Lord Curzon and Lord Milner – was dominated by Lloyd George. He used the same means as during the war. He continued a 'War Cabinet', meetings of a small number of chief ministers. He continued, too, his private secretariat, housed in the garden of No. 10 Downing Street and so called the 'garden suburb'. When, in 1919, the Committee of Imperial Defence was revived with its separate secretarial staff, the Cabinet nevertheless kept its own secretariat. New ministries survived the war – the Ministries of Labour, of Pensions, and the Air Ministry. Two new Ministries, of Health and of Transport, were set up in 1919.

Not only new departments of State, but the wider activities of older departments and of new public agencies betokened a general increase in State action. The civil service grew in size and importance, doubling in total numbers between 1914 and 1923 and going on increasing thereafter. In spite of (or possibly because of) virtual control by the Government of such industries as coal-mining, railways, and shipping during the war, no measures of formal nationalization were taken during these years, though they were much canvassed. New areas of official encouragement and activity were opened up by the Department of Scientific and Industrial Research (dating from 1916), the Medical Research Council (1920), and the University Grants Committee (1919). The Forestry Commission, to plan and carry out afforestation of crown lands and other additional areas, represented a new anxiety to conserve and develop the country's natural resources. The public service corporation, soon to become a much-favoured alternative to private enterprise and to nationalization, had not yet won political favour, although the model of the Port of London Authority dated from 1908. Instead, opinion preferred bodies with more limited powers, such as the Electricity Commission of 1919, to coordinate rather than run the new growing electrical industry. The British Broadcasting Company was formed under licence at the end of 1922 and given a monopoly of transmission. Powerful agencies were viewed with considerable distrust.

Even the terminology of government and administration changed in a significant way. Until after 1914 not one

department of State was called a 'Ministry'. Secretaries of
State had 'Offices' (the Home Office, Foreign Office, etc.)
and there were 'Boards' of Admiralty, Trade, Local
Government, Education. The war brought 'Ministries' of
Munitions, Labour, Pensions, Air. 'Ministries' rapidly
multiplied after the war, and some former 'Boards' (of
Agriculture and Education) now became 'Ministries'. The
change implied a new image of government, in which politicians and their 'departments' of expert administrators
jointly shaped and pursued policies. This image contrasted
sharply with that common before 1914 when

> the academic theory of the constitution had regarded the high
> places of Government as 'offices' – bundles of legal powers to be
> exercised in turn by individual politicians; not as 'departments',
> organizations of experts pursuing their own altruistic and implac-
> able course.[1]

It may be added that the use and meaning of the term
'administration' suffered comparable decline. Edmund
Burke in 1766 could write *A Short Account of a Late Short
Administration*, referring to the Government of Lord Rock-
ingham. Since 1914 this once general term for government
(including policy-making) has come to be more and more
restricted to the activities of bureaucracy and officialdom,
suitably abbreviated to simply 'admin.'

The post-war political scene was set not merely by the
continuation, until October 1922, of the Coalition Government and the ascendancy of Lloyd George but also by the
emergence of new alignments of forces on the Left, in opposition to the Coalition. The Labour Party, split by the outbreak of war, was healing its wounds. Arthur Henderson
had left the Government in 1917, and thereafter worked for
reunification of the 'pacifist' wing (led by J. Ramsay Mac-

1. W. J. M. Mackenzie, in *British Government since 1918* (1950), p. 58.
It may be a token of further evolution that in 1964 the Ministry of
Education became the 'Department of Education and Science'.

Donald and Philip Snowden) with the rest (led by Henderson and J. R. Clynes). In February 1918 the Party adopted a new Constitution which transformed it from an association of Socialist groups and trade unions into a national party, with constituency branches and individual members, as well as strong trade-union backing. Its programme, *Labour and the New Social Order*, written mainly by the Fabian Sidney Webb, aimed at 'the socialization of industry' and 'planned cooperation in production and distribution for the benefit of all who participate by hand or by brain'. In 1920 the Trades Union Congress also reorganized itself, creating a General Council to wield executive power between congresses and so give the movement greater continuity of policy and action. It became still more closely associated with the reorganized Labour Party through the National Joint Council (which later became the National Council of Labour), and in joint support of the *Daily Herald*, which, in 1919, resumed daily publication as the Party's main organ of publicity. Of the fifty-nine Labour members in the new Parliament, fifty-eight were trade unionists.

Politics were strongly affected by the fact of the Bolshevik Revolution. Only now, indeed, did Marxism become a significant force in British politics. Marxist groups had existed since the formation of Henry Hyndman's Social Democratic Federation in the 1880s. But the existence of a revolutionary Marxist government in Russia exerted new compulsions on Socialists to take a stand for or against the principles of Marxism. This pressure was intensified when, in 1920–1, an independent Communist Party of Great Britain came into existence. When it sought affiliation with the Labour Party it was firmly rebuffed: and the Labour Party Annual Conference of 1924 decided that not only could the Communist Party not be affiliated, but no member of it could stand as a Labour candidate in local or parliamentary elections, or even be eligible for individual membership of the Labour Party. The Communist Party readily adhered to the Third International (Comintern) now operating from Moscow. Thus was the schism between Communism and Socialism made absolute in Britain. While individual members of the Labour Party – even leading Fabians such as G. B. Shaw or the Webbs – acquired great enthusiasm for the experiments of the Soviet Union, and while Labour remained much more sympathetic than Conservatism towards seeking good relations with Russia, the Labour Party kept officially and firmly aloof from Communist aims and methods.

The critical year of transition from war to peace, from full mobilization to demobilization, was the year 1919. While the peacemakers met at Paris to settle the affairs of the world, the Government at home wrestled with social unrest and impending upheaval. The great influenza epidemic, which had struck Britain in the summer of 1918, reached its height by the end of that year and produced a new outbreak during the first three months of 1919. Coming at that moment it added greatly to human misery. In England and Wales 150,000 people died of it, more than 15,000 of them in London alone. In January 1919 Winston Churchill, as Secretary of State for War, had to reverse abruptly the procedure of demobilization, in face of serious demonstrations among the troops and in London. Within a year more than 4 million men were released from the services. Reabsorption of most of them into civil employment was made possible by the economic boom of 1919. Women, however, were often discharged from jobs in industry to make way for ex-servicemen.

The prospect of unemployment caused by rapid demobilization and the end of war-production provoked strikes and riots in Glasgow. The aim was a general strike for a forty-hour week to absorb all available labour in jobs. Led by William Gallacher, David Kirkwood, and Emanuel Shinwell, and representing not the beginning of revolution but only the last flicker of Clydeside revolts, the movement was quelled by troops and police. Other strikes followed sporadically till the end of the year; but the workers as a whole turned increasingly to normal political action and constitutional agitation in search of remedies for their distress. It was the more tragic that the employers and the politicians did not seize this opportunity to tackle the basic causes of economic instability and distress, and modernize the structure of industry.

The Government was committed to 'decontrols', the speedy removal of that effective but often unwelcome regulation of economic activity which had come into existence during the war and which might have been used beneficiently to reshape the post-war economy. During 1919 the controls of trade and shipping were allowed to end. Rationing of food and most price controls ended by 1920. The official date for the end of the war was fixed for 10 January 1920. Factories and stores of 'war surplus' goods were sold off. The Government made every show of its conviction that 'business is business', and that Governments ought to get out of business now that it was 'business as usual'. There was, indeed, considerable consolidation and integration in certain sectors of the economy. The 'Big Five' banks took final shape. The Railways Act of 1921 brought into being the four consolidated railway systems of the inter-war period, which replaced the old companies on 1 January 1923. But the whole climate of opinion in this respect, as in many others, was in favour of a 'return' to normalcy, which meant to freer competitive enterprise and a minimum of political direction.

The economic and social consequences, as soon as the brief boom was over, were disastrous. There was a mania for speculation, especially in the purchase of Lancashire cotton-mills, in shipbuilding and shipping, and in engineering industries: those businesses, in short, in which pre-war Britain had been eminently prosperous. Dreams of easy prosperity diverted capital away from the industries most in need of re-equipment or expansion. Inflation followed, the Government encouraging it rather than seeking to check it until April 1920, when it was too late. Prices rose fast during 1919 and 1920. In March 1920 the price index stood at 323, as against 100 in July 1914. Wages rose too, but more slowly, and for many workers real wages went down as compared with pre-war levels. This helped to focus the attention of trade unionists on collective bargaining for higher wages, rather than on long-term plans for nationalization or shorter hours. Some of the idealism went out of politics, which relapsed to a more earthy struggle for profits or wages, position or power.

In the tactical manoeuvres which this kind of contest involved Lloyd George was a proven master. Faced with the threat of a coal-strike he set up a Coal Industry Commission, nearly half of it representing Labour, under a judge, Sir John Sankey, to investigate the whole industry. It presented an interim report in March and a second report, on nationalization, in June 1920. Lack of clear majority recommendations gave Lloyd George the chance he needed to escape from doing anything radical. A Coal Mines Act in 1919 and a Mining Industry Act in 1920 enacted the seven-hour day and introduced minor reforms and amenities. The coal-mines were left otherwise intact, to be a source of much bitterness and trouble in future years.

The National Industrial Conference that met in February 1919 was presented as a confrontation of employers and workers, coming together to advise an eager Government. It ended in July 1921, when the trade-union members resigned from it in disgust. Two other comparable devices worked better: the 'joint industrial councils' (or 'Whitley Councils') brought together employers' and workers' representatives to discuss not only wages and hours but also such wider industrial problems as production methods, training, and welfare; and the permanent court of arbitration, set up by the Industrial Courts Act of 1919, settled the dockworkers' claim for higher wages which was argued so powerfully by young Ernest Bevin.

It was little wonder that further strikes and threats of stoppages continued. Strikes of the police in 1918 and 1919 caused particular alarm. A sudden and solid railway strike in September 1920 lasted a week and produced dramatic governmental emergency-plans. During the same year, at Bevin's suggestion, Labour movements in general set up a 'Council of Action' to stop the war of intervention against Bolshevism in Russia. Dramatized by the refusal of London dockers to load munitions on the *Jolly George* destined for Polish armies fighting the Russians, the campaign helped to check further intervention. Bevin, as Foreign Secretary a quarter-century later, held credit with the Russians for his action with the dockers in 1920. Faced with the threat of joint action of miners, railwaymen, and transport workers in the 'Triple Alliance', the Government passed an Emergency Powers Act which virtually restored its war-time emergency authority.

The reasons for unrest were more economic and social than political. Prices were high. The acute housing shortage continued long after the Prime Minister's promise of 'homes fit for heroes', and led to many rackets and hardships. During the slump of 1921 unemployment went up to more than 2,170,000. The Government's housing scheme, though not adequate to existing needs, established the notion that housing is a social problem, to be tackled on a national scale by getting houses built. By the Unemployment Insurance Acts of 1920-2, social insurance was extended so as to provide uncovenanted benefits ('the dole'): a step which broke from the strict theory of 'insurance', but which in an

unforeseen way was to become the humane basis for relief
and amelioration for millions in face of mass unemployment.
Here, too, a notion of social obligation for welfare was established, though the Government failed to appreciate or to
tackle the problems of structural unemployment, which now
became chronic in the shipbuilding, mining, and some
heavy industries. Instead of public works and schemes of
imaginative reconstruction, authority applied the economies
of the 'Geddes axe'. Instead of striving to stimulate and
expand international trade, the life-blood of Britain's recovery, it passed in 1921 the Safeguarding of Industries Act,
which imposed on various imports, chiefly from Germany,
duties of 33⅓ per cent. This reversion to tariffs caused fresh
frictions between the already restive Liberals and the Conservative majority within the Coalition. But the accumulated tensions which led to its downfall in October 1922 may
be best considered after examining two other highly controversial sets of issues of these years: the troubles in Ireland
and India, and indeed the reshaping of the Empire; and the
Peace Settlement in Europe and the Near East. These
aroused ancient fears and violent passions, and enticed
Britain further into the morass of violence.

TIMES OF TROUBLES: IRELAND AND INDIA

The 'Coupon Election' of December 1918 opened a new
phase in the Irish Question. When the extremist Sinn Fein
party, strengthened in its appeal by the Easter rising of 1916
and by British attitudes to Ireland during the war, won
every seat outside Ulster except four, half its successful
candidates were in prison. The Sinn Fein representatives
refused to sit at Westminster, constituted themselves a
separate Irish parliament (the *Dáil Eireann*) in Dublin, and
declared Ireland to be an independent Republic. In January they tried to gain formal recognition from the peace-

makers in Paris. Though their claim was no wilder than some that were accepted, they failed.

Henceforth the Party of Arthur Griffith, Michael Collins, and Eamon De Valera represented the main forces making for Irish autonomy. De Valera, President of the Party since 1917, and of the *Dáil* in 1919 (as soon as he escaped from Lincoln jail), was destined to be the focal point of the movement's political unity. American-born, of an Irish mother and a Spanish father, his visit to the United States in 1919 was a personal triumph, though his austere and aloof personality aroused little spontaneous warmth. Inside Ireland the forces aligned for battle, and her worst 'time of troubles' began. The days of John Redmond's Irish Nationalist Party, with its Parnellite aims of Home Rule, were over. Now the destiny of Ireland, like that of the world, was to be determined by war.

Collins's Irish Volunteers turned themselves into the Irish Republican Army (I.R.A.). Armed with smuggled rifles and home-made grenades, it was secretly assisted by members of the staffs of the railways, post office, and even police. Loyal members of the Royal Irish Constabulary (R.I.C.) and their families suffered boycott, ambushes, and assassinations. They were reinforced by recruits from among English ex-servicemen, paid ten shillings a day, and known as the 'Black and Tans' because of their khaki uniforms and black belts. A special division, recruited from ex-officers, was paid a pound a day. These troops were organized to crush the Irish insurrection by whatever means. They were not expected to be gentle or just in their methods. They were meant to meet terror with counter-terror, and they did not fail in their duty. It was the framers of policy, rather than its executants, who must bear most responsibility for the excesses and brutalities that resulted.

The civil war began at Easter 1920, with I.R.A. raids on barracks and income-tax offices all over Ireland. It soon assumed all the features of guerrilla warfare – ambushes, hostages, sabotage, betrayals, tortures, murders. Although both sides indulged in brutalities, the British Government inevitably incurred the greater opprobrium for using such methods.

Meanwhile, at the end of 1920, the Government of Ireland Act partitioned the country into the six counties of Ulster (which, as Northern Ireland, remained part of the United Kingdom) and the other Ireland of rebellion and terror. Each was equipped with a parliament, but the Act was ignored by the south. Fighting went on, with the Ulster Special Constabulary officially recognized and paid by the British Government, and the Irish Republican Government in the south acting more and more as an effective alternative to British administration. During the winter of 1920–1 martial law was declared in eight of the southern counties. In December the 'Black and Tans' burned the city of Cork. Opinion in England at last began to harden against continuance of the war, and anxiety to make a truce intensified during the spring of 1921.

On 24 May elections for the two parliaments duly took place. Again all but four of the 128 seats in the south were won by Sinn Fein, which treated them as new elections to the *Dáil*. The four, representing Trinity College, Dublin, thus ludicrously constituted the legal parliament of Southern Ireland under the Act of 1920. In the north the Unionists returned forty members, the Sinn Fein and Nationalists twelve, and the Belfast Parliament formally opened its session on 22 June. King George V, in his speech in Belfast, appealed for truce with the approval (albeit the last-minute approval) of Lloyd George. Two days later Lloyd George invited Mr De Valera and Sir James Craig (Prime Minister of Northern Ireland) to a conference in London, promising a safe conduct for all who came. It took place in the Mansion House, and a truce was made effective on 11 July.

Lloyd George proposed Dominion status for Ireland, so keeping it within the Empire, and freedom for Northern Ireland to determine its own relationship to the new Dominion. He and De Valera engaged in a lengthy correspondence during the summer (all duly published in the Press), and the situation in Ireland deteriorated meanwhile. The conference to negotiate a treaty met in London in October 1921. No Ulster representatives attended, though the issue of Ulster haunted the meetings: that, and the question of Irish relations with the Empire. What was eventually signed on 6 December was not a treaty but 'Articles of Agreement for a Treaty'. It called Ireland the 'Irish Free State', with the status of a Dominion within the British Empire similar to that of Canada. In Northern Ireland the arrangements envisaged in the Government of Ireland Act of 1920 were to persist for one month after ratification of the new Treaty, and during that month Northern Ireland could keep its existing status if it wished by contracting out of the Free State.

The *Dáil* ratified the Treaty by only sixty-four votes to fifty-seven; both houses of Parliament in London approved it by large majorities; there was little doubt that Northern Ireland would, in due course, exercise its right to contract out. But during 1922 this strife-torn land was to suffer the last agony: a civil war between extremists and moderates among the nationalists themselves, as soon as the unifying force of British military occupation was withdrawn. De Valera formed a new Republican Party, backed by the most intransigent elements of the I.R.A. which now included some Irish-Americans. It fought the elections, held in June, with considerable disorder. The pro-treaty party of Collins won fifty-eight seats, the anti-treaty party of De Valera thirty-five seats, the latter claiming that the only solution now would be to form a coalition government. When this idea was rejected civil war was intensified. With the battle of the Four Courts in Dublin at the end of June it assumed a pattern of open warfare between the Provisional Government of the Irish Free State and republican rebels against its authority. It was a war fought mainly by isolated gunmen in attacks on persons or property. It degenerated into criminal looting, violence, and terrorism. Eminent leaders died in these months: Arthur Griffith in August, of heart failure, and Michael Collins in the same month, shot through the skull. Power passed to newer leaders – W. T. Cosgrave, who became President of the *Dáil*, and Kevin O'Higgins, who became minister of home affairs.

By the end of April 1922 De Valera suspended all 'offensive operations'. Civil war died down, although I.R.A. bands continued sporadic operations for the next forty years. On 6 December the Irish Free State came into formal existence, Northern Ireland immediately contracted out, and the last British troops left Dublin. It was a crude settlement to have cost so much, and Lloyd George's reputation never recovered from his means of attaining it.

The negotiations with Ireland marked a change in the formal designation of the Empire as a whole. The original 'Articles of Agreement for a Treaty' referred to 'the Community of Nations known as the British Empire'. The Constitution of the Irish Free State, in 1922, described it as 'a co-equal member of the Community of Nations forming the British Commonwealth of Nations'. This last description had come into use during the war to describe the relationship between Great Britain and the self-governing Dominions. At the Paris peace conference in 1919 the Dominions and India were separately represented and individually became signatories of the Covenant and members of the League of Nations. The phrase matched well the new conception of a free association of equal partners, and was meant to reassure Irish susceptibilities. When Dominions

accepted Mandates to administer non-self-governing territories, as did Australia, New Zealand, and South Africa,
their own autonomy could hardly be in doubt. Even so, it
was 1926 before an Imperial Conference defined the relationship, and 1931 before the Statute of Westminster gave
statutory effect to the definition.[1]

Meanwhile next to Ireland it was India that began to set
the pattern of future developments, both in nationalist agitation for self-government and in British reactions to such
demands. In August 1917, as a sop to swelling Indian
nationalism, Edwin Montagu, Secretary of State for India,
had proclaimed that the British aim for India was 'responsible government . . . as an integral part of the British
Empire'. The Montagu–Chelmsford Report of 1918 made
proposals which were embodied in the Government of India
Act of 1919. The Act remodelled provincial governments
on the principle of 'dyarchy' – that is, conferring certain
powers on ministers responsible to elected legislative councils, but reserving other specified powers (over police,
justice, and most finance) for the Governor and his officials.
Centrally it produced a similar divided system, a two-
chamber legislature largely elected, but with extensive
powers reserved for the Viceroy and his Executive Council.
The concessions to responsible government were too slight
to satisfy the demands of the Congress Party led by
Mahatma Gandhi. India, too, entered her time of troubles.

The Amritsar Massacre of 13 April 1919 gave Gandhi the
ideal conditions in which to launch his ingenious campaign
of non-violent civil disobedience. After a mob had murdered
four Europeans an unarmed crowd gathered in an enclosed
garden. When it failed to disperse, Brigadier-General
R. E. H. Dyer ordered his troops to fire. By shooting and
panic, 379 people died and more than thrice that number
were wounded. Gandhi's campaign, meant to be strictly

1. See pp. 103 and 149.

limited to civil disobedience and boycott, was always liable
to get out of hand and provoke violence. When, in 1922,
Gandhi called it off the Government sentenced him to six
years in prison. But throughout the decade of the twenties,
disorder, communal riots, and strikes remained endemic in
India, and more stable government seemed unattainable
without a fresh start. Gandhi in prison was far from im-
potent to dislocate government.

In Palestine and Egypt, as well as in Ireland and India,
Britain was encountering the first advancing breakers of the
great tide of nationalism that was to dominate world history
for the next half-century. In Palestine she encountered the
intractability of the Arab–Jewish conflict which was to in-
tensify as time went on. In Egypt, formally a British protectorate, there was a revolt in March 1919. Failing to
reach an agreed settlement, Britain in 1922 unilaterally
recognized Egyptian independence, subject to provisos
about defence and the Suez Canal. Still it was impossible to
negotiate a treaty. By the end of 1924 she was tightening her
control over the country in face of threatened disorder. So,
as in Ireland and India, Britain experienced early forms of
that type of revolutionary warfare which later defeated
ruling administrations in Indo-China, Indonesia, Algeria,
Cyprus, and elsewhere. Guerrilla partisan bands, operating
amid a sympathetic or terrorized civilian population,
acquire great capacities for endurance and for inflicting
heavy losses. Resolute strategies of civil disobedience, boycott, and sabotage were to prove the backbone of resistance
movements. In 1920 their full potentialities were still hardly
appreciated. Nor had appropriate and effective methods,
either of suppression or of 'decolonization', been evolved
and perfected. Meanwhile in Paris, both by what was conceded and by what was withheld, the peacemakers were
creating a settlement in which these very forces of disruptive nationalism would gain in ferocity.

The Treaty of Versailles, Hitler taught the world, was a *Diktat*, a settlement imposed by force upon a helpless Germany by brutal victors. Britain and France went to the Conference, indeed, as the veteran allies which had at last triumphed. They shared a common purpose of trying to extirpate the aggressive militarism of Germany which, they believed, had inflicted so much suffering upon Europe. But they differed considerably about the best means of doing this, about how to reconcile this aim with the many other purposes now in the minds of the allied Powers, and about how far they could recoup their own losses from the vanquished without spreading fresh chaos in Europe. They were also much overshadowed by the presence of President Woodrow Wilson of the United States, commander of giant forces and resources with whom they had perforce to keep on good terms and who liked to enunciate general principles for a peace settlement with which they could not fully agree. He, together with Lloyd George, whose popular mandate had just been overwhelmingly renewed in the 'Coupon Election', and Georges Clemenceau, the French Premier revered in his country as the 'Father of Victory', constituted the 'Big Three'. Their concerted wills prevailed throughout the Paris Conference.

But even they, apparent arbiters of the destinies of much of mankind, were more powerless than they seemed. They were hemmed in by circumstances – by the clamour of their peoples for a speedy settlement which would let them return to the ways of peace, by the exigencies of material conditions, since much of Europe was devastated by war and many Europeans were starving, by the divergences of purpose between them, which must somehow be compromised before the treaties were signed. They were hampered – if not bound – by the impulsive promises they had made in the heat of the battle to their own peoples, to allies, even to enemies. They were limited, above all, by their own characters and position, and the arts of power by which they must seek to remain in charge of their States.

Clemenceau felt bound by France's past – by her bitter experience of two German invasions within his own lifetime, by the fearful blood-letting she had just suffered, and by his resolve that this must never happen again. So he appeared as the man of vengeance, 'the Tiger', restlessly demanding cast-iron guarantees against German resurgence, the fullest extraction of compensations ('reparations', as the world was soon to know them), the deepest humiliation of Germany.

Wilson felt bound by the principles of the 'Fourteen Points' which he had first enunciated, in January 1918, as a statement of allied peace-aims. He believed them to be the foundations of a just peace and they had been accepted, with some reservations, by France and Britain. He felt bound, above all, by the dictates of his own conscience – his inner voice which told him that national self-determination had become a moral principle that men would ignore at their peril, and that the Covenant of the League of Nations, which he insisted on having included in each peace treaty with former enemy States, was the supreme hope of mankind. He was bound, in fact, so tightly by the democratic constitutional requirements of the United States that he failed to get the treaty (and with it the Covenant) ratified by the Senate. But this inherent weakness was not foreseen in 1919, when his presence in Paris seemed the warranty of sanity and justice in the new order.

And Lloyd George – by what and whom was he bound? His large electoral majority of December gave him a free hand at home. His mental agility and diplomatic dexterity gave him great natural advantages in dealing with the aged and bitter Clemenceau and the more slow-moving Wilson –

though neither, as a tough bargainer of slender scruple, could be lightly disregarded. The separate representation of the Dominions at the Conference, giving him the asset of colleagues such as General Smuts of South Africa, made for a company congenial to his views. Adopting a view which lay somewhere midway between the nationalistic realism of the French and the vague idealism of the Americans, he could gain much of what he wanted under the guise of statesmanlike endeavours to bring his two allies into closer agreement. All the natural advantages seemed to lie on his side.

Yet even Lloyd George, as a peacemaker, was not entirely blessed. He, too, had his grave weaknesses and vulnerabilities. He was not insensitive to the mass hysteria and clamorous hatreds of the popular Press at home. He had to endure the undermining attacks of Lord Northcliffe, deeply resentful that the Prime Minister had excluded him from the delegation to the Conference. The troubles in Ireland and India, gathering around his head, caused some embarrassment and impatience to get home. He had scant sympathy with the abstract moralizing of Wilson, yet had to try to win over the President to compromising with the grim realities of Europe. He discovered less orthodox ways of disconcerting Clemenceau. ‘When I saw he was going to be nasty,’ he told Lord Riddell, ‘I always went for him as soon as possible. If you butted in like that, the old boy was quite disconcerted.’ In organization the Conference lacked clear priorities and well-defined, agreed purposes. Balfour called it a ‘rough and tumble affair’, and in the event matters were as often decided by force of circumstance or fortune, as by deliberate concerted agreement. Peacemaking, like warmaking, got out of hand.

The whole process of peacemaking was confined neither to the Paris Conference nor to the Treaty of Versailles, eventually signed with Germany on 28 June 1919. Within a year treaties were also signed with Austria (Saint-Germain), Bulgaria (Neuilly), Hungary (Trianon). The treaty of Sèvres, signed with Turkey in 1920, was rejected and the settlement reached at Lausanne after long fighting did not come into force until August 1924. Just as Poland, by going on fighting the Bolsheviks in 1919, won for itself an extended eastern frontier, so Mustafa Kemal, the new nationalist leader of defeated Turkey, refused to accept Greek occupation of half of Anatolia and was checked only by an ultimatum from Lloyd George in 1922 (the Chanak crisis). Fighting went on in some part of Europe or the Near East throughout the four years of peacemaking, and deliberate violence continued to reap some rewards. In 1923 Italy's new Fascist dictator, Benito Mussolini, sent warships to bombard and occupy the Greek island of Corfu. Although he was induced to withdraw his troops from Corfu, Greece had to pay Italy an indemnity. The example and the lessons of violent action were not lost on the new national States of Europe and the Near East, as resentful of Big Power patronage as they were jealous of one another. The auspices for the inauguration of Wilson's new world were not good.

What did Britain gain and lose from the settlement as a whole? Over Germany she gained immediate naval supremacy, and at the Washington Conference (1921-2) she entered into agreements with the world's other major naval Powers (the United States, Japan, France, and Italy), which stabilized a balance of power in the Pacific for the next twenty years. The ending of the Japanese alliance and the agreed limitations on naval strengths have been described as pointing 'to the end of the naval supremacy of the *Pax Britannica*, gracefully accepted by a poorer, less ardent Britain, imaginatively exploited by the rival thrust of America'. Her naval power in the Atlantic and the Mediterranean was to be challenged again, within fifteen years, by the Rome–Berlin Axis of Mussolini and Hitler; just as

Anglo-American strength in the Pacific was to be challenged by the rise of Japan. For the moment, however, she gained naval security.

Although repudiating territorial annexations, Britain gained 'Mandates', under League auspices, to administer most of Germany's former African colonies (large parts of Tanganyika, the Cameroons, and Togoland), and large areas of the Near East now freed from Turkish rule (Iraq, Transjordan, and Palestine). British Dominions also gained Mandates: the Union of South Africa for German South-West Africa, Australia and New Zealand for several of Germany's Pacific Islands. Such Mandates were all granted subject to varying degrees of accountability, but to the defeated nations the difference from outright annexation seemed slender.

It was soon to become a cause for reasonable doubt whether being a Mandatory Power was an advantage or a liability. The British Mandate over Palestine, specially conditioned by the undertaking of 1917 to establish 'a national home for the Jewish people', was to prove yet another recurrent source of warfare and violence and of international embarrassment until after the Second World War.[1] There were particularly serious clashes between Jews and Arabs in 1921 and again in 1929, British troops and police being engaged in trying to maintain order. Palestine, like Ireland, set the new pattern of irregular terrorist warfare.

Economically it is even more difficult to determine whether, on balance, Britain gained or lost from the settlement. No quantity of reparations could make good her immense material losses. Only the speedy revival of her own national economy, and of the world trade on which it depended, could do that. And just as the impoverishment and (in 1923) the temporary economic collapse of Germany destroyed one of Britain's best pre-war customers, so the

1. See above, p. 56.

nationalist fragmentation of Europe impeded the general revival of international trade. Efforts to exact reparations – in which France rather than Britain took the lead – were to prove especially disastrous for all. They led in March 1921 to allied occupation of the three towns of Düsseldorf, Duisberg, and Ruhrort on the east of the Rhine; to a catastrophic fall in the value of the German mark during the remainder of 1921 and 1922; and to Franco-Belgian occupation of the Ruhr in January 1923. Because these actions were taken without Britain's support, reparations became a constant source of friction and distrust between France and Britain, on whose continuing collaboration the preservation of the whole settlement, as already suggested, ultimately depended. The currency crash in Germany brought about a profound social upheaval, ruining whole classes and encouraging mass hysteria, and was a big landmark on the road to Hitlerism. Since Germany financed both her payments and her recovery by lavish foreign loans on which Hitler defaulted, it is even debatable whether, in the end, Germany paid out more than she appropriated from foreign creditors.

The wisdom of British policy about reparations did nothing to save her from the effects of either French political annoyance or German economic collapse. Nor did it lessen the remarkable effect of the blistering indictment of *The Economic Consequences of the Peace*, written and published in a white heat of indignation at the end of 1919 by the chief Treasury representative at the Conference, John Maynard Keynes. Keynes resigned from his post to write it. Its memorable descriptions of the personalities and scenes at the Conference, and his brilliant attack on the reparations policies made it world-famous. Both in Great Britain and America it did much to build up the belief – later so valuable to Hitlerian propaganda – that the peacemakers were foolish, their only policy vindictiveness, and the Treaty of

Versailles entirely evil. Even this by-product of the settlement had disastrous repercussions, and Sir Arthur Salter later recorded the view that 'on the whole his most famous book, brilliant and sincere as it was, did more harm than good; and that he was most in error when he achieved his most dramatic public success'.[1]

The political climax of the first five post-war years was marked by a sequence of acute governmental crises in 1922–23. Bonar Law's withdrawal from office in 1921 because of ill-health weakened Lloyd George's Government. The Chanak crisis of 1922 caused the resignation of Curzon as Foreign Secretary and angered many Conservatives. On 19 October 1922 a fateful meeting of the Conservatives was held at the Carlton Club, to force the issue and to wreck the Coalition in order to prevent Lloyd George wrecking the Conservative Party as he had already split the Liberals. Its outcome was decided by the appearance of Bonar Law, restored to better health. He attacked the Coalition. Since without his support it was doomed, Lloyd George resigned.[2]

Bonar Law, elected Conservative leader on 23 October, formed a Cabinet of sixteen that included Stanley Baldwin as Chancellor of the Exchequer, Curzon as Foreign Secretary, and Leopold Amery as First Lord of the Admiralty. Baldwin, who thus made his entry into high office, had entered Parliament in 1908, but he reached Cabinet rank only in 1921, at the age of fifty-three. Drawing his wealth from heavy industry but his satisfactions from country life, he was a quiet and not very impressive man, in sharp contrast with the dynamic, reckless, and vociferous ministers

1. Sir Arthur Salter, *Personality in Politics* (1942), p. 142. For an almost equally brilliant French counterblast to Keynes's book, see Étienne Mantoux, *The Carthaginian Peace, or The Economic Consequences of Mr Keynes* (1946); and for criticism of it, Sir Roy Harrod, *The Life of John Maynard Keynes* (1951).

2. Lord Beaverbrook, *The Decline and Fall of Lloyd George* (1963), has given a racy account of these events.

who had prevailed under Lloyd George. His arrival in power marked the dawn of a new age in British politics: more modest and moderate, placatory to the point of sleepiness, and at times mild to the point of inertia.

The keynote of the new age was already sounded in the general election of November 1922. Bonar Law obtained the dissolution of Parliament and appealed for 'tranquillity and freedom from adventures and commitments both at home and abroad'. Even the elections were quiet, by contrast with 1918, and nobody raised issues of principle. The polling returned 345 Conservatives, almost equal numbers of Asquithian and Georgian Liberals, and 142 Labour members. The latter elected, as leader of the Parliamentary Labour Party, James Ramsay MacDonald. MacDonald had been leader in 1914, but his war-time 'pacifism' and his post-war failure to get elected had relegated him to some obscurity.[1] Handsome and eloquent, his flexible voice enhanced by a rich Scottish brogue, with great charm but an air of sad and lofty pride, he was hardly the obvious leader of working-class Socialism. But as the parliamentary spokesman and organizer of the Labour Party at the moment of its massive electoral success he was an almost natural choice. With his entry on to the stage, simultaneously with Baldwin's accession to the Exchequer, the political forces of the next decade were taking shape.

At the beginning of 1923 Baldwin and Montague Norman, the governor of the Bank of England, negotiated the funding of the British war-debt to the United States. Both the terms and Baldwin's handling of them were controversial, but won him public attention. In May 1923 Baldwin (rather than Curzon, who was a peer) was invited by

1. It is necessary, here and elsewhere, to speak of MacDonald's war-time attitudes in inverted commas; for although they were indeed widely misunderstood, it was the misunderstanding of them which mattered politically: see Lord Elton, *The Life of James Ramsay MacDonald*, vol. I, *1866–1919* (1939), pp. 242–341.

King George V to form a Government. He made few changes in the existing team, but introduced as Minister of Health Neville Chamberlain, son of Joseph and half-brother of Austen. Chamberlain steered through an important Housing Act designed to encourage speedier building of small houses by private enterprise. So emerged the third future Prime Minister of the inter-war years.

Baldwin made protection, as a remedy for unemployment, a central issue of his policy. This abrupt resurgence of an old but still lively issue, uniting the Conservatives yet dividing them sharply from the Liberals and most of Labour, has been variously adjudged a blunder of Baldwin's or a master-stroke of electoral tactics. In November Parliament was again dissolved, and he fought the December elections on the single issue of protection. The Conservative majority dropped to 258, the Liberals (now reunited on free trade) gained 159 seats, and Labour won 191 – a spread of seats that brought Labour within reach of forming its first minority Government in January 1924. If Baldwin's overriding aim was to unite his party he paid a high price for its unity. Yet he had got unity, and a weak Labour ministry was no bad prelude to a return of Conservative ministries.

THE WASTE LAND

The thought and the culture of the first five post-war years inevitably reflected the violence of war and the equal violence of reaction against war. English culture had been as profoundly shattered by the experience as had Britain's economy or her international position. It seems likely that public life at all levels suffered a deterioration of standards and a decline of taste. But such tendencies are difficult to prove or to assess, and there was a propensity, already noted, to see pre-war conditions in rosier hue than they had ever merited. It may be that the contrast lay less with pre-war realities than with post-war hopes. Certainly the belief became widespread that the 'Coupon Election' had been a political racket, that the post-war House of Commons was filled with 'a lot of hard-faced men who look as if they have done very well out of the war' – it was Baldwin's own phrase – or, in Sir Harold Nicolson's variant, 'the most unintelligent body of public-school boys which even the Mother of Parliaments has known'. Certainly, too, public life was in many ways very unedifying. The activities of a Horatio Bottomley were strange comment on the world that was to have been made safe for democracy: clearly it had been made profitable for plausible rascals. The mass-circulation 'Yellow Press', descendant of pre-war papers stimulated to wilder excesses by the war years, blossomed anew and reached ever-higher figures of 'registered readers'. In June 1922 Lloyd George's 'sale of honours' in return for generous contributions to party funds became an open scandal. The debate in Parliament led to a Royal Commission and legislation, and contributed to the downfall of the Coalition. As long before as 1916, Lloyd George's reckless promise of a peerage even before consulting the King had led to sharp royal rebukes. But earlier still – in 1912-13 – the 'Marconi Scandal', involving Lloyd George, had aroused allegations that ministers abused their office to make big gains on the Stock Exchange. It led to libel actions and a parliamentary committee of inquiry; and as a modern biographer of Bonar Law remarked of Sir Rufus Isaacs and Lloyd George, 'it is quite certain now that no Minister who behaved as they did would survive for a day'.[1]

However one now assesses the change of tone in public life that followed the war, the change in social manners and morals was then apparent and was much commented upon. The emancipation of women took a multitude of forms:

1. Robert Blake, *The Unknown Prime Minister* (1955), p. 147: see also Frances Donaldson, *The Marconi Scandal* (1962).

from lighter clothing and shorter hair and skirts to more open indulgence in drink, tobacco, and cosmetics, from insistence on smaller families to easier facilities for divorce. Even male dress became brighter, more varied, and much less conventional. But the extent and significance of the new social freedoms may easily be exaggerated. The riotous 'bright young things' depicted by Noël Coward and satirized by Evelyn Waugh got reported in the Press, but were never more than small coteries of society. The 'flapper' to whom Mr Baldwin at last extended the vote in 1928 was a more attractive and less inhibited (if not notably more intelligent) successor to the young Edwardian ladies who had so strenuously agitated for this vote. They, like many more portentous writers and artists of the time, merely liked to 'shock'.

Forty years later the reaction provoked by the social morals, manners, and fashions of the early twenties is by no means one of outrage at immodesty. As the 'schoolboy shape' of female fashions of the earlier twenties changed into the 'schoolgirl shape' of the later twenties, one marvels at how restricted they were in their modernity, how lacking in robust dissipations. Even their wildness was brittle, their cult of self-indulgence as synthetic as the cocktails at their interminable parties, or the jazz played in the night-clubs. People who are anxiously frivolous or self-consciously out to shock soon become tedious. It was not long before they got tired of themselves. The great majority of people, of course, adopted sensibly the greater freedom now available in dress, manners, and movement, but were much too preoccupied with either personal problems (such as housing shortage or lack of jobs) or merely the routine of ordinary life to behave very differently from usual. Divorces, for example, which (excluding separations) had averaged 823 a year in 1910–12, averaged 3,619 a year in 1920–2: a significant yet not startling increase, all things considered. They rose to 7,955 in

1939. This was chiefly because the Matrimonial Causes Act of 1937 added to adultery three further grounds for divorce in England and Wales – wilful desertion, cruelty, and incurable insanity.

These changes of mood and ethos matched closely the current notions of psychology and philosophy, as well as current tastes and trends in literature. Frivolity and self-indulgence were a natural, perhaps inevitable, post-war mood. The whole civil population, no less than the armed forces, had experienced long strain, deprivation, and severities. Freudian psychology, or more correctly the popular version of it concerning sex and inhibitions, was seized upon eagerly. To get rid of your repressions was taken to mean abandoning self-restraint. Much unhappiness, as well as some happiness, resulted. The writings of Havelock Ellis, whose seven volumes on *Studies in the Psychology of Sex* came out between 1897 and 1927, caused tremendous controversy because of their 'shamelessness' of discussion. The novels of D. H. Lawrence and Aldous Huxley supported the same trend, and the new psychology encouraged experiments with a 'stream of consciousness'. James Joyce, in his *Ulysses* (1922), and Virginia Woolf, queen of the literary 'Bloomsbury Set', in her *Mrs Dalloway* (1925) and *To the Lighthouse* (1927), were the most successful practitioners of the art. Biographics, set upon a new path by the irreverent brilliance of Lytton Strachey, evolved deeper concern for psychological interpretation. Strachey's *Eminent Victorians* (1918) and *Queen Victoria* (1921) were frontal onslaughts on the idols of Victorian England. They also set out unashamedly to 'shock'. John Galsworthy's *Forsyte Saga* (1922) depicted the affluent middle class of England before 1914. In *A Modern Comedy* (1929) he described contrastingly the post-war generation. His plays of the twenties dealt discerningly with the economic and social problems of man in modern society.

The pre-war literary giants continued, at first, to dominate the scene – many of them surprisingly little affected, it seemed, by the intervening cataclysm. It was as if they, at least, meant to 'return to normalcy'. Between 1920 and 1924 appeared H. G. Wells's *Outline of History*, Hugh Walpole's *The Cathedral*, John Masefield's *Sard Harker*, E. M. Forster's *A Passage to India*, and perhaps the finest of all G. B. Shaw's plays, *St Joan*. The spate of war-books came mainly after 1924.

Apart from James Joyce, the lead of the literary *avant-garde* fell to the American-born T. S. Eliot. His *The Waste Land* (1922) and *The Hollow Men* (1925) are the poems *par excellence* of these early post-war years of desolation, disjointedness, and doubt. As irreverent as Strachey, as satirical as Shaw, as subtle as Forster, he presented in a sequence of cinema-like flashes an image of the world of lost men. Even his strong anti-democratic views and his love of bathos were symptomatic of the years that gave birth to Italian Fascism. Here, men felt, was the authentic prophet of the age:

> I think we are in rats' alley
> Where the dead men lost their bones.

There was curiously little awareness, at first, that the scientists were making some of the most momentous experiments and discoveries of all time. In June 1919 Sir Ernest Rutherford published an account of his splitting the atom, 'the first artificial transmutation of matter'. Less than six months later the Astronomer Royal at the Royal Society confirmed, as proven true, the astronomical predictions made by Einstein, based on the theories of relativity and space–time continuum which he had first put forward in 1905. In biology the study of genetics and of the living cell began to make momentous progress. In all three fields scientists, with Englishmen prominent among them, reached points of break-through into new realms of thought and understanding. But as yet, by 1924, the impact of these advances was slight.

What affected men most immediately was technology rather than science: such technological derivatives of earlier scientific advance as the motor-car and the aeroplane, cinema and radio. In all such fields the United States held a strong lead, and these years began the process often called the 'Americanization' of English life and culture. Civilization was felt, quite correctly, to be advancing towards great new benefits of material wealth, mobility, transport, communication, and entertainment. Here – once the waste land had been crossed and its aridity overcome – were marvels enough to revive the nineteenth-century faith in progress. In 1919 two R.A.F. flyers flew the North Atlantic, and in 1922 crystal-set enthusiasts could pick up B.B.C. broadcasts. [1] But the discovery attracting most popular attention was not that of Rutherford or Einstein or even Marconi. It was the unearthing, in November 1922, of the tomb of King Tut-ankh-Amen at Thebes. It was full of ancient riches and came complete with a sensational curse upon its discoverers. The Press gave it full publicity, Egyptian styles became a craze, and thousands knew about 'King Tut' who knew nothing of relativity.

1. The mood and atmosphere of the time are recaptured in Asa Briggs, *The Birth of Broadcasting* (1961) and, more informally, in S. Hibberd, *This – is London* (1950).

CHAPTER FOUR

From MacDonald to MacDonald, 1924–9

YEARS OF PROMISE

THE first Labour Government, headed by MacDonald, took office in January 1924. The second, also led by MacDonald, took office in June 1929. The time between these two events was a strange interlude in British national life and in Britain's internal and Commonwealth relations. After the phase of anguished settlement and aftermath which ended in the gloom of 1923, these years came as a time of hope and promise. The waste land, it seemed, had at last been traversed. The most outstanding features of the new landscape were, in economic life, a growing prosperity despite persistent mass unemployment; in politics, a mood of conciliation and pacification marred by the General Strike of 1926; in external relations, an era of better feeling and firmer cooperation, of efforts to establish good relations with Germany and the Soviet Union, marred by outbursts of animosity. We, knowing the outcome and the sequel to this checkered era of promise, must ask whether the signs of better times to come were only a mirage. If they were, why did they seem so substantial and so real at the time? Did men clutch too avidly at straws – at any sign, however slight, that beyond the waste land lay a promised land? Or were the leaders of Britain the hollow men, with real prospects almost within their grasp, which by folly or worse they threw away?

The results of the general election of December 1923, which gave the Labour Party its first chance to assume office, were explicable in many ways. Baldwin's abrupt decision to dissolve and to make protectionism the issue gave advantages to both the opposition parties; Labour, much heartened by its impressive gains in the elections of 1922, made a concerted and spirited national effort; Labour's appeal was strengthened by the feeling that, if its programme differed little from that of the Liberals in concrete proposals, it would carry them out much more reliably than the party of Lloyd George. But among all such explanations must be included the freakish working of the British electoral system. As compared with the previous general election of 1922, the Conservatives now won 38·1 per cent of the total vote as against 38·2 per cent; Labour won 30·5 per cent as against 29·5 per cent. Yet the new House contained eighty-seven fewer Conservatives, and forty-nine more Labour members. A very small swing of votes in the country was magnified into a large swing of seats in the House. The personnel in the Commons changed little: 421 had sat in the previous House. But now Labour with 191 members and the Liberals with 159 could together heavily outnumber the 258 Conservatives, and it was only a matter of time before Baldwin would be defeated and obliged to resign.

It happened on 21 January 1924, and the next day Ramsay MacDonald, son of a Scots farm labourer, kissed hands as Prime Minister and First Lord of the Treasury. Labour took office. 'He wishes to do the right thing,' commented King George V in his diary that evening. 'Today 23 years ago dear Grandmama died. I wonder what she would have thought of a Labour Government!' Whatever Queen Victoria would have thought, people at the time nursed both hopes and fears that were much exaggerated. The Clydesider, David Kirkwood, remarked that: 'Bishops, financiers, lawyers, and all the polite spongers upon the working classes know that this is the beginning of the end.' If so, it was a very mild and gentle beginning. The need for Liberal support in order to survive precluded any specifically socialist legislation. So did the sheer inexperience of the Labour ministers. The Prime Minister had no previous ministerial experience at all. Among his colleagues, only Henderson and Haldane had previously been in a Cabinet. MacDonald decided that the first necessity was an apprenticeship in power, and he used his minority position for this purpose. His decision to wear Court Dress on ceremonial occasions caused a strange outcry in the party – perhaps because it did symbolize the Government's determination to follow established constitutional practices even in such trivialities. At the Albert Hall meeting before taking office MacDonald put it in a phrase: ' "One step enough for me." (*Laughter.*) One step! Yes, my friends, on one condition – that it leads to the next step! (*Cheers.*)'

The ministry was to last only nine months, and the 'next step' was not to come until 1929. Meanwhile Labour in office contributed in two important ways to the new mood of hopefulness which began to prevail. In home affairs it tackled housing and unemployment – the two social evils that were undoubtedly the most urgent: in foreign affairs MacDonald, as his own Foreign Secretary, pursued a policy of pacification.

John Wheatley, the only Clydesider in the Cabinet, was Minister of Health. His Conservative predecessor, Neville Chamberlain, had started to subsidize the building of houses of a certain size, and had extended rent restrictions. But the housing shortage remained acute, prices high, the building trades disorganized; and Chamberlain's small subsidized houses were condemned as 'rabbit hutches'. Wheatley and his able Parliamentary Secretary, Arthur Greenwood, tackled the housing problem imaginatively and with vigour. They prepared a programme to produce $2\frac{1}{2}$ million houses by 1939. The Housing Act eventually became law in August 1924. It was a great personal triumph for Wheatley, and the main domestic achievement of the first Labour Government.

Unemployment proved a more intractable problem. Though figures of unemployed had fallen far below the peak of May 1921, they seemed to have stabilized at over 1 million. In 1924 it was still hoped to reduce this figure drastically, éspecially in those 'distressed areas' where industries in deep slump meant very high local figures of unemployed. The reasons for the stubbornness of this great social problem were appreciated only in later years, and they have been already indicated (see Chapter 2). In 1924 the need for more generous poor relief was met by extending unemployment benefits and by amending the Insurance Acts in several ways. Payments went up from twelve to fifteen shillings a week for women, from fifteen to eighteen for men, and the children's allowance was doubled to two shillings. But as regards more radical efforts to tackle unemployment as a chronic economic problem, the Party was at sixes and sevens. Especially as regards the crucial device of public works financed by central funds, its leaders were deeply divided. A scheme for a national system of electricity supply was somewhat hastily produced. Philip Snowden as Chancellor of the Exchequer fulfilled Beatrice Webb's fears of the previous December – 'chicken-hearted and will try to cut down expenditure – he even demurred to a programme of public works for the unemployed'. Snowden surprised many by his intense financial orthodoxy (three-ha'pence off sugar was not a very heroic fiscal measure); though Colonel Josiah Wedgwood, Labour's Chancellor of the Duchy of Lancaster, was making even more Gladstonian attacks against 'artificially creating work less useful than that which would be put in hand by the normal use of the taxpayers' money if left in their own pockets to spend'. The internal tension within the Labour Party between old-time individualistic radicalism and new-age socialism never mattered more than during its first brief spell of responsibility.

In foreign affairs it was a similar record of partial achievement and partial frustration. One aim was to get on to good terms with the Soviet Union. Normal diplomatic relations, severed since 1918, were restored in February. Then came negotiations about trade and finance, and treaties were signed in August. At the same time MacDonald agreed to the Dawes Plan for settling the vexed question of German reparations, still bedevilling Britain's relations with France and Germany alike. In September he attended the meeting of the Assembly of the League of Nations and took part in drafting, with the French Premier, Édouard Herriot, the 'Geneva Protocol' for the 'Pacific Settlement of International Disputes'. This agreement, unanimously recommended by the Assembly for acceptance by its member States, aimed to close gaps in the Covenant of the League which still left a door open for war. It tried to provide for automatic and compulsory recourse to arbitration. The French accepted it mainly because it sanctified the territorial settlement of 1919. The Labour Government did not ratify the Protocol before it fell, and in March 1925 Austen Chamberlain rejected it. It remained an epitaph – on a gravestone – to the new but brief mood of conciliation induced in 1924, which also produced the Locarno Pacts.[1]

It was over its relations with Communism that the Labour Party fell from power in October, and lost its majority in November. There were two characteristic incidents. In September the Attorney-General, Sir Patrick Hastings, withdrew a prosecution started against J. R. Campbell, acting-editor of the Communist paper, *The Workers' Weekly*, for alleged 'incitement to mutiny'. The Conservatives accused the Government of allowing political considerations to determine the withdrawal and moved a vote of censure. Hastings has shown in his *Autobiography* how MacDonald mishandled the affair until it inflated to a crisis. In the

1. See pp. 98–9.

political atmosphere already excited by attacks on Labour's desire to come to better terms with Communist Russia, the vote was carried by 364 votes to 198. MacDonald went to the country and new general elections took place in October (the third within two years, but the first to use radio for electioneering).

The second incident occurred four days before the poll. The copy of a letter, purporting to be signed by the Bolshevik Zinoviev and sent by the Third International to the still very tiny Communist Party of Britain, came into the hands of the *Daily Mail*. It was an exhortation to insurrection in Britain, and an immediate protest from the Foreign Office to the Soviet Government appeared to prove its authenticity, which the Soviet *chargé d'affaires* in his reply promptly denied. The truth about the 'Red Letter' remains uncertain. Internal evidence, and the felicity of its timing, arouse suspicion that it was a forgery. But in substance it was addressed not to the Labour Party but to the Communist Party, and indeed condemned MacDonald's Government for its bourgeois moderation. Only the excited atmosphere of the time, combined with MacDonald's hesitant handling of the affair, made it harm the Labour Party so much. The oppositions, and much of the Press, seized on it avidly, presented it hysterically, and showed little political scruple or sense of responsibility. Before the letter appeared in the Press Conservative propaganda had worked hard to equate the Labour Party with Communism. Having worked up a Red-spy mania, warning parents against 'plausible men and women who invite their children to attend Sunday Schools and join clubs' where they are 'taught to blow up bridges', Conservative leaflets added blandly: '... there are many Communists today in our so-called "Labour Party"; and so strong are they that even our Socialist Government must do their bidding'. The Zinoviev letter seems, in retrospect, too splendid and appro-

priate a climax to such propaganda to be entirely genuine.
Nor was the original of it ever produced.

The result of the election was so catastrophic for Labour
that it has been commonly attributed to the 'Red Letter'
scare. The Conservatives gained 161 seats and returned to
power with a backing of 419 members. Labour lost forty
seats. But again, as in 1923, the electoral system greatly distorted the shift of opinion and the crucial factor was the
decline in Liberal votes. Labour gained 33 per cent of the
poll and well over a million votes more than in 1923. The
true picture is that both parties gained, in votes and even
seats, at the expense of the Liberals. It was the Liberals,
dropping sharply from 159 to 40 seats, who were perman-
ently affected. Henceforth they became decisively the third
party in the State. What the 'Red Letter' scare may have
done was to drive some who had previously abstained and
some who had previously voted Liberal to vote Conservative. But it hardly determined a Conservative victory. Reduction in the number of triangular contests (with seventy-
five more Labour candidates in the field, and 115 fewer
Liberal, than in 1923) possibly did as much as the famous
'Red Letter' to ensure Conservative majority in the
Commons. At least political apathy had been smashed,
even if political responsibility had not increased.

The Labour Government resigned on 4 November. One
effect of the whole experience on the Labour Party was to
reinforce its hostility to the Communists. The Labour Party
Conference in 1925 reaffirmed, by nearly 3 million votes to
321,000, that individual Communists could not legally be
members of the Labour Party. Another effect was to give it
an excellent weapon against any future repetition of stunts
just before elections: public opinion remained sensitive to
suggestions of planned panic. A result of Labour's first
tenure of office was the departure from the Party of the
Independent Labour Party (I.L.P.) of James Maxton, now

convinced that Labour had failed for lack of courage. In Sir Patrick Hastings's view the spectacle of Labour in office for most of a year brought about a 'revolution in political thought' whereby to be a Labour man became 'if not respectable, at least permissible'. The band of missionary zealots was being converted into a responsible political party, recognized as a future component not only of British parliamentary life but of actual government.

Its successor, led by Stanley Baldwin, was so strongly based on a majority in the Commons that it lasted for nearly the full parliamentary term of five years. Winston Churchill was its Chancellor of the Exchequer, Austen Chamberlain its Foreign Secretary. Neville Chamberlain was back at the Ministry of Health and Lord Birkenhead was Secretary of State for India. It did not lack brilliance. But the tone imposed by Baldwin was, in his own words, 'Give peace in our time, O Lord!' It scrapped treaties with Russia and the Geneva Protocol. Baldwin remarked, 'I do not myself know what the word "Internationalism" means. All I know is that when I hear it employed it is a bad thing for this country.' Such bland insularity was not typical, however, of the foreign policy pursued by his Foreign Secretary. Coinciding with Herriot and Briand in France, and in Germany with Gustav Stresemann, who sought to guide his country back to good terms with its neighbours through 'fulfilment' of the already revised settlement of Versailles, Austen Chamberlain became identified with the 'spirit of Locarno'. In this he continued and developed MacDonald's work at Geneva.

The *rapprochement* between Britain, France, and Germany came to its climax in the Locarno Treaties, whereby the Franco-German frontier was guaranteed by Britain and Italy. It sprang from a new pattern of relations in Europe. Germany, freed from the real burden of reparations by the Dawes Plan of 1924 and the large American loans which followed it, enjoyed economic recovery and prosperity. France, still anxious about her national security but reconciled to lack of solid territorial safeguards, found the diplomatic reassurances of Locarno more acceptable. With Russia still the great outcast Power, it was only prudent to bring a resurgent Germany into closer association with her neighbours, and in 1926 she was admitted as a member of the League of Nations. In Italy Mussolini, the Fascist dictator, was still consolidating his own position internally, and had not yet embarked on adventures in expansion. To this lull Chamberlain's policy contributed, and from it the Baldwin Government benefited.

At home a gradual improvement of economic conditions and a temporary easing of unemployment figures to slightly below the 1 million level contributed a good deal to the sense of national recovery. The Government's financial policy was not imaginative. Churchill, led by his advisers at the Treasury to pursue a policy of 'deflation', in 1925 returned to the gold standard, restoring the pound sterling to its pre-war value. This caused considerable strain on the economy. It hampered British exports, which tended to be over-priced in world markets at a time of severe competition. It was the symbol of Conservative devotion to rigid financial orthodoxy, ridiculed by Maynard Keynes in his brilliant little pamphlet, *The Economic Consequences of Mr Churchill*. It helped to keep unemployment high in British export trades even in the later 1920s, when other countries enjoyed an industrial boom. It exposed Britain more nakedly to the effects of the crash on Wall Street in 1929. It was in some ways the last flicker of the dying hope that salvation could be found by going back – that 'recovery' and 'normalcy' referred to pre-1914 conditions. A large number of other countries returned to gold within the next year or two, but not all at pre-war parities. It was a decision of the City, not of industry. The Bank of England, to prevent loss of gold, had to keep up high interest-rates. This, in turn, kept up the burden of national debt charges, and so of taxation. It hampered enterprise. It ignored the structural changes brought about in Britain, and in world trade, by events of the previous decade. It particularly hit the coal-miners, as both Keynes and Ernest Bevin predicted in 1925, and so contributed to the situation which produced the General Strike.

When Baldwin took office the King urged him to 'combat the idea of anything like class war'. So far as his own even temper and good nature, an empirical approach and a reluctance to do anything spectacular could serve this end, Baldwin would loyally serve it. The mood was fostered by the conversations between the industrialist Sir Alfred Mond and the T.U.C. leader Ben Turner aimed at seeking peace in industry. The 'Locarno spirit' spread to industrial relations. But neither Baldwin nor his Cabinet had any coherent philosophy, still less any concrete policy, with which to work actively for social pacification. 'He would sniff and snuff at problems,' writes Sir Harold Nicolson, 'like an elderly spaniel.' The most systematic action came from Neville Chamberlain as Minister of Health. His achievements in these years give him a place among the founders of the Welfare State, and earned him a reputation which in 1937 was to carry him to the Premiership. His series of 'connected reforms' in poor law, national insurance, and rating involved twenty-five separate Acts of Parliament. In aggregate they carried out a complete overhaul and systematization of local government and of its relations with the Ministry of Health. They brought all the health, insurance, and poor law services into one scheme, extended health insurance and pensions schemes, and concluded several minor measures, such as those for smoke abatement and the sale of proprietary medicines. Its major Acts were the Pensions Act (1925), a Rating Act (1925), and the Local Government Act (1929).

These measures amounted to a new basis, cautiously but

successfully laid, for subsequent transition to the Welfare State. Other measures of the Baldwin Government helped towards the same end, even if no ministers then foresaw or wanted this as their larger consequence. They added to the machinery of public services, while broadening the democratic basis of the State, and form one of the strands of real continuity in English political and administrative development between the wars. In 1926 the Central Electricity Board was set up by the Electricity Supply Act, accountable to the Minister of Transport but empowered to plan and produce a national power supply. In the same year the British Broadcasting Company was replaced by the British Broadcasting Corporation, chartered as a public corporation. In 1928 a new Franchise Act extended the vote to women at the same age as to men (twenty-one), and so completed the trend to universal suffrage with what came to be known as Baldwin's 'votes for flappers'. These piecemeal and moderate foreshadowings of a more fully social-democratic State, so characteristic both in their cautiousness and in their recognition of the need to move with the times, were in strange contrast to the violent animosities aroused by the General Strike. Yet without these Baldwinian placatory gestures, might not the General Strike have had more catastrophic results? Before examining that great landmark in British social history of the twentieth century, it will be convenient to glance at Baldwinism in the British Empire, where its characteristics already noted in home affairs had a very close counterpart.

LIBERAL EMPIRE

The Constitution of the Irish Free State in 1922 described it as 'a co-equal member of the Community of Nations forming the British Commonwealth of Nations'.[1] The years

1. See p. 73.

between 1924 and 1929 were a formative period in the history of this new 'Commonwealth' which was rapidly – and often *de facto* before it was *de jure* – replacing the older concepts of the 'British Empire'. There was a double trend towards accepting the complete autonomy of the white Dominions (i.e. the Irish Free State, Canada, Australia, New Zealand, and the Union of South Africa), and also towards varying degrees of devolution of responsibility and delegation of power to the governments of the other major components of the Empire (e.g. India, Ceylon, Malaya).

The autonomy of the Dominions in foreign policy had already been largely conceded by their separate representation at the peace conference in 1919, their separate membership of the League of Nations, and the conferment of mandates on Australia, New Zealand, and South Africa. It had been emphasized in 1922 over the Chanak incident, when Lloyd George found Canada and South Africa unwilling to give military backing to British diplomacy; and again in 1925, when it was specified that Britain's obligations under the Locarno Pacts did not extend to the Dominions or to India. As early as 1922, Canada had negotiated a treaty with the United States on her own, and in 1926 she appointed a Canadian Minister in Washington. All these changes of practice, together with the virtually complete autonomy exercised by the Dominions over their internal affairs and with the swelling demand for greater self-government and even independence for India, led to the question of a new 'Constitution' for the Empire.

Balfour, as Chairman of the oddly named Inter-Imperial Relations Committee, produced for the Imperial Conference of 1926 a formula which was to become the doctrine of the new liberal 'Commonwealth of Nations'. While refusing to try to lay down a new Constitution for the Empire, Balfour framed the famous definition of Dominion status which was adopted by the Conference.

They are autonomous communities within the British Empire, equal in status, in no way subordinate one to another in any aspect of their domestic or external affairs, though united by a common allegiance to the Crown, and freely associated as members of the British Commonwealth of Nations.

As Great Britain was itself included in this description, the formula revolutionized the former 'mother country' theory of Empire. It was explained that: 'Equality of status so far as Great Britain and the Dominions are concerned is thus the root principle governing our inter-imperial relations.' This highly egalitarian theory had two consequences, both momentous for the future development of the Commonwealth. It created a special category of States, enjoying 'Dominion status', which meant complete self-government and autonomy but also continuing membership of this new community 'united by a common allegiance to the Crown'. It thus became possible for other parts of the Empire, as yet deficient in such status, to aim at achieving national independence *within* the Commonwealth (like Canada) instead of by leaving it (like the United States). 'Dominion status' could become an aspiration of colonial territories wishing to keep the advantages of the connexion with Britain. The second consequence was that, since the new egalitarian theory had far outrun realities, Great Britain had to be accorded in fact that special position within the Commonwealth which her history, resources, population, and geographical position conferred upon her. Despite mere 'equality of status' with the Dominions, she had to bear the main burden of imperial defence and foreign policy, she had the lion's share of investment and trade. Equality of function or 'stature' could not accompany equality of status. From these two consequences of the 1926 doctrine much of the subsequent development of the Commonwealth was to flow.

The Conference was rash enough to assert that the

position of the self-governing communities had 'as regards all vital matters, reached its full development'. It was wrong, as events of the next decade were soon to show. But that cautious Commonwealth statesmen made so rash an assertion in 1926 is itself a symptom of the new feeling in the world at that time. Things had reached a turning-point; many of the grimmer features of the past had gone for good; a new age lay ahead. The British Empire Exhibition at Wembley in 1924 (repeated in 1925) reflected this sense of pride in progress. *The Times*, adept at expressing mid-Victorian sentiments in a twentieth-century context, struck the characteristic note in its leader about the opening of the Wembley Exhibition:

Many a young man of our cities will find it difficult to walk past the oversea pavilions – with their suggestion of adventure, and space, and a happy life under the open skies of the bush, the prairie, and the veld – without feeling that almost irresistible tugging at the heartstrings which drew the pioneers of old to cross the oceans and to blaze the trail for those who followed. But, when it comes to hard facts, it is no use for our young men to go, and it is no use our sending them, unless we first find markets for their produce.

The Empire was facing 'hard facts', though British statesmen were somewhat perplexed as to how they should be handled.

Other common concerns were arising, too, to keep the Commonwealth together. The agenda of the Imperial Conferences of these years included discussion of trade and aviation. In 1925 the Imperial Economic Committee was set up to study and promote trade and marketing within the Commonwealth. The Imperial Shipping Committee dated from 1920. Imperial Economic Conferences began to be held, parallel to but less regularly than the political conferences (held roughly every four years from 1887 onwards). Trade with the countries of the Commonwealth remained a high proportion of British trade. Before 1914 some 35 per cent of Britain's home-produced exports went to the Empire: between 1919 and 1926 more than 38 per cent did so. India had always played an exceptionally large part in the British trading system; her agricultural production matching her demand for manufactured goods, especially textiles. India and other mainly agricultural countries with which the British traded could now find other sources of supply and were themselves becoming more fully industrialized. Imperial trade and investment therefore bristled with problems, studied but not very actively tackled in these years. In 1926, however, the Empire Marketing Board was set up, to promote imperial trade by scientific research and publicity.

Aviation had dramatic effects on a community as widely dispersed geographically as the British Commonwealth. Imperial Airways, with a government subsidy, was set up in 1924. Its regular weekly service to India began in 1929, and during the next decade it pioneered routes to all other parts of the Commonwealth. The remarkable personal appeal of the royal family, lent a new undertone by the long and critical illness of George V in 1928–9, and by the empire tours of Edward, Prince of Wales, throughout the twenties, gave the Crown even greater psychological reality as a focus of 'common allegiance'.

Within India itself these were years of preparation for greater storms to come. Under Lord Reading as Viceroy (1921–6) tensions were relaxed. His successor, Lord Irwin (later Lord Halifax), was confronted with the dilemmas of the Simon Commission. The Commission of Inquiry into the working of the 1919 Constitution represented all shades of British opinion, but it included no Indians. Its chairman, the able Liberal lawyer Sir John Simon, conducted his work with skill, impartiality, and speed. Gandhi, whose influence had spread during the years since 1921, decided to boycott all its inquiries. Lord Irwin issued a message to Indians, proposing equal Dominion status as the natural culmination for India's constitutional progress. The Simon Report, envisaging a federal solution to India's constitutional complexities, became the basis for the first Round Table Conference in 1930. That, too, was boycotted by Gandhi and the Congress Party. But when the Conference adopted a Liberal programme based mainly on the Simon Report, Lord Irwin induced Gandhi to accept it and to call off his civil disobedience campaign. Gandhi, indeed, came round to Irwin's view of India's destiny and, as Irwin informed the King, agreed that independence 'in association with Great Britain' would be 'the highest form in which it can be attained'. It was a great turning-point in relations between the two countries.

The connexion with India, and the urge to keep open a secure route of communication between Britain and the Indian Ocean via the Middle East and the Suez Canal, affected British relations with Egypt and the Sudan. During the war Britain had declared a protectorate over Egypt. After experience of clashes with the raw nationalist movement led by the Wafd Party, in 1922 she unilaterally declared Egypt independent, subject to four important reservations about security of communications, defence against foreign aggression, the protection of foreign interests and of minorities, and the Sudan. Repeated attempts thereafter to make a treaty agreement failed because the Wafd refused to accept the reservations. When in 1924 the Governor-General of the Sudan was murdered, Britain insisted on the withdrawal of Egyptian troops from the Sudan. In 1926 the Wafd leader, Saad Pasha Zaghlul, died, and was succeeded by Mustapha Nahas Pasha. The constitution of 1923 worked badly, and unsatisfactory stalemate endured until the treaty of 1936.

In the Sinn Fein party of Ireland, the Congress party of India, and the Wafd of Egypt, British administration encountered militant varieties of the new nationalist movements of under-developed countries, destined to become still more active and still more successful after the Second World War. As yet most British colonial territories hardly knew such movements, though they began to come into existence. The Ceylon National Congress dated from 1919, and some constitutional concessions were made to it in 1923. By 1931 a new Constitution, based on the proposals of the Donoughmore Commission of 1927–8, was brought into effect. It may serve as prototype of the direction and devices of developments towards more responsible self-government in the dependent territories.

The members of the Commonwealth enjoying full 'Dominion status' had parliamentary systems modelled to a greater or less extent on the British system. In dependent territories the most common pattern was a Governor responsible to the British Government, aided by an Executive Council, and in a few cases a Legislative Assembly composed partly of nominated (official) members, partly of members elected on a very restrictive franchise. The latter systems could be liberalized in several different ways and to subtly different extents. The Governor could be told to conform increasingly to the wishes of the Executive Council, the Council could be made in various ways accountable to the Assembly, the Assembly could be strengthened in its elected members, and the franchise on which they were elected could be widened. In the leading instance of Ceylon nationalist demands originally took the form of asking for a higher proportion of elected members of the Legislative Council, and their election for territorial constituencies rather than by communities. Fragmentary concessions led, by 1927, to a certain divorce of power from responsibility, which the Donoughmore Commission tried to remedy. It could be remedied only by giving more responsibility to Ceylonese ministers and by greatly enlarging the electorate. Both were done by 1931, and virtual universal suffrage was

introduced for election of fifty members of the new State
Council.

The flexible if complex pattern of government exempli-
fied in Ceylon was later adopted and adapted for other
colonies, especially in Africa. Together with the vista of
ultimate Dominion status, this system made possible the
advance, on a broad front yet at differing rates, towards full
self-government and independence. It was in the twenties
that this evolutionary path first became clear. The image of
a new 'Liberal Empire' was just emerging, sometimes
empirically and smoothly, sometimes only with wasteful
frictional heat. But there was one type of colonial territory
to which this pattern could hardly be applied: to multi-
racial communities with a minority of European settlers,
such as Kenya (created in 1920 from the East Africa Protectorate) and Rhodesia. In Kenya the 10,000 white settlers
wanted 'responsible government' for themselves, but could
not envisage sharing responsibility or power with the
3 million Africans and 23,000 Indians in the colony. In
1923 the Colonial Office declared that the interest of the
native population must always be 'paramount', thus ruling
out the idea of granting 'responsible government' to the
settlers alone. On the spot the settlers remained predomi-
nant in power, and an acute problem was shelved until a
generation later.

GENERAL STRIKE

The General Strike of 1926 is one of the most controversial
and significant events of the inter-war years. To the making
of the situation which produced it converged most of the
industrial dilemmas, political party feuds, and social schisms
of post-war Britain. From it flowed many of the constituent
elements in the industrial and parliamentary history of the
following decade. From its oddly haphazard beginnings,

through its tortuous course, to its inconsequential outcome, it affected almost every family in the land from the Royal Family down; even party feuds in Bolshevik Russia, it is claimed, were greatly influenced by its failure.

There are two crucial questions: why it happened at all, and why it acquired this outstanding significance. It was not the climax of general industrial unrest in 1925–6. It was brought about by a coal-miners' strike, and the coal industry was 'the cockpit of the industrial struggle'. Between 1911 and 1945 the miners, who constituted little more than 6 per cent of the industrial workers, provided nearly 42 per cent of all strikers. Persistent crisis in the industry most basic to the prosperity of pre-1914 Britain naturally had repercussions on the whole economy. Not only was the Miners' Federation one of the strongest trade unions, but it had once formed the 'Triple Industrial Alliance' with the Railwaymen and the Transport Workers. The Alliance was a potentially formidable instrument for either industrial battles or political pressure.

The Alliance, however, had known bitter defeat on 15 April 1921, remembered among trade unionists as 'Black Friday'. A strike called by the Triple Alliance was countered by Lloyd George's Coalition Government with vigorous emergency measures and a show of military force. In considerable confusion the union leaders called off the strike. The miners had to resume work on the mine-owners' terms. The incident earned for the Alliance the name of the 'Cripple Alliance', and made way for an alternative voice of the mass of trade unionists, the General Council of the Trades Union Congress.

A second memorable moment, known in contrast as 'Red Friday' (31 July 1925), was a more immediate prelude to the events of 1926. The mine-owners proposed severe cuts in wages and gave notice that they were terminating the National Wages agreement of 1924, made when French occupation of the Ruhr had eliminated German competition in coal. The return to the gold standard at pre-war parity had meanwhile, as already shown, deepened the crisis in the mining industry. The Miners' Federation, guided by its president Herbert Smith and its secretary, the former Baptist preacher, Arthur James Cook, refused to discuss the owners' terms. It put its case in the hands of the General Council of the T.U.C. while Baldwin set up a Court of Inquiry. The deadlock was ended by Baldwin giving way and granting a subsidy until May 1926, to allow time for a full inquiry into the industry. But the Government also set about preparing plans, and an unofficial 'Organization for the Maintenance of Supplies' (O.M.S.), to meet the threat of a general strike, came into being. Thus one important effect of Red Friday was that in 1926 the Government was as well prepared to counter strike action as it had been on Black Friday. The union leaders, on the other hand, dared not risk another Black Friday. The clash became unavoidable because of such changes of mood and circumstance.

To conduct the promised inquiry Baldwin set up a four-man Commission under Sir Herbert Samuel. Its members had two things in common: none represented labour and none had any experience or special knowledge of the coal industry. Its unanimous report of March 1926 included long-term proposals sympathetic to the miners, but short-term recommendations (reduced rates of pay and no subsidy) which the unions felt compelled to reject. Triangular discussions ensued. Lord Birkenhead wrote: 'It would be possible to say without exaggeration of the miners' leaders that they were the stupidest men in England, if we had not had frequent occasion to meet the owners.' On this remark, the comment of Mr L. S. Amery was: 'He omitted the prior claim of the Government itself, whose financial policy was so largely responsible for creating the situation in which both sides found themselves, and whose inhibitions and internal divisions forbade the obvious remedies that might have eased it.'

As the miners' contention had always been that even existing wages were too low for a decent standard of living, they would not budge on that point. Their strike began on 26 April. The owners, whom Neville Chamberlain described as 'not a prepossessing crowd', would not hear of a national minimum wage and demanded district agreements and wage-cuts. The aim of the General Council of the T.U.C., as of Baldwin himself, was to prevent a general strike. But positions had now been taken, postures struck; and the T.U.C. called a 'partial' national stoppage to support the miners' cause, to begin at midnight on Monday 3 May. It was not, and was not meant to be, a 'general strike', but only a selective sympathetic strike. It extended, however, to all forms of transport, the main heavy industries, the building and printing trades, gas and electricity workers. Other unions were kept in reserve as a 'second line'. It was clearly aimed to put pressure on the Government, which retaliated by vigorous measures to ensure essential public services. The country had stumbled into strife.

One feature of the whole story was the element of fatality. At moments of decision something apparently fortuitous or even farcical would intervene. On the Sunday evening before the strike began, last-minute feverish efforts of the T.U.C. and the Government to prevent it were stultified by two such events. The printers' 'chapels' of the *Daily Mail* refused, on their own initiative, to print an editorial which they held to be an incitement to strike-breaking. George Isaacs, secretary of the National Society of Operative Printers and Assistants, tried in vain to get the men to print it. News of the refusal was brought to the Cabinet (by Churchill, according to Bevin). It produced an immediate stiffening of attitude and a stern demand to the T.U.C. delegates to repudiate the printers' 'overt act' of interfering

with freedom of the Press, and withdraw its strike instructions. The delegates, taken completely aback by this new
turn of events, retired to draft a repudiation of the printers.
When they returned to present it to Baldwin they found all
the lights out, the Cabinet room empty; and Baldwin retired to bed. He explained later, to a friend, that he had
done all he could and there was nowhere else to go. In so
casual a way did the great event come to pass. Yet behind
the casualness lay the exasperations of tired men, the con-
flicting pressures of firebrands and moderates, the legacy of
distrusts (was it not the *Daily Mail* that had produced the
'Red Letter' scare two years before?). It was the product of
all post-war industrial strife and of its residual exasperations.

For the Government it was a threat to the Constitution; for the
General Council a tiger to be ridden; for some alarmists (or opti-
mists) the dawn of revolution. Now tens of thousands of British
citizens were to confound all these views by finding the strike the
most enjoyable time of their lives.[1]

The 'general' strike lasted nine days, from 3 to 12 May.
During that time the Government's emergency plans came
into operation with surprising smoothness and effect.
People got to work somehow, on foot or in a strange assortment of vehicles. Outside the big towns the population was
little affected. In the big towns, amid a mixture of good-
humoured neighbourly help and stern Governmental provision, people carried on. Mr Amery remarked many years
later that the strike was thirty years too late: the existence
of radio (with some 2 million regular listeners) and of large
numbers of private cars made the shortage of Press and of
public transport a minor inconvenience, not the paralysing
weapon envisaged by the myth-makers of revolutionary
syndicalism.[2] There were countless local riots and spontane-

1. Julian Symons, *The General Strike* (1957), p. 53.
2. The strike helped to define the position of the B.B.C. in national
life: see A. Briggs, *The Birth of Broadcasting*, pp. 360-84.

ous acts of violence, but both the Government and the T.U.C. strove to restrain the militants. These disturbances were never coordinated, and remained mere 'rumblings before a storm that never broke'. Perhaps Baldwin's greatest act of wisdom was now, having prepared, to let things take their course and to restrain the few members of his Cabinet (including Churchill and Sir William Joynson-Hicks the Home Secretary) who wanted more dramatic actions. Churchill he preoccupied with editing the new official *British Gazette* – 'the cleverest thing I ever did', Baldwin later chuckled: 'otherwise he would have wanted to shoot someone'.

To the million mine-workers already on strike were added more than another million men. When the strike was called off nine days later there was no evidence of a substantial return to work meanwhile. This degree of workers' solidarity after years of severe unemployment was impressive. Much of the drive and direction that were provided for the strike came from the vigorous founder and general secretary of the Transport and General Workers' Union, Ernest Bevin. He was a member of the General Council, and so far as it was saved from being a fiasco it was chiefly his doing. But if it was not a fiasco, neither was it a success. It gave an impressive demonstration of support for the miners' cause, and probably on balance public opinion was warmly sympathetic to that cause. But the Sorelian myth of the 'General Strike', of 'direct action' on a scale great enough to coerce Governments and paralyse nations, was not one accepted by the mass of British opinion, nor even by the organized workers themselves. It was a method not at all compatible with democratic government or parliamentary procedure, and efforts by MacDonald and others to argue this had been brusquely brushed aside. In embarking on even a 'partial General Strike', or what the T.U.C. insisted on calling a 'National Strike' of sympathy, the General Council had gone further than public opinion would readily go. This predicament, between sympathy for the miners and reluctance to undermine democracy and challenge a parliamentary Government, was painful to most citizens. In the end their choice would be in little doubt.

The deadlock was broken by the intervention of Sir Herbert Samuel, acting entirely personally and negotiating in secret with the T.U.C. leaders. When the miners refused his proposed basis for resuming negotiations the T.U.C. called off the General Strike because they felt 'not justified in permitting the unions to continue the sacrifice for another day'. Since Samuel had acted in a private and unofficial capacity, the Government could insist that it was uncommitted. This made the outcome a test for Baldwin's capacity to restrain his more fire-eating colleagues. Perhaps it was because he ruled that the crisis passed without reaching the brink of civil war: though *The Times* commented, in its back-handed way, 'Mr Baldwin is infinitely more valuable for what he is than for anything in particular that he does.' In Russia the advocates of world revolution were discredited, and soon were to suffer Stalinist purges in preparation for 'building socialism in one country'. In Britain, at least, 'direct action' aimed at producing revolution was now popularly discredited and parliamentary government was fortified anew.[1]

The General Strike was called off on 12 May. The miners' strike went on, amid increasing hardship, for another six months. The General Council had gained no terms

1. There is a large and still growing literature on these events. The main sources are Alan Bullock, *The Life and Times of Ernest Bevin*, vol. I (1960); G. G. Eastwood, *George Isaacs* (1952); L. S. Amery, *My Political Life*, vol. II (1953); Viscount Samuel, *Memoirs* (1945); A. W. Baldwin, *My Father: The True Story* (1955). See also R. P. Arnot, *The Miners: Years of Struggle* (1953), and the lively journalistic account by Julian Symons, *The General Strike* (1957). Much is still obscure and open to contrary interpretations.

at all for either the miners or those who struck in support of them. Many were victimized for having taken part in it. The two or three days after 12 May were almost more dangerous than the nine days before it, because of widespread anger with the T.U.C. and the 'betrayal'. The number on strike increased by 100,000 within the twenty-four hours after its nominal 'end'. Tempers were dangerously frayed. But the plight of the miners was irretrievable. When at last their strike was ended they forfeited everything they had fought for: national agreements, shorter hours, better wages. The miners had lost some £60 million in wages. The strike had drained the funds of the unions, and made support of strike action impossible for some time to come. Union membership, too, fell off, and numbers affiliated to the T.U.C. declined even more sharply. As if to perpetuate this moment of trade-union weakness and debility, the Government passed in 1927 the Trade Disputes and Trade Union Act, making all sympathetic strikes illegal and attacking the political use of union funds. The measure was important in two ways. By its apparent vindictiveness it undid much of the good achieved by Baldwin's policy of moderation during the strike; it embittered class and party feelings unnecessarily. It also gave the Labour Party a mission to repeal the Act as soon as it had a clear majority – a pledge which it fulfilled in 1946.

The whole drama, tragic and comic by turns, evoked deep loyalties and strong passions. Few of the leaders in public life, in any sphere, came out of it with unblemished credit. If each side had its wild men, fortunately each also had its moderates. Civil leaders now, like military leaders in the Great War, fumbled and stumbled until events themselves took charge. The real hero – if there was one at all – was the ordinary citizen: whether the policemen and strikers who good-naturedly played football matches, or the soldiers and volunteer students who braved the jeers (and worse) but carried on, or the miners who endured so much hardship bravely and with surprisingly little malice. In this harsh test of endurance for democracy in Britain the ordinary citizen won: which was just what should be if national disruption were to be averted. The reward of good sense among so many millions of people was not appreciated at the time. What died in 1926, though nobody noticed, was the myth of syndicalist revolution as the road to better times. The idea no longer lurked in English minds, as it had lurked in some before 1926, that one real good big strike would change everything. That idea was now, in the idiom of the time, 'debunked'. What gained new life, though again nobody noticed, was parliamentary socialism and the prospect of building a democratic Welfare State. The cost to the nation, the *Economist* calculated, was £300–£400 million.

THE CONDITION OF THE PEOPLE

Nobody supposed, until the later twenties, that it made sense in the context of British parliamentary politics to talk of 'Left' and 'Right'. Appropriate to European semicircular assemblies, where a party's conservatism could be measured by how far round to the right of the central rostrum it normally sat, the terms had no natural relevance in the two-sided face-to-face assembly at Westminster. A party sat on the Speaker's right if it was in office, on his left if it was in opposition: Labour, when in office, was on his 'Right'. Like the British rule of elections that the man at the top of the poll gets in, what mattered in Parliament was whether you were in or out of office. It was allegedly H. G. Wells who, in 1927, first used in print the word 'Leftism'. Certainly in these years the terms first gained the general currency which they have kept ever since.

The implications which the terms imported were ideological. But the ideology of 'Leftism' was far from clear in the misty climate of English politics. It did not coincide with party divisions. To the Communists it implied the class-war, and its adoption in these years reflects the class-war language of the General Strike. To others its essence became sympathy for the under-dog – in this instance the British miners, but soon to include all believed to be victims of injustice, even Sacco and Vanzetti in Massachusetts. In protest against the judicial ill-treatment of these two Italian Communists, there was a demonstration of some 200,000 people in Hyde Park on 22 August 1927. When they were executed the next day, after being reprieved from the death-sentence since 1921, the mood of bitter grief among millions who had never even seen them was intense. Such protests, occurring in many countries and usually associated with the Communist Third International ('Comintern'), were often led by local Communist Parties. There emerged a new pattern of 'the Left', to become increasingly familiar during the thirties with the rise of 'Popular Fronts': an alliance of Communists, Socialists, trade unionists, Radicals, and some Liberals, as well as numbers of individual 'do-gooders', united only in protest against real or alleged injustices. The Communists always strove to claim leadership and any credit or publicity available. It was commonly easier to get unity, however superficial and temporary, on a highly charged emotional issue of foreign affairs than on domestic matters where the component groups had divergent interests, and opinions were more solidly based. Internationalism of various kinds – pacifism, disarmament, the 'outlawing of war', federalism – became a favourite concept of the new 'Left', which by reaction drove many of the 'Right' into postures of more assertive nationalism and insularity. Sensitivity to human suffering and courage in attacking injustice were the strength of the new 'Left': a claim to monopolize righteousness and an undiscriminating 'under-doggery' were its failings.

The long-term importance of the new concept was that it blurred the really important distinction between the Communists, pledged to fight the class-war with revolutionary weapons and for revolutionary ends, and the Labour Party and the T.U.C., which were committed to parliamentary democratic methods and to improving the conditions of the workers within the framework of capitalist society. This blurring suited the aims of the still small Communist Party, and played into the hands of the more extreme 'Right', who were anxious to daub all opponents with a red brush. It is not surprising that these same years brought the rise of small Fascist organizations, modelled on Mussolini's party in Italy but not yet banded together under Sir Oswald Mosley. They eagerly offered their services as special constables during the strike; their offer was seldom accepted.

The strongest pulls of polarity were not to come until the thirties. It needed not only a general strike but also an economic slump to excite Communists and Fascists to their greatest efforts. Meanwhile, in 1928 and 1929, economic conditions and social life took a turn for the better, and the years of promise and hope, so gravely interrupted by the strike, moved into their milder autumnal days. British life went on in a minor key, its most controversial issues fairly sedate and high-level, like the controversy about the revised Prayer Book.

The Church Assembly of the Church of England produced a revised Prayer Book, which was immediately attacked by Low Churchmen and evangelicals as disturbingly Anglo-Catholic or even Papist. The House of Lords accepted it, but in the Commons it was vigorously attacked by the Home Secretary, Sir William Joynson-Hicks, and by Sir Thomas Inskip. The Commons rejected it. The controversy raised the whole issue of establishment, for the State was preventing the Church from conducting its internal concerns as it wished. A compromise was reached whereby bishops, in their own dioceses, authorized certain parts of the book to be used by incumbents. Thus 'levels' of Churchmanship remained as diversified as they had been before, and war between Church and State was side-stepped. One unexpected consequence was the welcome given by some Anglican clergy to the American 'Buchmanite' movement; they saw in the high-pressure revivalist methods of the so-called 'Oxford Group' one way of offsetting the ritualism of the High Church party. Another essay in religious revivalism of these years, also deriving from America, was the Four Square Gospel Alliance of Aimee Semple McPherson. But Anglicans did not back her, a spectacular meeting in the Albert Hall was a failure, and the more muted tones of religious life in England held their own.

It is not easy to assess the place of the Churches in British life of the twenties. There was much talk of their failure to attract or to hold the loyalties of the younger generation. The rise of 'the Left' was, in some measure, indication of this. The new thought of the time – whether its prophet was Marx or Freud or Einstein – seemed to erode religious faith as the Churches had always preached it. Agnosticism was fashionable, and the leaders of literary taste went in for 'debunking'. The war books that suddenly became popular in 1929 were works such as the German Erich Maria Remarque's *All Quiet on the Western Front*, Robert Graves's *Goodbye to All That*, and R. C. Sherriff's play *Journey's End*. Most war books now became anti-war books.

Church attendance in general certainly declined, although the Roman Catholic community in England was growing steadily and made a few sensational converts among former Anglicans. The Church of Scotland and the United Free Church reunited in 1929, and Presbyterianism gained greatly in strength thereby. The three main Methodist churches worked for union and gained it by 1932. But indifference remained a common attitude. The Archbishop

of Canterbury until 1928 was Randall Davidson, an eccle-
siastical Baldwin in his gifts for reconciliation and compromises of moderation. His intervention in the General
Strike, though limited in its effect because he was not
allowed to broadcast, was an appeal on behalf of all the
Churches in England for a negotiated settlement. It caused
the Government embarrassment, and so was given little
publicity. But it helped to set the Church of England on the
path towards active concern for social justice which William
Temple, who in 1929 became Archbishop of York, was to
pursue more energetically still. Such men showed that the
established Church did not irretrievably 'belong to the
Right'. Though churchgoing tended to decline, from 1924
onwards the broadcasting of religious services brought religious worship and preaching into many homes, and not
only on Sundays. A popular parson like 'Dick' Sheppard,
vicar of St Martin-in-the-Fields, owed his vast following to
success as a radio personality. Taking churchmen of all
denominations, divisions of attitude among them were not
notably different from those within the country as a whole:
and perplexity was more in evidence than fanaticism.

In countless ways the texture of social life was changing,
sometimes almost imperceptibly, sometimes spectacularly,
and people's interests and pursuits changed with it. The
population of the United Kingdom grew by nearly 5 per
cent during the twenties.[1] Emigration overseas from Great
Britain declined, from 256,000 in 1923 (its post-war peak)
to only 92,000 in 1930, and many returned to offset those
going. Within Britain the population gravitated heavily to
the Home Counties around London, and to south-eastern
England in general, away from Lancashire, South Wales,
and other 'depressed areas'. 'Greater London' grew
dramatically to more than 8 millions by 1931: an increase of
9·7 per cent since 1921. It now included a fifth of the whole

1. See p. 19.

population of England and Wales. Growth was fastest in
the 'outer ring' of suburbs and new housing estates, dormi-
tory areas for the city from which large armies of commuters
put still greater strain on already congested transport
services.

Although much of the new housing was unplanned, and
'ribbon development' spoiled many of the roads of Britain,
the London County Council and other big cities planned
large housing estates which far exceeded, in size and social
importance, any previous rehousing schemes. Thus Becon-
tree in Essex, begun by the L.C.C. in 1921, housed more
than 80,000 people by 1930. Birmingham, Bristol, Liverpool, and other large cities embarked on similar enterprises.
Many of these schemes suffered from lack of imagination as
well as from lack of experience or money. As with so many
'council houses' everywhere, minimum standards of den-
sity, size, and amenities were rarely accompanied by ideas
of elegance, attractiveness, or even community life. The 'age
of the masses', of which social philosophers increasingly
wrote, took visible form in immense, dreary new suburbs
and impersonal estates.

The masses, wherever they lived and whatever their occupations, were catered for in countless new ways. Apart from
the methods of 'mass-production', increasingly adopted in
factories, many consumer goods standardized in quality,
price, and packaging filled the multiple stores and, above
all, Woolworth's. By bulk purchase, small profit-margins,
and speedy turnover, Woolworth's conveyed the economic
benefits of cheap mass-production to the working-class
housewife more vividly than any other medium. Introduction of the system of hire-purchase made it possible
for small wage-earners to buy more costly goods such as
furniture, sewing-machines, bicycles, and the new vacuum-
cleaners.

The organizations which employed people, and whose

policies affected so much of their lives, were coming to be
more often very large-scale concerns. On one hand, the
growth and activity of various public or non-profit-making
organizations were features of the twenties: local authorities,
building societies, cooperative societies, and public-utility
companies or corporations of an ever-increasing variety. It
was estimated that public property as a proportion of all
property rose from between 6 and 8 per cent before 1914 to
between 8 and 12 per cent in 1932-4. On the other hand,
giant concerns in industry increased in number and became
even more gigantic. Some continued since before 1914
(J. and P. Coats in sewing cotton, Portland cement, Shell
oil); the new industries were often dominated by a few very
large firms (Courtauld's and British Celanese in rayons,
Austin and Morris in motor-cars); and the two largest com-
bines of all dated from these years – Imperial Chemical
Industries (I.C.I.) from 1926, and Unilever, a combination
of British and Dutch concerns in the thriving industry of
soap and vegetable oils, from 1929. In its sectors of most
vigorous growth British industry was dominated by large
and dynamic organizations, linked closely with world economy and susceptible to world trends, no less than in its
traditional and more vulnerable industries. By such means
were the methods of mass production and the markets of
mass consumption linked together.

Popular entertainments, too, reached a more 'massive'
scale. Sport assumed a new dimension with the growth of
amateur football leagues playing their Saturday afternoon
matches, with the immense popularity of professional football (the first cup final at Wembley, held in 1923, was
attended by the King and stormed by some 200,000 of his
subjects), and the rapid growth of greyhound race-tracks at
Wembley, White City, and scores of other centres during
the later twenties. 'Community singing' became popular.
The cinema (wherein silent films were succeeded by

'talkies' after 1929) assumed a big place in English life. By 1929 there were some 3,000 cinemas, and as the British film industry was then just beginning to assert itself in productivity as against the ubiquitous American movie industry the box-office was large throughout the decade. From 1923 on, radio competed with the cinemas, dogs, and the pubs to entertain the working man and his wife. Perhaps because of counter-attractions, but also because of the high taxation of spirits, sobriety increased. Convictions for drunkenness had been 189,000 in 1913; in 1930, with a larger urban population, there were only 53,000.

Already the popular Press had come to aim at entertainment almost as much as at giving news, information, or even views. In the mid twenties the popular papers waged a circulation-war: their weapons at first offers of free insurance for registered readers, then large cash prizes in competitions, finally free gifts on a lavish scale. Mass circulations raised advertising revenue. When the Betting Act stopped some cash prizes the *Daily Herald* set the pace in gift offers. They proved costly, so a truce was called to free gifts in February 1932. J. S. Elias, managing director of Odhams Press which produced the *Daily Herald*, set a new vogue a year later by offering a four-guinea presentation edition of works of Dickens, in sixteen handsome volumes, for only eleven shillings plus coupons cut from the *Herald*. There was an immense response. When the Press barons protested Elias admitted that the net cost of the volumes, mass produced, *was* only eleven shillings. Thereupon the *Daily Mail, Daily Express*, and *News Chronicle* all produced rival sets of Dickens, offering sixteen handsome volumes for only ten shillings. In all, 11 million copies of Dickens were sold, at very small cost to the papers. In 1933 the *Daily Express* was first to top the 2 million mark for daily circulation. So was democracy educated in Britain.

Social life was revolutionized by the coming of the

internal-combustion engine in millions on to the streets. In place of the vanishing horse came buses, lorries, vans, family cars, motor-cycles: nearly 1 million of them by 1922, more than 2¼ millions by 1930. Road safety became a national concern, and chaos on the King's highway, especially in the areas of denser population and at holiday times, became a permanent feature of English life in the twentieth century. The immense amounts of time and money spent on leisure pursuits were cause for frequent lamentation by moralists. It explained the decline in churchgoing, it contrasted ill with prevalent poverty and unemployment, it distorted the economy; but the condition of the people, still raw from the aftermath of war and the strains of civil strife, finding new modes of leisure and pleasure that were unsophisticated, lent itself too strongly to such expenditures to be checked by moralizing or reproach. In view of the still greater economic crisis impending, it was well, perhaps, that the people should know this brief time of relaxation.

When Baldwin perforce went to the country in May 1929 the two looming issues were, inevitably, unemployment and peace. Employment had been at a high level since 1927, but even so the official rate of unemployment was at best 9 or 10 per cent, and the actual number of people out of work (as against the official figure of those within the insurance scheme) was alarmingly large. There was a 'hard core' of at least a million men at any one moment unemployed. The hopes for international peace, however, seemed rosier. In 1928 internationalist ideology reached a climax in the Briand–Kellogg Pact for the 'renunciation of war', signed by fifteen States, including Britain. Since the agreement did not rule out wars of self-defence, or indeed the possibility of aggression without a declaration of war, it availed little. But it voiced the general yearning to 'outlaw war'; it was accepted eventually by sixty-five States; and Britain had made clear before signing it that she reserved the right to defend 'certain regions of the world the welfare and integrity of which constitute a special and vital interest for our peace and safety'. (The United States, similarly, had reiterated the Monroe Doctrine.) Baldwin had, however, broken off diplomatic and trading relations with the Soviet Union in May 1927, after the ill-conceived raid on the London offices of Arcos Ltd, the British company responsible for trade with Russia.

The Conservatives fought the election with the slogan of 'Safety First', accompanied by innumerable posters of Baldwin's face. The electorate was the largest ever, swollen to nearly 29 million by the 'flapper vote'. After a dull campaign the result was indecisive. Labour, with 288 seats, became the largest party in the House. The Conservatives held 260, Liberals 59. Again the electoral system worked erratically. The Conservatives had polled nearly 300,000 more votes than Labour, though they had twenty-eight fewer seats. Labour could be outvoted by the other two parties collaborating. In a sense nobody had 'won'. But since His Majesty's Government had to be carried on after Baldwin's resignation on 4 June, Ramsay MacDonald again formed a Labour Government. Nearly all its principal members had held office before. Snowden returned to the Exchequer, but J. R. Clynes became Home Secretary and Arthur Henderson (with young Hugh Dalton as his Under Secretary) took charge of foreign affairs. The two chief novelties were the first British woman Cabinet Minister, Miss Margaret Bondfield as Minister of Labour, and the benign George Lansbury, who, as a congenial Minister of Works, instituted 'Lansbury's Lido' in Hyde Park. It was a moderate ministry, lacking representatives of the 'Leftist' wing of the Labour Party but including a few former Liberals and clearly depending for survival on some of those moderate men of all opinions who resisted violent change. It survived for just over two years, buffeted by the blizzard of the world economic crisis. Hugh Dalton's verdict was apt enough:

The Second Labour Government's record abroad is a moderate success story, not lacking courage and skill. Its record at home is a hard-luck story, with failure almost unredeemed either by courage or skill.[1]

Unfitted by its nature to offer heroic measures or to exact drastic remedies, the second Labour Government was the victim both of circumstances and of its own inadequacies, as will be shown below.[2]

1. H. Dalton, *Call Back Yesterday* (1953), p. 259.
2. See pp. 132–41.

PART II

FROM WORLD CRISIS
TO WORLD WAR
(1930–45)

CHAPTER FIVE

National Government and Economic Crisis, 1930–5

THE ROAD TO NATIONAL GOVERNMENT

THE ironic position of the Labour Government was that most of its energies had to be dedicated to making the capitalist economy work better. The crisis of August 1931 which brought it to an end was a convergence of crises, political and personal as well as economic. It can be understood only by considering each of these separate developments and then examining their convergence.

The economic crisis was in one sense endemic since before 1914 and more openly operative since 1919. It was a British segment and variant of the Great Depression which shattered the world's economy between 1929 and 1932. There is still room for wide difference of judgement about its causes but some of its salient features are undeniable. One was the long-term secular trend towards low prices of primary products (mainly foodstuffs and raw materials for manufactures) which made it more and more difficult for nations mainly engaged in producing primary goods to afford to import manufactured goods. Another was the severe dislocation of characteristic nineteenth-century patterns of world trade and investment by a host of new developments: the industrialization of great new Powers such as the United States and Japan, the virtual exclusion of Russia from world markets, the dislocation of international trade by the world war and of investments and loans by the tangle of war debts and reparations. To these world-wide trends Britain was especially susceptible by reason of its once pre-eminent role in the world economy, its severe losses during the war, and its post-war reliance on the old basic industries of coal, shipbuilding, and textiles (see above, Chapter 3).

Whatever the British economy endured in these years must, therefore, be seen as largely (but not entirely) the result of world tendencies, of difficulties only partially within her own competence to handle. The wisdom or folly of the policies which Governments adopted must be judged in awareness of this fact, yet by reference to the particular social and economic ills brought upon the country by these trends. The economic depression, like the two great wars, had a quality of fatality – an impersonal calamity as if it were not of human creation – which bred despair and intensified fears. Governments might have done wiser things, performed and demanded greater exertions, done what they did more opportunely or more skilfully: they were unlikely, given the total situation of Britain, to be able to save the country from severe loss, suffering, and disruption. They made some mistakes, and mistakes in these circumstances could be very costly.

The crisis, as has been seen, first affected Britain in the form of persistent and endemic unemployment. No Government of the twenties found a way of reducing the figure of the registered unemployed below the one-million mark. Among various reasons for this failure was the reliance of the British economy upon an international trade which had not recovered from its war-time disorganization and which, from the beginning of 1929 until 1934, steadily shrank in amount and in value. This shrinkage was in part due to deliberate policies – to tariffs which obstructed trade, to financial policies which hampered exports. It was, even more, the result of a general *malaise* of the economy of the world. It was closely related to a steep fall in world prices between 1929 and 1932, which the

World Economic Survey of the League of Nations explained like this:

It is so far-reaching and complete that it is unlikely to have been produced by any single cause. The variety and contradictory nature of the explanations offered, even in expert circles, leads in itself to a suspicion that the causes are complex and not fully understood. It is not only the monetary mechanism but the whole economic organization of the world that has been affected, and it is unlikely that any single weakness would have caused such a general collapse.[1]

Internally, as internationally, low prices meant low incomes, unemployment, and inadequate purchasing power.

This being so, what did British Governments do about it? They did not, for some time, appreciate the real reasons for the crisis, nor of course did they at first appreciate its scale and severity. This was because the economic blizzard first hit Britain in the curious form of the crash on Wall Street at the end of October 1929 – only a few months after MacDonald resumed the Premiership. The breakdown on the stock exchange in New York was the bursting of a bubble of speculation. It shattered the monetary and credit system of the western world. American loans to Europe – on which so much of Germany's recovery had relied – abruptly and completely stopped. A drying up of purchasing power all over the world resulted in a catastrophic fall in prices. In Germany, most nakedly exposed to the crisis, registered unemployed rose in number from less than 2 millions in 1929 to a peak of more than 6 millions in March 1932. In Great Britain the number of actual unemployed rose to more than $3\frac{1}{4}$ millions in 1931, and to a peak of $3\frac{3}{4}$ millions by September 1932. This meant that between 6 and 7 million people were 'living on the dole'. This was the national and human tragedy that men in authority and power seemed helpless to do much about.

1. *Survey*, 1931/2, p. 115.

The Labour Government inaugurated a modest programme of public works: the right policy, but too limited in scope. It passed the Development (Loan Guarantees and Grants) Act and the Colonial Development Act, both in 1929. J. H. Thomas of the N.U.R. as Lord Privy Seal was commissioned to act as 'Minister of Employment'. His public works schemes of 1929 cost £42 million, the utmost permitted by the austerely orthodox Snowden at the Exchequer. Sir Oswald Mosley, former Conservative M.P. and now Chancellor of the Duchy of Lancaster, drew up a plan of action. It included measures to increase purchasing power and to finance development; but it, too, was blocked by Snowden, and in May 1930 Mosley resigned in protest to form his 'New Party' along with John Strachey and eventually to become Britain's leading Fascist. It won little support and did nothing to induce Labour to launch a vigorous attack on unemployment. Instead the Government continued palliatives, putting more money into the Unemployment Insurance Fund, and passing a Bill which extended 'transitional benefits' to more unemployed people. It transferred from the claimants of relief to the officials the onus of proof whether the claimants were 'genuinely seeking work'. Such ameliorations, however desirable, did not add up to a policy. The Government passed a few other constructive measures which belonged to the continuous story of previous and subsequent measures: such as the Housing Act (1930), which provided subsidies for slum clearance, and the Agricultural Marketing Act (1931), which provided for marketing boards of producers to grade and sell agricultural produce. It attempted others – notably an Education Bill to raise the school-leaving age to fifteen, which was defeated by the Lords. It lacked the drive and the parliamentary backing to dominate the adverse circumstances which accompanied its whole existence, and fell apart in disagreements about its own policies.

It was only a matter of time before it was defeated, and what defeated it was the financial crisis of March 1931. At this great turning-point in the inter-war years the world economic crisis led straight into the British political crisis. It also happened to be a moment of personal crisis for the leaderships of the two major parties.

On the Conservative side, 1930 was a year of realignment of forces. Lords Beaverbrook and Rothermere had for some months run a protectionist campaign and formed a United Empire Party. Its central idea was free trade within the Empire, with a tariff wall round the Empire against the rest of the world. The two press barons, having forced out J. C. C. Davidson from the chairmanship of the Party in favour of Neville Chamberlain, gunned Baldwin. But Baldwin hit back. In March 1931 he made a frontal assault on them which became memorable:

Their methods are direct falsehood, misrepresentation, half-truths, the alteration of the speaker's meaning by putting sentences apart from the context, suppression, and editorial criticism of speeches which are not reported in the paper. . . . What the proprietorship of these papers is aiming at is power, but power without responsibility – the prerogative of the harlot throughout the ages.

Baldwin was reaffirmed in his position as party leader. Meanwhile, two months before, Churchill had resigned from his place in the Conservative Party's 'shadow cabinet' because of disagreements about British policy in India. By these devious ways the order of succession to leadership was laid down, and it was ordained that when Baldwin went in 1937 it was Chamberlain, not Churchill, who inherited the unenviable task of meeting the resurgence of Germany under Hitler.

In February 1931 the Conservative opposition tabled a vote of censure on the Government for extravagance. A Liberal amendment asked for a committee of inquiry. This was accepted by the Government, which proceeded to set up a Committee on National Expenditure under Sir George May of the Prudential Assurance Company. Matters came to a climax in July. Unemployment figures rose to more than 2¾ millions; the Macmillan Committee on Finance and Industry issued its report, which documented the country's economic dilemmas; Germany's acute financial crisis led to a conference in London; at the end of the month, immediately after Parliament went into recess, the May Committee produced its Report showing the grave financial plight of the nation. It foresaw a deficit of £120 million, and the need for £24 million of new taxation as well as for economies of some £96 million, more than two-thirds of these being cuts in outlay on the unemployed. The picture was probably too gloomy, the economies proposed alarmist. But it shook confidence, at home and abroad, in Britain's financial solvency. To check the drain on its gold reserves the Bank of England had to raise £80 million credits in Paris and New York. But reserves went on draining away. On 11 August Ramsay MacDonald returned to London from holiday in Scotland to face from the rulers of the Bank of England warnings of an imminent financial crisis. By 23 August the Labour Government came to an end – petering out in disarray like the hopes of the twenties themselves. This crisis of August and September 1931, which gave rise to the National Government, deserves closer consideration as a historic landmark.

THE CRISIS OF 1931

Who made the National Government? The men who 'killed' the second Labour Government and who thereafter, presumably, manipulated the crisis of August? But do these include the King and Ramsay MacDonald himself, as well as Baldwin, Neville Chamberlain, and Sir Herbert Samuel, who more directly gained from it? Do they include the bankers and financiers, those sinister 'City interests' allegedly plotting against Labour in power? So much has been written about the great crisis, some of it highly speculative and prejudiced, that even now the issue remains controversial and, in some respects, obscure. One certainty is that most of the theories of what happened are mutually incompatible, and most are more lurid than the actual events. [1]

The sequence of events was as follows. On Monday 24 August the King accepted the resignation of the Labour Government and invited Ramsay MacDonald to form a National Government in order to deal with the financial emergency. The new Cabinet was formed by 25 August; it included both Baldwin and Samuel. The Labour Party members, besides MacDonald, were Snowden, Thomas, and Lord Sankey. The Conservatives, in addition to Baldwin, were Neville Chamberlain, Sir Samuel Hoare, and Sir Philip Cunliffe-Lister. The two Liberal members held key posts – Samuel the Home Office, Lord Reading the Foreign Office. Lloyd George, official leader of the Liberal Party, was too ill to take office. It was not, Samuel noted, 'a Coalition in the ordinary sense of the term, but a co-operation of individuals'.

On 27 August the Labour Movement's three committees (T.U.C. General Council, National Executive of the Labour Party, and Consultative Committee of the Parliamentary Labour Party) produced a joint manifesto denouncing and repudiating the new coalition. Next day the

1. The fullest and most balanced account of the crisis is by R. Bassett, *Nineteen Thirty-One: Political Crisis* (1958). Much valuable new material was first published in H. Nicolson, *King George V: His Life and Reign* (1952). Remaining gaps are mainly due to unavailability of MacDonald's papers and the lack of a full, good biography of him. The account here given is based primarily on Bassett, Nicolson, Viscount Samuel, *Memoirs* (1945), Sir H. Clay, *Lord Norman* (1957). For the proposal to form a 'National Government', see p. 138.

Parliamentary Labour Party endorsed this attitude. At the same time the Conservative and Liberal Parties decided to support the National Government.

On 8 September the new Government appeared before the House of Commons to seek a vote of confidence. The Prime Minister presented a message from the King, read by the Speaker.

The present condition of the National finances, in the opinion of His Majesty's Ministers, calls for the imposition of additional taxation, and for the effecting of economies in public expenditure. His Majesty recommends the matter to the consideration of his faithful Commons, and trusts they will make provision accordingly.

MacDonald explained both the financial crisis and the case for forming a National Government. The Government got its vote of confidence, only 12 Labour members supporting it and 242 voting against it. It presented an emergency budget, and on 21 September left the gold standard. At the ensuing general election (27 October) the National Government won an overwhelming majority – 554 out of the 615 seats. The vote for Conservatives went up by more than 3 millions as compared with 1929; the Liberal vote declined by roughly the same number. Labour lost some $1\frac{3}{4}$ million votes, and mustered only fifty-two seats.

The crisis split both the Labour and Liberal parties, 'National Labourites' and 'Liberal Nationals' becoming distinct from the old parties. But whereas the result marked yet another milestone in the disintegration and downhill trend of the Liberal Party, the bulk of Labour went into opposition with only a handful of its parliamentary leaders back in the House. Among them were only three ex-ministers – George Lansbury (who took over the leadership of the party), C. R. Attlee, and Stafford Cripps. The landslide was so great that the opposition, stunned and bitter, turned readily to personal recriminations, charges of 'betrayal', and sinister explanations. MacDonald, on the basis of this new 'mandate', reconstructed his National Government in November. Neville Chamberlain replaced Snowden at the Exchequer, Sir John Simon replaced Lord Reading at the Foreign Office. Otherwise, the composition was little different. This Government ruled until June 1935.

Left opinion as a whole, especially trade-union opinion, first concentrated its dismay against the handful of former Labour leaders – MacDonald, Snowden, Thomas – whom it accused of a great 'betrayal'. This was the personal crisis. It was exacerbated by old dissensions within the party. MacDonald had been out of step with the majority during the Great War and even during the General Strike; Snowden's financial policies had been notoriously 'orthodox' and 'reactionary'; Thomas, despite his immense *bonhomie* and undoubted drive, was suspected of being a political time-server, overfond of flesh-pots and of power. They were formally expelled from the Labour Party before the election. There was much cynical comment that although the National Government had allegedly been formed to save the country from ruin by keeping the pound on gold, on 21 September (that is, less than a month later) it went off the gold standard without ill effect. There was indignation that the economies which Snowden imposed in order to balance his budget were at the expense of teachers, police, and armed services as well as the unemployed – the sections least able or likely to hit back. It could be retorted, however, that neither step could have been taken by the much weaker Labour Government without shaking confidence and encountering even greater difficulties. Even so, rumours of pay-cuts precipitated mutiny at Invergordon in mid-September – an entirely bloodless affair which came as a useful diversion of public attention.

Some of the recriminations glanced off the Prime Minister on to the King himself. The National Government was described by Professor Harold Laski, soon after the election, as 'born of a Palace Revolution'. The phrase, as well as the idea, stuck until, twenty years later, the notions on which it rested were disproven by evidence published by Sir Harold Nicolson. The unprecedented political situation of August left the constitutional position very complex. But there is no evidence at all that the King behaved with any constitutional impropriety: indeed, it was his duty and function, as a constitutional monarch, to solve the political crisis as quickly and satisfactorily as he could. When Mac-Donald had warned the King of the possible collapse of the Labour Government because of internal disagreements the King decided that the proper procedure was to consult the leaders of the Conservative and Liberal Oppositions. By chance it was Sir Herbert Samuel whom he saw first, and Samuel urged that

The best solution would be if Mr Ramsay MacDonald, either with his present, or with a reconstituted Labour Cabinet, could propose the economies required. If he failed to secure the support of a sufficient number of his colleagues, then the best alternative would be a National Government composed of members of the three parties. It would be preferable that Mr MacDonald should remain Prime Minister in such a National Government.[1]

Baldwin was received that afternoon, and approved the idea too. Far from the National Government being either a long-hatched plot of MacDonald's or something forced upon the parties by the King, it emerged with complete constitutional propriety from the monarch's necessary consultations with the three party leaders. If it came from any one person, it came from Samuel. The King's Private Secretary recorded at the time: 'It was after the King's interview with Sir Herbert Samuel that H.M. became convinced of the necessity for the National Government.' This is borne out from other sources, including Samuel himself.

1. Sir Harold Nicolson, *King George V*, p. 461.

When all party leaders urged a National Government the King had no alternative but to accept.

The hidden historical continuities between the course of the General Strike in 1926 and the crisis five years later are beginning to appear. There was a strikingly similar alignment of personalities – MacDonald and Thomas as anxious as Baldwin to find a moderate compromise solution, the King himself eager for anything likely to preserve national unity, Samuel as the mediator and the initiator of an ingenious way out of the predicament. There is even a parallel in the part played by sheer chance. It happened that, on 27 July 1931, the official Liberal leader, Lloyd George, fell seriously ill. Had he, instead of the deputy leader, Samuel, been received by the King on 23 August, would the proposal for a National Government have been mooted at all? In September when, in Nicolson's phrase, Lloyd George was still 'an irritable and puckish convalescent at Churt', his sympathies certainly lay with Henderson and the Labour opposition. He even proposed that he be taken in an ambulance to Buckingham Palace to confer with the King, MacDonald, and Baldwin, and was strongly against a joint manifesto in the elections. Had Lloyd George been up and about, what different twist might events have taken? In the circumstances his illness further splintered the Liberals, for thereafter besides the Samuelites and the Simonites there was the Lloyd George family group equipped with ample political funds.

Fresh constitutional problems were involved in the elections. The original coalition rested on the express understanding that when the immediate crisis had passed each party would resume its independence of action. After the decision to go off gold it became arguable that the National Government should now go to the electorate with a joint appeal. But if so, what appeal? Any reference to the issue of protection split the coalition. The formula eventually found on 5 October was a joint request for 'a doctor's mandate': a blank cheque to do whatever seemed best to remedy the country's ills. But a general election in Britain does not, in principle, give 'mandates' to any government. It elects a House of Commons which is but one organ of a composite, sovereign, Parliament. Thereafter it is for Parliament, in its exercise of sovereignty, to decide what shall be done. All such dubieties, however, were swept away by the rush of events in the autumn of 1931. At least the notion of a 'doctor's mandate' was an honest admission that nobody knew just what should or could be done next. It was the expression of that empiricism in politics which was the real common ground of the party leaders of 1931.

The repercussions of the crisis on political parties and personal attitudes may be seen as in some ways an adjustment in British political life to the new force of 'Leftism' which, as already shown, was then only a few years old. This force, emotional as well as ideological, cut across existing party formations. The I.L.P. was much more 'Leftist' in spirit than the whole Parliamentary Labour Party, and in 1932 duly split off from it. Individuals, notably MacDonald, Snowden, and Thomas, were in general less filled with this spirit than were such men as Henderson, Lansbury, or Bevin. MacDonald on the new 'Right' of Labour had much in common with a moderate Conservative like Baldwin, as is demonstrated throughout the twenties and thirties by the strong continuities and affinities between the measures which they supported. A 'Right-wing' Conservative like Churchill gave as much anxiety and trouble to Baldwin as did a 'Left-wing' Labourite, like Maxton, to Ramsay MacDonald. It was to the interests of the shrinking and enfeebled centre party, the Liberals, to draw together kindred spirits from the new Left and the new Right, and insert themselves as part of a national coalition. To explain the event in such terms is not to suggest sinister plots or even, at all moments, conscious calculation. Politicians in moments of crisis are apt to be guided as much by instinct and intuition as by guile and deliberate calculation. The centripetal pulls exercised by the circumstances of 1931, which threw up the phenomenon of the National Government, operated in all three parties. But they operated only through certain individuals and groups within them. How strong was the centripetal pull may be seen from the fate of the eccentric extremes: neither the Communists nor Mosley's 'New Party' could attract votes enough to return a single representative to Westminster.

FAMILY AFFAIRS

In the twenties MacDonald and Baldwin had alternated in office: in the thirties they shared it simultaneously. In the twenties it had been MacDonald who was in the ascendant, in the thirties it was Baldwin who reached the apex of his career in his handling of the supreme British 'family affair', the abdication crisis of 1936. The partnership continued as MacDonald, Baldwin and Co. until 7 June 1935; thereafter it continued as Baldwin, MacDonald and Co. Like a sedate and leisurely firm of comfortable family solicitors, they conducted the business affairs of Great Britain and the Commonwealth with mild, unhurried manners, facing no issue until it was clamant, seeking no decision until it was overdue. Their ways, unlike the ways of the harsh, brash bosses of rival concerns, were civilized and humane, if a trifle old-fashioned. History may come, more and more, to see them as Tweedledum and Tweedledee – presiding jointly over British national life in one of its peculiarly unheroic periods.

Given the new universal suffrage and therefore the efforts of parties to depict, in Press and on Radio, public images acceptable or detestable to the masses, it is perhaps to be expected that neither man matched with reality his popular *persona*. The Left came to think of MacDonald, the moving Scottish orator who had captured the hearts of Labour in its early days and won respect during the war by the sincerity of his 'pacifism', as the arch-betrayer, a vainglorious lover of pomp and power over-beloved by duchesses. With his great natural charm went, naturally enough, a good endowment of vanity; it may be that he was too easily weighed down or stampeded by the complexities of the economic condition of the country. Likewise the public image of Stanley Baldwin, the stolid pipe-smoking country-lover, with pigs and the goodly earthiness of old England as a warranty of simple honesty, concealed an astute if sometimes lethargic politician, sensitive and with intelligence far above the 'plain man' level. His temperament gave him a Micawber-like streak, since he preferred things to sort themselves out rather than be 'settled' by him; and he was always prepared to await the event rather than forestall it. But he was also capable, in crisis, of intensive energy and concentration. His son, A. W. Baldwin, wrote of him after his death: 'far from being bovine, he was endowed by nature with a battery highly charged with vigilant nerves'. He was no showman and hated the whole apparatus of publicity – a disadvantage for a party leader in the twentieth century, or perhaps in any other.

It is very incongruous, in an age of genuine villains such as Hitler or Stalin, that two such personalities as MacDonald and Baldwin should feature in political demonology. Just as MacDonald, to the Left, was the lost leader and the arch-traitor of Labour ('Labour's Love Lost'), so Baldwin, to the backbenchers of the Right, became the arch-betrayer of democracy. He was the man who clung to office at the cost of letting Britain drift ill-armed towards war. Even his authorized biographer, G. M. Young, failed to rescue Baldwin from this charge; and though it has been fully and carefully analysed and the worst crudities of it removed, he has not been acquitted of the charge of considerable inertia in face of mounting danger.[1] But the significant fact is the eagerness of opinion between the wars (and since) to find scapegoats, to believe in the black political treachery of former heroes. Perhaps super-villainy was more readily believed of men once held to be greater than they were, one excess nourishing the other. What many, imbued with the passions of the time, could least forgive either man was his incorrigible moderation. Neither was well fitted, by temperament or character, to deal with inexorable national crisis. Each broke down in health by reason of his efforts to ride the storm. Limitations of character, rather than treachery, may come to be seen as the most important feature of the MacDonald–Baldwin partnership.

The 'family affairs' which they handled fell into two broad categories: domestic issues, economic and social, dominated by the repercussions of the world economic depression; and affairs of the Commonwealth, seen by both as naturally linked with the domestic problems of the United Kingdom and with efforts to solve them. The natural conservative remedy for economic slump was protection and economy: so Walter Runciman at the Board of Trade took power to impose duties on imported manufactured goods, while Sir John Gilmour at the Ministry of Agriculture was given similar authority to obstruct the import of fresh fruit, vegetables, and flowers. The move to frame a general tariff met with such opposition within the

1. G. M. Young, *Stanley Baldwin* (1952), made poor use of scanty materials; A. W. Baldwin, *My Father: The True Story* (1955), redresses the former bias, but is too full of filial piety to be objective. The best analysis is R. Bassett's article in *The Cambridge Journal*, vol. II, No. 2, November 1948, on 'Telling the Truth to the People: Myth of the Baldwin "Confession".' See also Lord Boothby, *My Yesterday, Your Tomorrow* (1962).

Cabinet from Liberal and some Labour members that MacDonald issued his famous 'agreement to differ'. Dissentient ministers were allowed to remain within the ministry; in return for thus submitting to majority wishes, they were given freedom to oppose tariffs publicly. This breach of the very basis of cabinet government – of all its principles of collective responsibility and solidarity – was avowedly exceptional and redeemed only by its avowal.

On this basis, in March 1932, the Import Duties Act, promoted by Neville Chamberlain, imposed a general 10 per cent customs duty on most imports, with explicit exemptions for scheduled goods and on all goods from within the Empire. That summer an Imperial Economic Conference met in Ottawa. The Ottawa agreements, embodying a notion of 'Empire free trade' which meant tariffs against non-Commonwealth countries and a complex tangle of tariff bargains even within the Commonwealth, was too much for the free-traders. In September 1932 Snowden, Samuel, and Sinclair resigned. The ranks of National Labour (MacDonald, Thomas, Sankey) and of Liberal Nationals (the Simonites) were so greatly thinned that the National Government was henceforth predominantly and more blatantly a Conservative Government, dominated in its economic and social policies as much by Neville Chamberlain as by Baldwin.

By 1933 economic recovery was beginning, and it continued till 1935. Unemployment fell from its peak of nearly 3 millions in the winter of 1932-3; by July 1935 it fell for the first time below 2 millions. The index of production, from a base-line of 100 in 1929, fell to 84 in 1931 but rose to 93 in 1933, and to 110 in 1935. While imports were maintained, exports declined, making for certain 'depressed areas' where industry was especially dependent on the export trades, even when other industries, such as the building trades, stimulated by the housing boom, were flourishing. There was a growth of new industries: chemicals, rayon, cars, and radio. The cost of living fell, so that those in continuous employment were, in general, better off. The burden of recovery was carried unduly by the unemployed, and by those foreign producers whose goods Britain imported more cheaply than ever. World commodity prices fell more than export prices, so that Britain's imports cost her only two-thirds of their former cost. It is likely that these favourable terms of trade did more to maintain her standard of living than any deliberate measures of government policy.

Policy concerned itself mainly with the regulation of currency and of trade. Currency was 'managed' by the introduction of the Exchange Equalization Fund in 1932, and the formation of the sterling bloc consisting of Britain, the Dominions, and Scandinavia. Between 1932 and 1935 Britain made trade agreements with seventeen other countries outside the Commonwealth, ranging from Argentina to the Soviet Union. These usually agreed quotas of imports in return for concessions to Britain's exports. Collectively they altered the pattern of British trade in favour of the Dominions. British farmers were not only protected by tariffs and quotas but were also helped by specialized marketing boards and by subsidies. Marketing boards were set up for milk, bacon, potatoes, and hops. Acreage subsidies were given for such crops as barley, oats, and sugar beet.

The largest single factor in industrial recovery was probably the building boom. It was a boom partly in building private dwellings, partly in commercial and industrial building. Dwellings built by local authorities (mainly 'Council houses') ran fairly steadily at about 75,000 a year. The building of private houses and flats ran at some 200,000 a year in the early thirties, then rose to well over 350,000 a year. This boom accounted for a large share of the increase in employment, spreading as it did to the materials industries and to furniture-making and other trades. Financed mainly with the help of building societies or by local authorities, the new houses were cheap enough to effect a real rise in the standard of living. Connected closely with a rapid rise in the number of families (and not merely of people), with the migration of population and industry, with the rise in real incomes largely due to the favourable terms of trade, and with rising standards of consumption and expectation of good living standards, the rehousing of the British people in these years was the most encouraging feature of an otherwise bleak social scene.

This rosy prosperity in some sectors of the economy contrasted, however, with black despair in others. Contrasts sharpened between high, rising incomes of those fully employed in expanding sectors and the long-term idleness and deepening poverty of families in the 'depressed areas'. Official figures of registered unemployed reflected less than the truth. At the depth of the slump, in September 1932, between 6 and 7 million people were 'living on the dole'. Even in 1934, with recovery well started, massive unemployment persisted in some areas – most notoriously on the Tyne and Tees and in the Welsh valleys. In general, it was the unskilled workers who suffered most severely; though the skilled worker, in idleness, eventually lost skill and self-respect and more readily became disillusioned and rebellious. Long-term unemployment brought acute psychological and social problems, no less than economic loss.

That it did not cause more political disruption was due partly to the impermanent status of most of 'the unemployed', partly to the system of relief. For all the criticisms levied against it and the occasional severities and injustices in its administration, the 'dole' did much to prevent real destitution. The actuarial calculations of unemployment insurance were totally upset by the depression, and the means tests applied before grant of assistance were haphazard and variable. Reduction in assistance because of earnings of other members of the family created fearful domestic problems and provoked bitter protests. It was bad enough for a father to be interminably out of work when his son or daughter could find a job: it was intolerable when their earnings led to a reduction in his own meagre 'dole', and so to yet greater dependence on his children.

The Government repeatedly tinkered with legislation to try to relieve the unemployed as thriftily as possible. At the moment of crisis in September 1931 it had cut unemployment benefits by 10 per cent and introduced a means test. Assistance was then transferred from the Public Assistance Committees of local authorities to a statutory commission, the Unemployment Assistance Board (U.A.B.). In 1934 it consolidated the system of insurance and assistance in the Unemployment Act, which thus became a landmark in the growth of the Welfare State. But the scales of relief payments, uniform and national, due to operate from January 1935, aroused such widespread protests that they had to be hastily revised and postponed until November 1936. The U.A.B. was, from the start, endowed with a bad reputation among the workers, and the Government got no political credit from the large sums eventually expended on relief. In 1934, too, it passed a Special Areas Act, aimed partly at the transfer of workers to more prosperous areas, such as to the motor-industries of the Midlands or the light industries of the South, and partly at the promotion of new industries in the Special Areas. The Commissioners appointed to carry out the schemes accomplished little. The greatest recovery came from a natural convalescence and revival of the economy.

Perhaps concentration of mass unemployment in certain 'depressed areas' helped somewhat to soften awareness of the contrast between poverty and prosperity. Even so, these were the years when the terrible social paradox of 'poverty amid plenty' impinged most acutely on the national conscience: a fact of constant relevance to the national mood which brought into being the Welfare State after 1945.[1] On the short run it fed the flames of political activism of both Left and Right, which flared up into the Communist and Fascist disorders of 1934. The pace was set by the British Union of Fascists, founded in 1932 by Sir Oswald Mosley in imitation of Mussolini's Blackshirts. The movement organized large meetings and a private force of blackshirted members to suppress any opposition at them. The Communists were equally prepared to resort to brute force. Open violence became common. In June 1934 a mass meeting of the Fascists held at Olympia, in London, produced flagrant brutalities on a scale that shocked opinion in both country and Parliament. The Press, hitherto reporting Mosley's meetings as headline news and in a few cases even showing them favour, decided to withhold publicity. The 'Night of the Long Knives' in Germany, when Hitler and his henchmen purged their party, revealed more of the nature of Fascism. Communist heckling and counter-demonstrations, especially in the East End of London, eventually roused a lethargic Government to take more vigorous measures against the growing threat to public order. The Incitement to Disaffection Act of 1934 and the Public Order Act of 1936 both extended police powers, and so encountered bitter criticism as attacks on freedom, but the latter Bill suppressed the wearing of political uniforms and limited the holding of provocative processions.[2]

In the realm of imperial affairs the scene was dominated

1. See Chapter 8.
2. The prohibition affected the 'Greenshirt' movement of Social Credit, whose exotic 'Kibbo Kift Kindred' resembled Fascism more in style than in substance. It was active in the thirties, and in 1935 a Social Credit Government came to power in Alberta, Canada.

by two familiar sets of problems: Ireland and India. The Statute of Westminster, passed in 1931, gave formal recognition to a situation which already largely existed in fact: namely, that Dominions Governments could freely pass legislation that was repugnant to British laws applying to those Dominions, and that no British law applied to a Dominion without its consent. It implemented, constitutionally, Balfour's famous definition of Dominion status in 1926, and recognized the Crown 'as the symbol of the free association of the members of the British Commonwealth of Nations'. The Act solemnized and recorded the new era of Commonwealth relationships towards which Britain and the overseas nations had been moving since 1914, and which still had far to go before attaining specific definition or complete application. The first to take full advantage of the situation was Mr De Valera, who in 1932 succeeded the more moderate W. T. Cosgrave as Prime Minister of the Irish Free State. He proceeded to sever the remaining formal links with Britain: ousting the Governor-General, James MacNeill, abolishing the oath of allegiance to the Crown, removing the Treaty from its place in the Constitution of the Free State, ending appeals to the Judicial Committee of the Privy Council. In 1934–6 he took two more drastic steps. He abolished the Senate, and altered the law of Irish citizenship to distinguish Irish nationality from common British citizenship of the Empire. Ireland claimed, under the Statute of Westminster, to be still a member of the Commonwealth; though from 1932 onwards it was engaged in a tariff war with Britain, and De Valera's long-term aim was to make Eire a Republic and to keep only 'external association' with the Commonwealth – an aim he achieved, at last, in 1937. The Irish Republic contrived, with Irish logic, to confuse yet more profoundly the already intricate theory of Commonwealth relations.

Indian problems were no simpler. A series of Round

Table Conferences was held in the early thirties at which Gandhi demanded for India Dominion status in the fullest Irish sense. The anxiety of the National Government, now inclined to regard substantial independence for India as inevitable, was how to secure enough protection and representation for the different communities of India to forestall civil war. In 1935 it passed the Government of India Act, providing for an all-India federation and greater autonomy for the provincial governments. The latter provisions were carried out much more fully than the former, and the coming of war in 1939 deferred further attempts at a settlement. The Act of 1935, however, afforded a sound liberal basis on which later negotiations could begin, and made some contribution to the final agreements (see Chapter 8).

One final 'family affair' of these years calls for special comment. It was now that the monarchy won for itself that remarkable hold on the affections of the British people and on the imagination of the Commonwealth as a whole which enabled it to weather the storm that lay ahead. Already before 1931, as has been shown,[1] King George V, Queen Mary, and the Prince of Wales had created firm roles for the royal family in a post-war world of chronic instability and crisis. The Prince's tours of the Empire raised his popularity to great heights in the twenties. The Crown remained a focus of 'common allegiance' even after the Statute of Westminster and after Irish demolition of imperial ties. Two events based it, now, on even firmer foundations. One was the King's Christmas Day broadcasts to all peoples of the Commonwealth and Empire, the first of which was delivered in 1932. These enormously popular annual talks made the magic of monarchy felt in a more intimate way throughout the Commonwealth. The other event was the Silver Jubilee, celebrated in May 1935. It gave occasion at an anxious mo-

1. See p. 105.

ment in world affairs for reflective retrospect of national
fortunes since 1910. It also demonstrated the affectionate
popular esteem in which the King and Queen were held in
the Britain of 1935. 'I'd no idea they felt like that about me,'
remarked George V after a drive through the cheering East
End of London: 'I am beginning to think they must really
like me for myself.' Showing that he was 'just as much King
in Whitechapel as King in Whitehall', George V was cher-
ished, in a world fast declining into international dishonour
and collapse, as an embodiment of all the domestic and public virtues: in Sir Harold Nicolson's list, 'faith, duty, honesty,
courage, common sense, tolerance, decency, and truth'.
Plain, homely, human virtues, desperately needed in a
world where Hitler and Mussolini had cried havoc, and
were soon to let loose the dogs of war. His death, on
20 January 1936, was indeed like the passing of a whole
era of English history. He had perhaps, as his successor
remarked, waged 'a private war with the twentieth century',
but his very old-fashionedness had been his strength.

THE LOCUST YEARS

Throughout the years 1931–5 Stanley Baldwin was continuously in office, Churchill continuously excluded from
office. In November 1935, when Baldwin was triumphantly
returned in the elections, Churchill was equally persistently
excluded. They agreed in describing these years as 'years
that the locust hath eaten'. They were, as Churchill saw
and said at the time, but Baldwin only admitted later, a
time of tragically lost opportunities, of last chances never
seized. It was now that the fabric of international organization, and the essential sub-structure of confidence and
resolve, were alike eroded by a series of successful aggressions by the dictators, of futile protests by the democracies.
By 1935 the hopes of a decade before were completely

shattered. Prospects of peace hung by the thread of a general western rearmament speedy and massive enough to deter vainglorious tyrants from taking the final gamble of a general war. How did this terrible deterioration come about? And how far does responsibility for it lie at the door of the National Government?

The sequence of events can be briefly listed. In September 1931 Japan began the conquest of Manchuria. The Chinese Government appealed to the League of Nations, and to the United States as a signatory of the Briand–Kellogg Pact. Neither made a response prompt or decisive enough to give the Japanese any cause to halt or even to amend their plans of conquest. In December the Council of the League (of which Britain was a permanent member) postponed indefinitely any coercive measures against Japan. In 1932 fighting broke out in Shanghai between Chinese and Japanese forces, and truce was imposed by joint Anglo-American action. But the two countries did not follow it up, and in 1933 when Japan withdrew from the League and launched its attack on China proper the League did nothing and the United States did nothing.

Meanwhile, in January 1933, Hitler became Chancellor of Germany and proceeded to establish the National Socialist Party in dictatorial power, ruthlessly crushing all opposition. The Disarmament Conference, which had opened inauspiciously in February 1932 at Geneva, had already faced the brutal fact that Germany had been illegally rearming for some time. It resumed its meeting in March and again in October 1933, only to learn of Germany's withdrawal from both the Conference and membership of the League. Had it been possible for either the League or the major Powers to take firm action then, the tide might have turned. But nothing was done. In May 1934 the Disarmament Conference was adjourned indefinitely.

In 1935 Italy launched her premeditated attack on Abyssinia, a fellow-member of the League. Abyssinia's appeal to the League under Article 15 of the Covenant coincided, in March, with Hitler's adoption of conscription in Germany. Conscription had been expressly forbidden in the Treaty of Versailles. Britain, along with France, was busy trying to form the 'Stresa Front' with Italy against Germany, and at the Stresa Conference in April neither MacDonald nor his foreign secretary, Sir John Simon, cared to mention Abyssinia. MacDonald resigned, because of failing health, on 7 June, and was duly replaced by Baldwin. Simon was similarly replaced by Sir Samuel Hoare. At Geneva in September Hoare declared that Britain stood 'for the collective maintenance of the Covenant in its entirety; and particularly for steady, collective resistance to all acts of unprovoked aggression'. It was widely thought that British policy had swung back again to support 'collective security' implemented through the League, rather than following a stratagem of manipulating the balance of power such as was implied by Stresa. The following month, when Mussolini openly declared war on Abyssinia and the League pronounced Italy an aggressor and called for sanctions against it, it seemed, indeed, that the tide was turning. Japan's claims on Manchuria, Germany's claims to rearm and break free from the restrictions of the Versailles settlement, were both arguable. Mussolini's claim to Abyssinia was not even that. It rested on out-of-date grudges, dreams of avarice, and prefabricated excuses. The clear overt challenge to the principles of the League, in the form of open aggression against a fellow-member, was apparently to be met, at last, with some courage and resolve.

But the sequel, as the year 1935 drew to a close, proved how wrong such beliefs were. The National Government, now led by Baldwin, fought the elections of November partly on the strength of the nation's economic recovery since 1931, partly on the issue of foreign policy. It declared that the League would 'remain, as heretofore, the keystone of British foreign policy'. It promised that the Government would strive 'to uphold the Covenant and to maintain and increase the efficiency of the League'. It announced that it would begin a moderate programme of rearmament, while continuing to work and hope for a general limitation of armaments. Mr L. S. Amery's account of his talks with Hoare and Neville Chamberlain at the end of September reveals the half-heartedness of its two leading ministers. Of Chamberlain he wrote in his diary:

His whole view, like Sam's, was that we were bound to try out the League of Nations (in which he does not himself believe very much) for political reasons at home, and that there was no question of our going beyond the mildest of economic sanctions such as an embargo on the purchase of Italian goods or the sale of munitions to Italy. . . . If things became too serious the French would run out first, and we could show that we had done our best.[1]

It was the prevalence within ministerial circles of this attitude which doubtless explains the *dénouement* that startled the world. In mid November 1935 the National Government gained 432 seats, the Opposition only 180. Baldwin returned to power with Hoare as his foreign secretary. On 10 December the country learned that Hoare, on his way through Paris for a holiday in Switzerland, had agreed with M. Pierre Laval, the French Premier, to propose a settlement based on the surrender to Italy of very large parts of Abyssinian territory. The 'Hoare–Laval Pact' exploded any belief that the Government intended to work a system of collective security. The popular outcry was so great that Hoare, refusing to recant publicly, had to resign.[2] His

1. L. S. Amery, *My Political Life*, vol. III (1955), p. 174.
2. See for his own account, Viscount Templewood, *Nine Troubled Years* (1954), Part II; and Sir Anthony Eden, *Facing the Dictators* (1962).

replacement by Anthony Eden, publicly identified with genuine belief in the League system, alone saved Baldwin from party mutiny. Baldwin declared in the House, 'It is perfectly obvious now that the proposals are absolutely and completely dead.' He added, with his customary disarming frankness, that 'I was not expecting that deeper feeling which was manifested . . . in many parts of the country on what I may call the ground of conscience and honour.' But, then, what had become of collective ministerial responsibility? The truth was – though Baldwin did not then perceive it – that it simply was not possible, in the Europe of 1935, to switch foreign policies to and fro in this way without assuring the waiting dictators that Britain and France lacked the nerve and the will-power to defy them, whether separately or through collective action.

The main burden of responsibility for Britain's failure to put up effective resistance to the successive aggressions of Japan, Germany, and Italy must undoubtedly lie upon Baldwin, MacDonald, and their colleagues, who held power in these years. It is fruitless to try to apportion responsibility among friends and allies: ultimately the collapse of the League and the settlement of 1919 was, of course, the collective failure of all the peacemakers. But did not the responsibility, within a democracy such as Britain, lie to some extent also on the Opposition, and even on the nation as a whole? In a famous reply to Churchill, on 12 November 1936, Baldwin maintained that it did. He blamed the pacifist feeling which had existed strongly in the country in 1933 and 1934. He recalled that at the by-election at East Fulham, in October 1933, a National Government candidate advocating rearmament was heavily defeated by a Labour candidate opposed to rearmament, and a majority of 14,521 turned into a minority vote of 4,840. He declared that he had not seen any prospect, then, of getting a mandate for rearmament, and spoke now with an 'appalling frankness'. Rather than hold elections then, with the likelihood that they would return a large Labour majority opposed to rearmament, he had held on until the mood of the country could change. It had changed by the end of 1935. Then he did seek an electoral decision. It might reasonably be replied that Governments do not need 'mandates' to be responsible governments, and that Baldwin's emphasis on rearmament even in 1935 had not been so overwhelming. But in the course of this explanation Baldwin uttered two sentences that haunted him for the rest of his life, and smeared his reputation ever since.

Supposing I had gone to the country and said that Germany was rearming and that we must rearm, does anybody think that this pacific democracy would have rallied to that cry at that moment? I cannot think of anything that would have made the loss of the election from my point of view more certain.

The time he spoke of was 1933-4. In February 1933 the Oxford Union Society had passed its famous motion that 'this House will in no circumstances fight for its King and Country'. Peace societies of many kinds were holding large and enthusiastic meetings. Thinking about peace and security was very muddled, so that internationalist supporters of the League (committed, therefore, to collective sanctions against an aggressor) often thought of themselves as pacifists. Most relevant of all, for Baldwin's case, the Labour Party was led by George Lansbury, veteran spokesman and grandfather-figure of the idealistic Left; and the party-line was to oppose rearmament by a Conservative Government on the grounds that it could not be trusted, while urging vigorous support for collective action against aggression. Even apart from East Fulham, Baldwin had excuse enough for thinking of Labour as somewhat unrealistic in foreign policy.

His 'appalling frankness' speech came to be profoundly misunderstood, because it was taken to refer to his decision to hold an election at the end of 1935 – by which time, as has been seen, public opinion was becoming rather more aware of the unpalatable truth that collective security might need military power to provide it. But Baldwin was right about the prevalence of pacifism in 1933–4. Canon 'Dick' Sheppard, a radio preacher of immense appeal, founded the Peace Pledge Union in October 1934. Within a year 80,000 people pledged themselves on postcards not to fight in a war. It was widely held that arms bred war, and that disarmament had been prevented by the sinister machinations of armaments manufacturers, commonly called 'merchants of death'. The spate of anti-war literature of the later twenties[1] now bore fruit in a refusal to contemplate war, even to resist frontal aggression. Unilateral disarmament and individual conscientious refusal to fight were the only way.

At this point, too, the accumulated legacy of deep social distrust which had come down from the days of 'khaki' elections, 'red-letter' scares, the General Strike and indifference to mass unemployment, began to matter. The mutual suspicion it engendered explains, on one hand, Baldwin's inability to contemplate making way for a new Labour Government, and on the other the contention of the Left that a Conservative Government could not be trusted with massive armaments. Into the gap left by this mutual repulsion of the parties came a tide of absolute pacifism.

Absolute pacifism could be – though it not always was – a self-consistent and intellectually tenable position. So was a policy of resolute international collaboration to enforce existing treaty obligations and uphold, by means of overwhelming military power, the decisions of international organizations such as the League. Neither political party, however, held either of these views, though individuals such as George Lansbury at one extreme, Winston Churchill at

1. See p. 119.

the other, did hold them. While the Labour Party urged reliance upon collective security with disarmament, the Conservative Party resorted to independent national action outside the League, backed by only moderate and belated rearmament. Either Party's policy, consistently pursued, would probably have led to war and might have led to national defeat. What was in fact done was a muddle of measures – now supporting the League and now abandoning it, now enforcing sanctions severe enough to arouse Italian public resentment and solidify it in support of Mussolini, yet insufficient to impede his conquest of Abyssinia. An over-riding anxiety was to keep the two dictators apart, as they had been at the end of 1934, to prevent Hitler from making an ally out of Mussolini. Nothing could more completely have accomplished the opposite result than the measures actually taken.

On both sides policies were overmuch coloured by escapist and wishful thinking based on things it was fashionable (and comfortable) to believe: that dictators could be overthrown by economic means, and might indeed head for ruin spontaneously; that military might could not defy the moral opinion of the world; that political predicaments could be conjured away by finding the right ethical principle. Perhaps these ideas proved more pernicious than the simple longing for 'peace at any price'.

The amalgam of inconsistent ideas then most common in British opinion was clearly expressed by the results of a Peace Ballot held in the winter of 1934 and announced in June 1935. Between 10 and 11 million people endorsed the views that Britain should remain a member of the League, and that she should seek reduction in armaments, and even the all-round abolition of national military and naval aircraft, by international agreement. Similar numbers voted for collective coercion of an aggressor by 'economic and non-military measures'. But only some $6\frac{3}{4}$ millions supported further recourse to military measures against an aggressor, and more than 2¼ millions opposed this. The idea that Fascist dictators would submit to non-military coercion, when they knew that their opponents had no intention of resisting might with might, was a favourite belief in the thirties. In its shirking of unpalatable risks, its mental and moral inertia, the National Government fully represented the mass of British opinion in the 'Baldwin age'. Its real condemnation was that it did not give that initiative and leadership which a democracy never needs more desperately than when it is inclined to surrender to its own wishful thinking. C. R. Attlee's comment, many years later, had point: 'We didn't stop them re-arming. With their majority they could have done anything they wanted about armaments and putting our defences in proper shape – if they'd had the will.'

The Labour Party, in the autumn of 1935, took its first important step towards a more realistic policy under new leaders. The Party Conference at Brighton in October revealed an open split between those who opposed both sanctions and rearmament (Lansbury and Sir Stafford Cripps) and the bulk of the national executive, backed by the T.U.C., which favoured both with sober realization that they might lead to war.[1] When Lansbury put the case for Christian pacifism, and offered to resign from the leadership of the party because he disagreed with the official resolution supporting sanctions, his views were greeted with tremendous applause. But Ernest Bevin spoke next, for the resolution of the T.U.C. He spoke brutally, to sharpen the contrast with the sentiment to which Lansbury had appealed. He charged Lansbury with putting both himself and the Party in a false position by continuing as leader

1. For differing interpretations of this occasion, see Alan Bullock, *The Life and Times of Ernest Bevin*, vol. I (1960), pp. 562–74, and Raymond Postgate, *The Life of George Lansbury* (1951), pp. 291–305.

when his views conflicted with those of the majority – a position that it was now too late to retrieve by disavowing responsibility on grounds of private conscience. 'It is placing the Executive and the Movement in an absolutely wrong position to be taking your conscience round from body to body to be told what you ought to do with it.' And to Cripps, who had spoken of the League as the 'International Burglars' Union' likely to involve labour in a 'capitalist and imperialist war that sanctions may entail', Bevin retorted common-sensically, 'You cannot be in and out at the same time, not if you are honest.' Bevin won, and the vote in support of sanctions was carried by 2,168,000 votes to 102,000. The full implications were not yet generally seen or accepted. But a decisive step had been taken towards framing a more consistent, realistic policy. On 8 October Lansbury resigned from leadership, and was succeeded by Major C. R. Attlee. It was a turning-point in the history of Labour.

CHAPTER SIX

The Inclined Plane, 1936–9

YEAR OF ABDICATION

THE events described in the previous Chapter were a glum prelude to the grimmest and most crucial year since 1919. With the machinery and prestige of the League shattered, the rulers of Italy, Germany, and Japan proceeded with preparations for fresh conquests. The Governments of Britain and France were the two pillars by which any new system of security in western Europe could alone be held up. They had left the world in little doubt that they would prefer substantial concessions (preferably at the expense of other nations) to self-defence. Public opinion, still heavily defeatist and pacifist, liked to recall some of the 'frank confessions' of Stanley Baldwin which made the whole idea of meeting aggression by war seem preposterous. 'I think it is well for the man in the street to realize that there is no power on earth that can prevent him from being bombed ... The bomber will always get through' (1932). 'When you think of the defence of England, you no longer think of the chalk cliffs of Dover, you think of the Rhine. That is where our frontier lies' (1934). In March 1936 Hitler reoccupied the demilitarized zone of the Rhineland. He met with a revulsion of feeling among the French, but no opposition from either of the Governments whose security he thereby destroyed. Eight months later Mr Baldwin was remarking that rearmament only made war more likely: 'I am prepared to devote all our efforts ... to do what is necessary, but I am conscious all the time of the folly of all of us.'

When a British Prime Minister could so complacently

accept hostile occupation of an area that he had himself called Britain's modern frontier, and could admit that acquiring power wherewith to check such acts was pure folly, there had occurred a curious abdication of responsibility – almost of the will to survive. The year 1936, in this and in other senses, was a year of 'abdications'. By now other nations had found more dynamic and purposeful governments. The United States had found F. D. Roosevelt and his 'New Deal'; France and Spain found 'Popular Front' governments; Belgium had M. Paul van Zeeland's national administration; Germany had Hitler. Britain had a government slightly more exclusively Conservative than the one before.

The Labour Party at its Brighton Conference had begun to shape a new attitude and to find new leadership. But autumn 1935 was too late for it to influence policy in the crucial early months of 1936. It suffered from a *malaise* similar to that of the Conservatives, and is open to the same charge of doing 'too little too late'. One omen of the mounting ideological struggle was the formation, in May 1936, of the Left Book Club, a powerful intellectual influence during the next three years. Within a year it attracted 50,000 members, each of whom received monthly a book chosen by a committee consisting of the publisher Victor Gollancz, Professor Harold Laski, and Mr John Strachey (then an avowed Marxist). It was a landmark in the shaping of a self-conscious and more ideological 'Left'. Together with the publication of 'Pelican Books' and 'Penguin Specials' from 1937 onwards – many of them tracts for the times and dealing with international affairs in the form of sixpenny paper-backs by eminent authors – the Left Book Club met the needs of a newly alert, anxious, and receptive reading public. Its first offering, *Out of the Night: A Biologist's View of the Future*, by H. J. Muller, Professor of Zoology at Texas University, set the pace.

Describing future possibilities of artificial insemination, the author exclaimed: 'How many women, in an enlightened community devoid of superstitious taboos and of sex slavery, would be eager and proud to bear and rear a child of Lenin or of Darwin!' Fortunately some of its successors were more realistic.

In May 1936 the Italians captured the Abyssinian capital, Addis Ababa, and the Emperor Haile Selassie went into dignified exile while King Victor Emmanuel III of Italy was proclaimed Emperor of Ethiopia. In the autumn Mussolini and Hitler made the 'Rome–Berlin Axis', not a military alliance so much as an agreement to concert future aggressions. Germany and Japan signed an Anti-Comintern Pact, to which Italy, too, adhered a year later. These evidences that the three restless Powers meant to hunt as a pack produced no positive counter-action from Britain, France, or the United States. Britain, indeed, had made a naval treaty with Germany in 1935 and now proceeded, in January 1937, to the so-called 'Gentleman's Agreement' with Italy, accepting the *status quo* in the Mediterranean.

Little wonder that, faced with a Spanish Civil War in which Germany and, even more, Italy, flagrantly gave help to the rebels against the Popular Front Government, Britain and France found themselves expected to stand aside. The dictators helped to establish in power General Franco, whom they hoped to use to challenge both French security on land and British naval strength in the Mediterranean. The British and French Governments over-eagerly agreed to arrangements for non-intervention which all major Powers (including Germany, Italy, and the Soviet Union) signed by the end of August 1936. The agreement was, of course, soon infringed by the three Powers mentioned, the Soviet Union sending fighter planes to the republican Government, Italy sending considerable forces and equipment, Germany mainly aircraft, to the rebels. By the end of

1936 the rebels held most of northern and western Spain and Franco's Government was formally recognized by Germany and Italy. They expected a speedy victory. But in the new year Madrid held. The Government received help in the form of the International Brigade, recruited from mainly left-wing opponents of Fascism in several European countries, including Britain and France. The Spanish Civil War became international, and Spain became the ideological battlefield of Europe. Even at the end of 1937 the military situation was still a stalemate. Thereafter the extent of foreign help to General Franco became decisive, although his eventual victory was delayed until April 1939.

The effect of the Spanish Civil War on Britain was great. Sympathy undoubtedly lay mainly with the republican Government, though the extent of Communist influence on it was a frequent source of apprehension and doubt. The suspicion, fortified by the policy of strict non-intervention, that the British Government secretly wanted Franco to win, intensified existing schisms in public opinion. To go and fight for Spanish democracy was a call that evoked warm response in many young men thirsting for some such opportunity of action. It did much to turn the tide of absolute pacifism, and not only because it gave further proof of Fascist intentions and ruthlessness. It broke the spell, so powerfully cast by Baldwinian politics, of inertia, helplessness, drift. By giving people something to do that was accepted as positive, urgent, and right, it revived a sense of purpose in national politics. By infusing a spirit of class-warfare into political discussion it probably, in the short run, increased disunity in the country. But in longer terms it almost certainly made for a new unity as well as new coherence of purpose. This came about partly by the moral crisis and the heart-searching doubts it caused on all sides. The Left became war-minded, even militant. The Right became wedded to 'non-intervention', almost pacifism. The parliamentary parties were in some measure by-passed by the mass of new organizations – the Friends of Nationalist Spain who favoured Franco, the Friends of Spain, and many others, who opposed him. The Press divided almost equally, and hundreds of pamphlets and books appeared, expounding and passionately pleading. Such a commotion of opinion denoted something new.

At the end of 1936 attention was absorbed in one supreme, dramatic abdication – the abdication of the King. Edward VIII, long popular as Prince of Wales and still unmarried, succeeded his father in January. At his side, when the heralds proclaimed his accession, stood an American lady, Mrs Ernest Simpson. She had divorced one husband and hoped soon to divorce another. The King spent much of his free time in her company, especially on his Mediterranean 'sunshine cruise' that summer. Readers of the British Press hardly learned of her existence, for it – unlike the American Press – unanimously upheld complete self-censorship for nearly a year. British opinion therefore knew of their association only through foreign papers and gossip, and the countless rumours that increasingly circulated. Even the case of *Simpson* v. *Simpson*, at Ipswich Assizes on 27 October, in which she secured a decree *nisi* and thereby freedom to marry again after six months, was given minimal publicity. It was important for Baldwin, who had to tender official advice to the monarch on such matters as would affect the position of the monarchy, the Commonwealth, and the succession, to discover the King's intentions. On 20 October he had an informal talk with the King, but for nearly six weeks the crisis remained discreetly veiled. At a further meeting on 16 November Baldwin learned that the King intended to marry Mrs Simpson and was prepared to abdicate if need be, though he wished if possible to remain King. The Cabinet, strongly led by

Baldwin, wanted to prevent abdication but also to prevent the King's marrying Mrs Simpson. The compromise solution of a morganatic marriage which avoided the King's wife becoming Queen was ruled out because the Government refused to bring in the necessary legislation.

Baldwin had the situation well in hand before the public storm broke on 2 and 3 December. The Bishop of Bradford, Dr Blunt, made remarks at a diocesan conference about the King's need for God's grace. The Bishop unintentionally released the avalanche. Anxious editors took his remarks as the cue to make the news public in Britain. For the next week the public thought and talked of little else as the drama reached its climax. People took sides for the King or for Baldwin. Much opinion in Britain and in the Dominions was averse to having as Queen a lady with two previous husbands still living. The monarchy as George V had left it could not be reconciled in public imagery with other than complete stability, continuity, and 'respectability'. The King's decision to abdicate was given to Baldwin on 5 December, but he did not fully communicate it to the House of Commons until five days later. Baldwin's speech then was masterly in its combination of informality and political skill. He persuaded the House that his own solution, even his own handling of it all, was the only one conceivable. It was a masterpiece of casual persuasiveness. 'He may have his defects as a party leader or as an administrator,' wrote *The Times* leader-writer acidly, 'but in handling a great national problem . . . he has no comparable rival. . . .' Many found themselves wishing that the Prime Minister had shown equal strength of purpose and equal relentlessness in handling Heads of other States.

On 11 December a Declaration of Abdication Act was rushed through and the Duke of York became King as George VI. That evening Edward broadcast to the nation before going into self-imposed exile, later to marry 'the woman I love'. It was a tense and moving speech. It was soon apparent that the crisis had caused no lasting harm to the fabric of constitutional monarchy either in Britain or in the Commonwealth. The new King and Queen so perfectly reproduced the familiar pattern that the throne was unimpaired.

That the crisis could have got out of hand and rent the nation asunder is suggested by the noisy and ill-assorted supporters who rallied embarrassingly to the King: Sir Oswald Mosley, Mr Harry Pollitt, Lady Houston, Lords Beaverbrook and Rothermere, the *Catholic Times* and *Social Credit*, the romantically inclined of all ages who revelled in the drama of the choice before the King. Anyone listening to Baldwin's oration found it difficult to know just what choice the King was supposed to be making.

Not whether or no he should marry Mrs Simpson, morganatically or royally, because Mr Baldwin had said that was impossible; not whether or no he should abdicate, because Mr Baldwin had said no pressure was being brought to bear on him; not whether or no he should dispense with his present Ministers, and appoint others, or rule without Parliament, because Mr Baldwin said no constitutional issue had arisen. What, then, was he being called on to decide? No one quite knew.[1]

Baldwin's oratorical skill lay in adroitly confusing and smothering the issue, while giving every impression of clarifying it. When, for once, he chose not to abdicate responsibility but to display and deploy his full resources of ingenuity, agility, and relentlessness, it was another who had to abdicate. It was only a month since he had made his 'appalling frankness' speech, confessing an incapacity to change public opinion.[2]

1. Malcolm Muggeridge, *The Thirties (1930–1940) in Great Britain* (1940), p. 285.
2. For accounts of the crisis highly critical of Baldwin, see Compton Mackenzie, *Windsor Tapestry* (1938), and Malcolm Muggeridge, op. cit. For more favourable accounts see G. M. Young, *Stanley Baldwin* (1952),

THE CHAMBERLAIN ERA

Baldwin did not seek to remain in power for long after his triumphant handling of the abdication crisis. His version of 'National Government' (June 1935–May 1937) weathered its many storms with remarkable resilience. Sir Samuel Hoare, driven by popular fury from the Foreign Office in December 1935, was taken back to run the Admiralty six months later. The appointment of Sir Thomas Inskip of prayer-book fame as Minister for the Coordination of Defence inspired little confidence; and in May 1936 J. H. Thomas resigned from the Colonial Office amid scandal of a budget leakage. Ramsay MacDonald remained throughout as Lord President of the Council, and died six months after the ministry resigned in May 1937. Neville Chamberlain, Chancellor of the Exchequer, emerged as the strongest man in the Government and as heir-apparent to Baldwin. King George VI was crowned on 12 May 1937. On 27 May Baldwin made way for Chamberlain, who took office on the following day. Sir John Simon succeeded him as Chancellor of the Exchequer, Sir Samuel Hoare went to the Home Office, Anthony Eden remained at the Foreign Office, but only until February 1938.

On 10 June 1936 Chamberlain had already made clear his resolve to abandon sanctions, not only as applied against Italy but also as a measure he was prepared to adopt against

Chapter XXIV, and J. W. Wheeler-Bennett, *King George VI* (1958), Chapter VIII. For personal accounts, see Duke of Windsor, *A King's Story* (1951), and Duchess of Windsor, *The Heart has its Reasons* (1956). It is now known that Neville Chamberlain, months before the crisis, had drafted a memorandum of censure on the King, that it 'was discussed by an inner group of ministers, and Stanley Baldwin dissuaded them from sending it to the King' (Thomas Jones, *A Diary with Letters, 1931–1950* (1954), p. 371; which also contains other important details about the whole affair). On the part of the Press see *History of The Times, 1912–1920 and 1921–1948*, vol. IV (1952). The roles in the crisis of *The Times*, the B.B.C., and the Archbishop of Canterbury remain somewhat obscure.

any Power. Quaintly describing the hope of saving Abysinnia by continuing to apply sanctions against Italy as 'the very midsummer of madness', he asked: 'Is it not apparent that the policy of sanctions involves, I do not say war, but a risk of war?... Is it not also apparent from what has happened that, in the presence of such a risk, nations cannot be relied upon to proceed to the last extremity unless their vital interests are threatened?' Chamberlain, clearly, was going to be more impatient of shams than Baldwin. But was there not now a new danger, that this forceful man of narrow but strong-willed views would over-rate the chance of getting peace by timely concession?

Britain had known only two Prime Ministers since 1923: and Chamberlain was of their generation, being only three years younger than MacDonald, two years younger than Baldwin. Lacking their warmth and generosity of mind, he drew upon larger resources of energy, will-power, and precision of thought. His brusquer manner and rasping voice contrasted with their more mellifluous phrases and delivery. He was not born to suffer fools gladly, and had not the *panache* of his father, Joseph, or his half-brother, Austen. His ministerial career had revealed a civil-servant quality: he was an efficient and progressively minded administrator as Minister of Health (1924–9), a tough and resilient Chancellor of the Exchequer, not afraid of unpopularity (1931–7). Like his father, he had been Lord Mayor of Birmingham. Something of the *ethos* of that great commercial city hung around his approach to foreign policy, of which he had virtually no experience at all.

By experience and qualities alike Chamberlain was cast to be a vigorous, efficient Premier in home affairs. It was his personal tragedy to be Premier during three years in which, more than at any other time since 1918, international affairs assumed supreme national importance. 'Masterful, confident, and ruled by an instinct for order, he would give a lead, and perhaps impart an edge, on every question. His approach was arduously careful but his mind, once made up, hard to change. . . .' Forming a Government that looked, and at times was, a one-man affair, he drew upon himself the fire of the Opposition at a time when tempers were especially aroused by what Eden called 'the War of the Spanish obsession'. The civil war in Spain did not end until the spring of 1939, and formed a lurid background to the succession of *coups* and crises staged by the Rome–Berlin Axis. Again, the sequence of events need be only briefly recalled.

In July 1937 Japan began undeclared war on China – in effect a resumption, on a large scale, of the attack of 1931. Peking was evacuated and the Chinese were driven back to the line of the Yellow River. By the end of the year the Japanese had captured both Shanghai and the capital, Nanking. Although the League of Nations formally condemned Japan's action, neither Britain, France, nor the United States attempted to apply any sanctions. By October 1938 Canton fell. Chamberlain resolutely refused to take any action that might directly embroil Britain. In the Far East, given United States attitudes, he believed in peace at any price. In 1934 he had observed, with great prescience: 'U.S.A. will give us no undertaking to resist by force any action by Japan, short of an attack on Hawaii or Honolulu.'

In March 1938 Hitler moved against Austria. The Treaty of Versailles had forbidden union (*Anschluss*) between Germany and the new lopsided state of Austria. In July 1934 Austrian Nazis attempted a *coup* to prepare for German annexation. The plan was blocked by Italy. But Italy's pre-occupation with Abyssinia and Spain, and Germany's greatly enhanced military power, encouraged Hitler to make a fresh attempt in 1938. He assumed supreme command of all the armed forces of the *Reich*, so gaining absolute control over the Army lest it should obstruct his plans. On 12 March, despite concessions from the Austrian Chancellor, Schuschnigg, German troops marched in, occupied Vienna, and moved on to the Italian frontier at the Brenner Pass. Hitler, who was himself Austrian by birth, accomplished with little international protest his first aggression against an independent State and struck another blow at the Versailles Settlement. The frontier of Czechoslovakia now lay exposed to German advance from Austria. Along this border Germany began to hold military manoeuvres on a grand scale.

Meanwhile, in February 1938, Anthony Eden had resigned as Foreign Secretary in open disagreement with Chamberlain's foreign policy. Lord Cranborne, Eden's Under-Secretary of State and the future Lord Salisbury, resigned with him. Chamberlain got his way about 'appeasing' Italy only by threatening to resign himself. Henceforth it was more blatantly than ever a one-man Government, for Lord Halifax, who succeeded Eden, was known to agree with the Prime Minister. Accordingly, the spring and summer of 1938 were the hey-day of 'appeasement' as a policy for Britain. The word had not yet acquired the sinister sense it was soon to have. It still meant taking a certain initiative in working out, by agreement, settlements of outstanding international disputes.

Some such, indeed, were susceptible to patient negotiation, and in these Chamberlain was successful. One was Ireland. In May 1937 De Valera issued the text of a new Constitution of Eire, defined as a 'sovereign independent Democratic State'. It came into effect at the end of 1937, when the Irish Free State ceased to exist. Chamberlain accepted it and proceeded, in April 1938, to sign agreements which went far to placate Irish nationalist feeling on everything save partition. He surrendered the three Irish ports held by Britain since 1921. He ended the trade war. He accepted £10 million as a lump sum in payment of land annuities and other outstanding payments. Two years later Eamon De Valera wrote: 'You did more than any former British Statesman to make a true friendship between the peoples of our two countries possible.' It was a testimonial, from an unexpected source, that many former British statesmen would have coveted. Churchill's scornful attack on the agreements was less than just.

Less susceptible to 'appeasement' was the problem of Palestine. Britain, as the mandatory Power, found it increasingly impossible to keep the peace between the Arabs and the Jews. Jewish immigrants, seeking that 'national home' promised by A. J. Balfour in 1917, flowed into Palestine, especially after the European economic crisis and the Nazi persecution. By the end of 1934 there were some 300,000 Jews in Palestine, as compared with three times that number of Arabs. In 1936 there were riots, strikes, and outbursts of great violence. Arab terrorists attacked not only the Jews but also the British troops and police trying to keep order. The Jews took reprisals – on both. A Royal Commission, set up at the end of 1936, reported by the middle of 1937 and proposed a threefold partition of the territory into an Arab State, a Jewish State, and a mandated strip, including Jerusalem and Bethlehem, under British control. The proposal pleased nobody. A further Commission in 1938 rejected partition, and instead a Round Table Conference was summoned for early in 1939. It reached no agreement, civil war went on, and in May 1939 the Government issued a policy statement of its own. It proposed to allow regulated Jewish immigration for five years more, and thereafter to end it save with the consent of the Arabs. Then an independent Palestine would be set up, containing a large Jewish minority. Again, this proved no solution. Britain began world war in 1939 with a civil war on her hands in Palestine, just as in 1914 she had entered war with endemic civil war in Ireland.

Perhaps his success with Ireland, with negotiation of trade treaties between Britain, the United States, and Canada, and (relatively) in reaching some reconciliation with Mussolini, was itself to prove fatal, in that it made Chamberlain stubbornly resolved not to resist German attacks on Czechoslovakia in the autumn of 1938. 'You have only to look at the map,' he noted in March 1938, 'to see that nothing that France or we could do could possibly save Czechoslovakia from being overrun by the Germans, if they wanted to do it. . . . I have therefore abandoned any idea of giving guarantees to Czechoslovakia, or the French in connexion with her obligations to that country.'[1]

This being so, it was scarcely necessary, had he known it, for Hitler to stage the elaborate parade of indignation about alleged ill-treatment of Germans in the Sudetenland by the Czech Government. Hitler's strenuous efforts to justify his invasion of the most important industrial and strategic areas of the country by reference to minority-rights could have been spared. The only essential was to convince the British Prime Minister that Germany would go to war rather than forgo this aggression, and then France would be automatically paralysed and Britain sternly held back from taking any form of 'sanction' or reprisals. Nevertheless, on 24 March 1938 Chamberlain warned the House of Commons that if Britain's ally, France, became involved in war for the defence of Czechoslovakia the inexorable pressure of facts might well prove stronger than formal pronouncements. This somewhat cryptic declaration was widely held to imply a promise to stand by Czechoslovakia if France did the same.

Chamberlain's reactions to the mounting Sudeten crisis passed through three phases. First, he sent Lord Runciman to Prague to act as conciliator and adviser. When Hitler

1. Quoted in Keith Feiling, *The Life of Neville Chamberlain* (1946), pp. 347–8.

became more menacing he himself flew to Munich to meet
Hitler and seek a peaceful solution by mediation. He returned and conferred with the French Premier, Édouard
Daladier. Secondly, he agreed with Daladier a plan for
extensive cessions of territory by Czechoslovakia and forced
it upon a reluctant Czech Government. Thirdly, he flew to
Bad Godesberg for a second meeting with Hitler, only to
find the *Führer*'s new demands so inflated that he could
not accept them, but instead appealed to Mussolini to
bring about a new conference to save peace. On 29 September Chamberlain, Daladier, Hitler, and Mussolini met
and agreed terms to be imposed on the Czechs, in the
absence of any representative of either the victims or of the
Soviet Union, which had earlier offered support. Chamberlain flew back to London, to be welcomed with immense
enthusiasm as the man whose initiative had saved the world
from war.

The policy of 'appeasement', applied in this way to the
demands of the Fascist dictators, rested on an ultimate
fallacy: that their aims were limited to redressing specific
grievances, and once these were reasonably and willingly
conceded they would settle down peacefully. It meant
regarding their appetites as satiable, the grievances as
legitimate, their objectives as limited. If, as Churchill held,
none of these assumptions was true, then to make concessions was merely to strengthen both their appetites and
their means of satisfying them. Because he stubbornly clung
to fallacious views, Chamberlain was led into a false position. To mediate, as a sort of arbitrator, in the internal
affairs of a foreign State as did Runciman and, on his first
flight, Chamberlain, was in itself a doubtful procedure.
But till then he had acted on the principle that there was a
real dispute between the Czech Government and its internal
German minority which was endangering peace but which
could, by wise concession, be resolved. When Hitler, at

Berchtesgaden, insisted that the territories inhabited by Sudeten Germans must be ceded to Germany on the principle of 'self-determination', he avowed the real purpose of his whole policy – outright aggression – and destroyed the only reasonable basis for further British mediation. To go on, after that, to coerce a friendly Government into ceding territory to a hostile neighbour was an unwonted role for any British Prime Minister.

There can be no doubt that Europe stood on the brink of war in September 1938. Faced with the excessive German demands of the Godesberg Memorandum the new Czech Government, under General Syrovy, rejected the demands and ordered general mobilization. The French mobilized 600,000 reservists and held military consultations with the British general staff. In Berlin Hitler made still more violent speeches and pleaded, 'This is the last territorial claim I shall make in Europe.' The British Navy was mobilized, and on 28 September Chamberlain broadcast. 'How horrible, fantastic, incredible, it is that we should be digging trenches and trying on gas-masks here because of a quarrel in a faraway country between people of whom we know nothing.' It was the authentic voice of the insular-minded Birmingham business-man. He went to Munich the next morning, convinced that the House of Commons wanted peace at any price. He was shocked by Hitler's practice of what, twenty years later, was to become known as 'brinkmanship'. The result was the collective blackmail of the Czechoslovak Government into giving Hitler all he wanted. Next day Mr Duff Cooper, First Lord of the Admiralty, resigned in protest. The initial hysterical relief at escape from war soon began to give way to a mood of shame and renewed fear. The surviving rump of the Czechoslovak State could not resist further aggression. When it came, in March 1939, Hitler met with little difficulty in occupying Bohemia and Moravia, while

Hungary seized Ruthenia. Chamberlain was left with the humiliation of explaining that the guarantee he had given, six months earlier, could scarcely apply now to a State that had ceased to exist. It was the lowest point of in-effectual and humiliating British foreign policy.

But it also marked the end of appeasement. Hitler had now broken even his own promises, and none would ever again believe him. He had committed, the cynics suggested, what in Chamberlain's eyes was the final crime – he had openly tricked Chamberlain. Defence of his policy of appeasement, at the time and since, has normally followed two lines: that it was necessary to gain time, to catch up on the pace of German rearmament, before risking war without also courting defeat; and that only a policy of long patience, and of abundant proof that Hitler could not be checked without war, made it possible for Britain to go to war united and purged of the pacifism, the sentimentalities, and the fears which hamstrung her policy in the earlier 1930s.

The first of these lines of defence, which can be tested by such facts as the speed and scale of British rearmament programmes and the use made of the time gained, lays Chamberlain open to the charge that if he deliberately chose this policy he was buying time and security for Britain by consciously sacrificing allies and friends who had trusted him. The second, whether it is a later generalization or an allegedly conscious calculation made at the time, implies even greater division and confusion of opinion in Britain than existed in fact. Moreover, Chamberlain's constant concern before March 1939 was to argue that Hitler must be trusted to be reasonable – not that war with him must be taken as inevitable.

The adequacy of Britain's rearmament programmes in these years is a subject of controversy. The outline programme of 1935 had envisaged increasing the Royal Air Force to a level of parity with the new German *Luftwaffe*. The British Navy, too, was overhauled and reconditioned, and in 1939 Churchill found it overwhelmingly superior to the German in strength and in numbers. The Army was neglected, and was thought of as for home defence and imperial outpost garrisons, rather than for expeditionary forces. It was only partly mechanized and modernized. Expenditures on armed forces give some measure of the disparities. In 1938 Germany spent £1,710 million, a quarter of her national income, on armaments; Great Britain spent £358 million, a mere 7 per cent of her national income, and this was greater than France was spending. Britain's total expenditure on defence was hampered until after Munich by Treasury control, parliamentary economies, Opposition distrust, and pacifist public opinion. Only after Munich did rearmament accelerate, fed by lavish defence budgets: £580 million for 1939–40. The economy became geared to war-production. It was later revealed that whereas 2,827 planes had been produced in 1938, 7,940 were produced in 1939. Civil defence preparations, under the able direction of Sir John Anderson after October 1938, moved ahead fast. They included plans for evacuation of people from cities, providing air-raid shelters, distribution of civilian gas-masks, emergency fire and transport services, and a large scheme of voluntary organizations.

On the other hand, Germany did not waste the interlude after Munich: and she had gained immensely in strategic advantages, in destruction of the thirty-six Czech divisions and acquisition of the Skoda works and other Czech resources. The balance sheet of Munich remains very difficult to draw up. There are too many imponderables. But it is far from obvious that, save in convincing the British and Dominion Governments that appeasement was a failure, the balance of gain was in its favour. The Labour Party had stopped direct opposition to rearmament in July 1937, though pacifist groups and members remained active. After the *Anschluss* opinion hardened increasingly in support of rapid rearmament. Few now trusted Hitler. But as late as 10 March 1939, only five days before Hitler devoured the remainder of Czechoslovakia, Chamberlain announced his belief that 'Europe was settling down to a period of tranquillity'. The image of a clear-eyed, realistic Prime Minister, compelled to fresh concessions by a cringing democracy, is implausible.[1] Perhaps the wisest verdict was Ernest Bevin's in 1941. 'If anyone asks me who was responsible for the British policy leading up to the war, I will, as a Labour man myself, make a confession and say, "All of us." We refused absolutely to face the facts. . . . But what is the use of blaming anybody?'

The sequel to March 1939 was the outbreak of the Second World War in September 1939. During the intervening six months Germany digested her great gains, economic and strategic, in Czechoslovakia, and began to menace Poland. Chamberlain, now completely converted from appeasement and from the reluctance to give pledges of support which went naturally with it, pledged support to Poland, Greece, Rumania, and Turkey. The guarantee to Poland, given at the end of March, became the formal reason for Britain's

1. On the great controversy about appeasement in general, and Munich in particular, see J. Wheeler-Bennett, *Munich: Prologue to Tragedy* (1948), L. B. Namier, *Europe in Decay: A Study in Disintegration, 1936-1940* (1950), both hostile to it; compare more favourable verdicts in Keith Feiling, *The Life of Neville Chamberlain* (1946), and Lord Strang, *Britain in World Affairs* (1961), Part III. For a not impartial eye-witness account, see Winston S. Churchill, *The Second World War*, vol. I (1948), *The Gathering Storm*, Book I; and for a lively account, M. Gilbert and R. Gott, *The Appeasers* (1963).

declaration of war on Germany on 3 September. On
1 September, without declaring war and perhaps in the
hope of another Munich, Hitler sent his armoured divisions
and planes into Poland. On the Sunday morning when
Britain's declaration of war was sent, Chamberlain broadcast
to the nation. He summarized the position in a phrase:
'. . . a situation in which no word given by Germany's ruler
could be trusted, and no people or country could feel themselves safe, had become intolerable.'

But meanwhile British policy suffered yet another shock.
On 23 August the German and Soviet Governments signed
a non-aggression pact for ten years. Its real purpose was
contained in a secret protocol which defined spheres of
influence in eastern Europe. Germany was to have Lithuania
and western Poland, the Soviet Union was to have Finland,
Estonia, Latvia, the eastern part of Poland, and the
Rumanian province of Bessarabia. The Nazi–Soviet Pact
was, in one sense, Russia's Munich. She bought peace, and
time, at other nations' expense. She lost enormously in
world prestige and goodwill by this cynical deal with the
Government she had for long denounced as totally evil.
Hitler's conquest of Poland was so swift that the Soviet
Union had to accelerate its own plans. On 17 September it
began to occupy the eastern areas of Poland assigned to it
by the Pact. The German and Red Armies met at Brest
Litovsk. Poland was partitioned so that, by rearrangement,
Russia gained all three Baltic States and roughly half of
Poland. Hitler agreed, so as to have his hands free for
action in Western Europe.

Meantime, too, the Axis partners had not been idle in
making acquisitions. In April Italy attacked and occupied
Albania. The Soviet Union prepared for an attack on Finland, which it launched at the end of November. Britain
and France prepared to send aid to Finland, and the
League of Nations suddenly revived enough to condemn the

Soviet Union as an aggressor and expel it from membership. The Finnish war ended in March 1940, fortunately without spreading, but with concessions to Russia. Japan continued her private war in China, despite the advice given to members of the League by the Council of the League to apply separate sanctions against her. The Chinese did, however, receive technical aid from the Soviet Union. To so strangely tangled a skein had world diplomacy come. The only allied belligerents arrayed against Germany were Great Britain, France, and the Dominions (but not Eire). Italy was still at peace with Britain and France.

When war began Chamberlain reconstituted his Government. He reduced it in size, as a War Cabinet, to nine key ministers. He took in Winston Churchill at the Admiralty, Anthony Eden returned as Secretary of State for the Dominions. Though these changes were all to the good, the basic weakness was that the Prime Minister was still the man identified with appeasement and his closest colleagues were the 'men of Munich'. He clung to office until May 1940, carrying out several changes of individual ministers. Germany's invasion of Norway in April and Britain's failures in the campaign forced the issue. Country and Parliament needed a national leader of more inspiring stature and record, and a Government of wider talents to conduct the war. Labour agreed to serve in a National Government not led by Chamberlain. On 10 May he resigned and recommended that Churchill should succeed him. By agreement with Churchill he remained leader of the Conservative Party. So ended the phase that Churchill christened 'the Twilight War'. On 10 May also Hitler invaded the Low Countries.

THE SPIRIT OF THE THIRTIES

The decade which began with formation of one National Government in face of economic crisis ended with formation of another in face of military crisis. During the intervening years the economic crisis had, in large measure, receded as the military crisis grew. Within so brief a span the people of Britain knew deep economic depression and widespread distress, prolonged crises and intense anxieties, fumbling leadership and moments of national humiliation. Yet anyone who lived through that 'devil's decade' knows that it would be incorrect to depict the spirit of the thirties as one long agony of apprehension. They knew also considerable prosperity, much happiness, even some profoundly creative activity.

The essence of the spirit of the thirties was not apathy but inertia: an incorrigible *immobilisme* in State and society, a structural resistance to change, and especially to any radical improvement. Far from being apathetic, opinion of many kinds was exasperated and despondent, made so by repeated experience of inability to impose any effective control either on policies or on the sheer course of events. Consciences were deeply stirred, but they could find no outlet in constructive action. The sense of helplessness and drift that resulted may explain the escapist flavour of the most fashionable cults. What appealed most was 'getting away from it all'.

Some forms of 'getting away' were admirable and innocent, as healthy in spirit as they were health-giving in results. It was the great era of 'rambling' and of 'hiking'. The Youth Hostels Association, formed in 1930-1, provided nearly 300 hostels with beds for a shilling a night and by 1939 had more than 83,000 members. London Transport successfully catered for the urge with its 'Metroland' rambles, and at week-ends Green Line coaches dispersed countless parties of 'ramblers' into the Buckinghamshire countryside. Butlin holiday camps began. Other fashionable pastimes were less healthy, if hardly less strenuous: the football pools acquired some 10 million

regular participants. It was the age of the Granadas and
Odeons, the new big-scale cinema chains which did much,
by lengthy double-feature shows and organs rising from the
floor, to swell the numbers of cinema tickets sold weekly to
the 20 million mark. Money not spent on 'beer and baccy'
was often spent on the dogs at the greyhound stadiums, or
on watching the new oddity of all-in wrestling. On the
other hand, Radio gave millions very cheap entertainment
at home, ballet and Promenade Concerts remained immensely popular, and never before had the arts been so
widely available at such modest cost. Much else, indeed,
was unusually cheap: competition and price-cutting made
for cheap transport, cheap goods, free gifts. But many, of
course, had very little money to spend.

Much that was good went on regardless of – even in spite
of – the politicians and the national crises. Real national
income continued to rise after about 1925, and 'from the
beginning of the recovery the rate of increase was speeded
up, the late 1930s showing as much increase as the whole
of the period between 1913 and the mid-1930s'.[1] The index
of production (1929 = 100), which had risen to 110 by
1935, rose to 124 by 1937. The trends of the earlier thirties
were continued throughout the decade. Although unemployment figures dropped with rearmament, the position
suddenly worsened in 1938-9, when there were between
1,800,000 and 1,900,000 names on the official registers of
unemployed. There are signs that, but for the outbreak of war
in September 1939, renewed depression might have set in.

Total figures of unemployed had always concealed very
big variations between different industries, areas, and
types of worker. It continued to be the old industrial north
and the great nineteenth-century industries of coal, iron,
shipbuilding, and textiles that suffered most. The south,

1. S. Pollard, *The Development of the British Economy, 1914-1950* (1962),
p. 290.

especially the busy Home Counties of housing estates and streets of suburban villas, was the home of twentieth-century England. Here there concentrated many of the new light industries and an increasing proportion of the whole population. The contrast between depression and prosperity became, to a larger extent, the contrast between north and south. An acute literary observer, J. B. Priestley, in his *English Journey* (1934), found almost two nations. The expanding, comfortable, moderately prosperous world of suburbia loomed larger in national life. Walter Greenwood posed the bitter human problems of prolonged unemployment in his novel (and later play), *Love on the Dole* (1933). The 'condition of England question', as the nineteenth century had called it, returned as the foremost social concern. George Orwell's widely read *The Road to Wigan Pier* depicted depressed northern England: though a later critic could condemn it as 'an insult to Lancashire people, (in) that it lumped them all together with the low-class incompetents from whom he had drawn so many of his false impressions'.[1]

The cult of 'facts' – whether in the form of the documentary film, novel, or play, or in the form of 'social surveys' – perhaps betrayed less a scientific faith than a loss of all faith. The characteristic organization was *Mass Observation*, founded in 1937 'to study everyday behaviour in Britain'. It purported to present 'the science of ourselves'. Its production *Britain*, a 'Penguin Special' of 1939, consisted of highly impressionistic essays of consistent Leftist colour on such miscellaneous topics as astrology, public opinion about political issues, all-in wrestling, armistice day, and the popular dance 'the Lambeth Walk'. G. D. H. Cole, C. E. M. Joad, and other writers for Victor Gollancz wrote several 'Intelligent Man's Guides' on world chaos, or how to prevent war, or 'Guides' to philosophy, morals, politics,

1. Gerard Fay in *The Baldwin Age* (ed. John Raymond, 1960), p. 131.

economics, etc. There was no scarcity of information or of good advice, no lack of eager disseminators of both: what was still lacking was translation of thought into action. 'Town-planning,' adds Mr Muggeridge, 'flourished without abating ribbon-development; traffic was counted and classified, and road deaths increased; social surveys abounded, and what they had surveyed, continued.'

The Left, made fully self-conscious by the Spanish Civil War, dominated public opinion as befitted a country where the other levers of power were controlled by the Right. Of immense influence were the *New Statesman and Nation*, the Left Book Club, the *Left Review*, the ubiquitous and tireless G. D. H. and Margaret Cole, Harold Laski, Raymond Postgate, and their like. A monthly sixpenny journal, published by the latter from 1937 onwards, was even called *Fact*. It was consistently Leftist and dealt with such familiar themes as Pacifism and Socialism, the Army and prisons (by privates and ex-convicts) and trade-union history in – of course – a 'documentary' fashion. *Picture Post* (started in 1938) provided pictorial social documents. Facts always seemed to point one way.

One feature of the period in literature was the continuing predominance of writers of a much older generation or of a slightly older generation: on one hand, Shaw, Wells, Bennett, Galsworthy, Walpole, and, on the other, D. H. Lawrence, T. E. Lawrence, Aldous Huxley, J. B. Priestley. At a popular level writers effected striking adaptations to the changing moods. Noël Coward became the patriotic creator of *Cavalcade* (1931), which drew large middle-aged audiences to Drury Lane. Aldous Huxley was drawn into politics with *Brave New World* (1932) and out of it again into contemplation with *Ends and Means* (1937). Dorothy Sayers, who gave crime fiction a new literary excellence during the Baldwin era, turned to Christian apologetics with her plays *The Zeal of Thy House*

(1937) and *The Devil to Pay* (1939). The younger generation of novelists and poets, born before 1914 and formed by the inter-war years themselves, were just establishing their names before the Second World War came: Stephen Spender, Cecil Day Lewis, George Orwell, Louis MacNeice, W. H. Auden, and Christopher Isherwood. The new men were not, in all, a galaxy of great literary genius, though they voiced in sentiments and mode of expression the troubled, disjointed spirit of the decade. Meantime F. R. Leavis, in the pages of *Scrutiny*, set a new style of literary criticism that was to remain controversial and influential for the next thirty years.

In the special realm of historical learning and writing a few giant figures held the field: of an older tradition, G. M. Trevelyan; creator of a new precision, L. B. Namier; such craftsmen in the new art of writing economic history as R. H. Tawney and J. H. Clapham; such skilled synthesizers as the learned contributors to the fourteen-volume *Oxford History of England*. The mantle of more flippant historical writing and of mordant biography descended from Lytton Strachey to Philip Guedalla. At the opposite pole Arnold J. Toynbee embarked upon his monumental *Study of History*, received with infinitely more gravity before 1939 than it was by the time of its completion in the 1950s.

The thirties were not a time of prolific greatness in the arts, but neither did they lack original creative achievements. Functional architecture, largely under the inspiration of Walter Gropius and the 'Bauhaus' school, had considerable effect on the whole of British taste – an impact transmitted by E. Maxwell Fry and others. The decade knew also the monumental sculptures of Jacob Epstein, the delicate carvings of Eric Gill, and the subtle simplicity of Henry Moore; and the new phase in the career of Ralph Vaughan Williams that began with the ballet *Job* (1930) and comprised seven more great symphonies. In two spheres of activity, however, Britain led the world: in the development of economic and social theory associated with the names of Lord Keynes and Lord Beveridge, and in the continued advance of the physical sciences connected with Lord Rutherford and his colleagues and pupils of the Cavendish Laboratory. In both these fields what happened in Britain in the thirties did much to shape thought and social life of the fifties and sixties.

In economic and social ideas the early thirties were a seminal period. Men of all parties and of none, faced with the intractable problems of British industry, of depressed areas, of monetary policy, turned increasingly to the view that there must be more deliberate control and more rational planning of the nation's economic life. Arguments for 'rationalization' in industry, for a 'managed currency', for national economic plans, found support from all sides that had not been forthcoming before 1931. So ready were capitalists, conservatives, liberals, and non-party intellectuals to advocate various forms of direction and control [1] that it may be questioned whether the example of the Soviet Five-Year Plans helped or hindered acceptance of such ideas in Britain. It is likely that the enthusiastic claims made for the Five-Year Plans, combined with the still very lively phobias about Bolshevism, inhibited the growth of such ideas in some quarters. At the highest intellectual level John Maynard Keynes expounded revolutionary economic ideas, equipping economists with a new general theoretical framework and fresh methods of analysis with which to examine problems of unemployment, financial policy, and national planning. His *Treatise on Money* (1930) and his *General Theory of Employment, Interest and Money* (1936) were stimulated by the problems of his day, but had small effect

1. E.g. Sir A. Salter, *Recovery* (1932); Harold Macmillan, *Reconstruction: a plea for a national policy* (1933); *The Next Five Years: an Essay in Political Agreement* (1935).

on the measures adopted in the thirties. Orthodoxy prevailed, that economy, thrift, minimal public expenditure, and balanced budgets are at all times desirable. Thus the National Governments cut unemployment benefits and public expenditure in an effort to prevent unemployment. The gist of Keynes's theory was that 'in times of depression and unemployment it is desirable to encourage spending and lavishness'. The Government was doing the opposite. Keynesian doctrines, as adapted by Lord Beveridge and others, were to become the very foundation of post-war welfare legislation and policies for 'full employment'. Experience of the thirties gave them remarkable prestige and a favourable climate of opinion. It can even be argued that they were acclaimed too recklessly: they had had a contractionist side too, which made economy and thrift desirable in incipient inflation, and this was forgotten in the conditions of the fifties which were utterly different from those of the thirties.

Even more spectacular were the achievements of the natural sciences, especially of physics. Building on the achievement of Rutherford in 1919, and on further explorations of the structure of the atom conducted throughout the inter-war years, physicists not only laid the foundations of the Atomic Age but also developed important new fields – radio-physics, which led to the invention of radar and the extensive use in research and industry of radio-isotopes, and astro-physics which heralded the Space Age. In the biological sciences genetics made important advances, and the living cell began to reveal its microscopic complexities no less significantly than the atom. In Britain it was still mainly in universities that such pioneer research was conducted; but already important government-supported institutes also contributed, notably the Department of Scientific and Industrial Research and the Medical Research Council (dating from 1916 and 1920 respectively).

The discovery of penicillin by Sir Alexander Fleming in 1929 led to the highly successful use of it as an antibiotic after 1940.

There was virtually no expansion of Universities in the thirties. Two new foundations began at Oxford (St Peter's Hall in 1929, Nuffield College in 1937), none at Cambridge. Exeter and Hull University Colleges had been set up in the twenties, but none was added in the thirties. Reading, which became a University College in 1903, received full university status in 1926, but no new Universities were founded in this period. The numbers of full-time University students remained static at around 50,000; in 1938-9 it was actually some 500 lower than in 1935-6, because of a decline in numbers at the University of Wales. Neglect of higher education was a lamentable feature of the thirties. The fate of primary and secondary education in the period was symbolic of the fate of social services in general. The second Labour Government planned to raise the school-leaving age to fifteen in 1931. Thwarted by the slump and by failure to deal with the religious issue which caused opposition of the churches, the project was re-enacted in 1936, when the churches were placated with grants and the slump was receding. It was timed to come into force in September 1939. Then war held it up till the Butler Act of 1944 and the Labour Government's measures of 1947. Perhaps the period's most significant improvement was in the grammar schools. In 1923-4 there had been nearly 385,000 pupils in efficient secondary (grammar) schools: by 1938, there were nearly 545,000; but the number of State Scholarships, fixed at 200 in 1920, was still only 360 in 1938. The 'ladder of learning' was narrow, and it was pitched at a steep incline. Great opportunities were lost, here as in other spheres, during the thrifty thirties.

G. M. Trevelyan suggested that the Battle of Britain in

1940 was won not on the playing-fields of Eton but in the grammar schools of the thirties. Certainly the scholarship boys of the thirties, though a relatively small *élite*, were to assume important roles in public life after 1940. It has been pointed out that there is a tantalizing similarity between the growth of a University-educated generation and the increase in size of the Registrar-General's 'Social Class I', which includes professional and similar occupations. While one rose by 57 per cent, the other also rose by about 50 per cent. But which is determinant of the other? The truest focus may be to regard all these changes as but aspects of one overall transformation of British society in the twentieth century, most clearly marked by successive generations. The first decade of the century saw the coming to maturity of the first generation educated in the new free and compulsory elementary schools; the inter-war years brought the first main outflow from the new secondary schools, though as late as 1931 only one child in five aged between eleven and fourteen gained any secondary education at all; the post-war years have brought a new surge of University-educated men and women, urgently needed to run the services and sustain the advance of a modern technological and welfare society. The national system of education kept pace with – though perhaps several paces behind – the development of modern Britain: its advance helped, in turn, to make possible the next phase of growth. In this whole process there were two noteworthy characteristics. One was that the whole of this great 'silent revolution' was congested into a relatively short span of time – a single lifetime. The other was its uneven pace, bursts of activity being followed by phases of deceleration and even retrogression. The thirties, characteristically, belonged to the latter.

CHAPTER SEVEN

Waging World War, 1939–45

THE SEVEN PHASES OF WAR

WHEN Churchill assumed leadership of Britain and the Commonwealth in May 1940 the spirit of the thirties died. It died, visibly and audibly, in the great Commons debate of 8 May, which compelled Chamberlain's resignation. The mood of mental lassitude and moral fecklessness began to disperse, incongruously for a nation that so soon was to experience the physical powerlessness of Dunkirk and the peril of the Battle of Britain. Until then 'the twilight war' had still been haunted by something of the spirit of the thirties. The French called it the *drôle de guerre*, the Americans more downrightly 'the phoney war', for it was an international phenomenon. After all the excitement, the mounting tensions, the speedy fall of Poland, in the West nothing much happened. Hitler held out olive-branch offers to France and Britain in October, and again in November, less in expectation of their being accepted than in order to blame the Western Powers for any hardships Germans might suffer. Apart from occasional skirmishes in the Maginot Line and considerable activity at sea, the scene was uncannily quiet. Above all, there was no bombing. People had heard so much about the rigours and horrors of another war that reality seemed an anti-climax: which suited Hitler's purposes well enough.

Yet many sensed it was only the lull before a storm. The British Expeditionary Force took up positions at the north end of the Maginot Line. The Navy suffered serious losses by the sinking of the aircraft carrier *Courageous* and the battleship *Royal Oak* – reminders of the menace of the U-boats. Aircraft dropped leaflets over Germany. At home defence measures included black-out and rationing, evacuation from London and the extension of military conscription. The budget for 1940 provided £2,000 million for war purposes. The nation's fighting power grew fast, and on 4 April Chamberlain declared that by not attacking during the winter Hitler had 'missed the bus'. Five days later Hitler's troops invaded Denmark and landed at several places in Norway.

The second phase, the German *Blitzkrieg* offensive in the West which thus opened on 9 April 1940, lasted until October. It brought immense reverses: the landings and withdrawals of British forces in Norway by May; German conquest of the Low Countries in May and of France by mid-June; British retreat from the beaches of Dunkirk, between 26 May and 4 June; and the Battle of Britain for air superiority over the Channel coast during July–September. These cataclysmic events left an indelible mark on British national attitudes and sentiments. The swift sequence of disasters culminated in the dramatic appeal for hundreds of little ships to go out to the Dunkirk beaches and fetch home the quarter-million soldiers of the shattered Expeditionary Force. The country was left more defenceless in face of a European conqueror than at any time, perhaps, since 1066. But the weary, scattered forces were brought home, in a veritable epic of endurance, improvisation, and good luck, greatly aided by French rearguard resistance. Churchill, who had taken command in the midst of these disasters, offered nothing but 'blood, toil, tears, and sweat', but gave in return confidence in eventual victory. Bereft of her European allies, deserted by the new French Government of Marshal Pétain, who on 17 June besought Hitler for an armistice, but shielded by the Royal Navy and Royal Air Force and supported by the whole Commonwealth (except Eire, which alone remained neutral), Great Britain faced the full onslaught of Hitler's invasion plan, 'Operation Sea-lion'.

Invasion required establishment of air superiority over the Channel and Channel coast. This task was entrusted to the *Luftwaffe*, which on 10 July made its first heavy bombing raid on southern England. For a month bombing was concentrated on shipping and ports, for another month on airfields and London. But by mid-September, when the Battle of Britain had reached its climax, Hitler abandoned plans for invasion. He had failed to get air superiority. By the use of better fighter-planes directed to their points of interception by radar, and by the skill and sacrifice of many of her bravest pilots, Britain inflicted on the *Luftwaffe* losses on a scale it could not afford. During August and September it lost 1,244 planes and crews. The few hundred young pilots who won the battle were British and Dominion men, and also Czech, Polish, Belgian, and French. On 17 September 'Operation Sea-lion' was postponed indefinitely. 'Never in the field of human conflict,' said Churchill, 'was so much owed by so many to so few.'

Even so, throughout late autumn and winter, German planes continued to bomb London and the larger industrial cities. Civilians found themselves almost as much in the 'front line' in the bombed cities of Britain as had the Belgian or French refugees, crowding the roads in front of Hitler's invading armies. Yet just as, between the wars, British people had escaped the worst of the horrors that befell Europe – actual invasion, violent revolution, secret police terror, and concentration camps – so now, too, they were spared the ultimate disaster of invasion, mass-refugee movements, enemy occupation. It was perhaps a sense of this relative good fortune, of miraculous hair-breadth escape from total disaster, that turned the defeat of Dunkirk into a source of high morale. The great surge of public confidence in Churchill as a national leader dispelled both doubts and fears. Henceforth the mass of the people did not contemplate defeat. When the road to survival was firmly indicated they set out resolutely and unitedly along it, with no delusions that it might be short or painless. The long sense of frustration and futility in the thirties bore some benefits at last, in the pent-up energies now released and the strength of purpose unanimously achieved.

Morale rose, too, with a few timely victories against the weaker Axis partner, Italy. Mussolini had waited to declare war until June 1940, when France was clearly in collapse. In September Marshal Graziani invaded Egypt from Libya. In December General Wavell counter-attacked, pushed the Italians 500 miles west to Benghazi, and took 130,000 prisoners with very small losses to himself. He then withdrew to Egypt, leaving a small Australian garrison to hold Tobruk. From Kenya and the Sudan, however, two British columns advanced against Mussolini's East African Empire. By May 1941 they took Eritrea, Italian Somaliland, and Abyssinia, avenging Mussolini's defiance of the League only five years before. In November a dashing British air-attack from the carrier *Illustrious* on the naval base at Taranto knocked out three Italian battleships; and in March naval units inflicted heavy losses on the Italian Fleet off Cape Matapan in southern Greece.

The third phase of the war, which began in the winter of 1940 after the Battle of Britain, thus brought some crumbs of comfort. But the year 1941, in general, was one of big disasters. Although Italy suffered more reverses in the Balkans when she attacked Greece and Yugoslavia, German intervention quickly brought the expulsion of British troops from Greece and even Crete, and Axis occupation of the whole of the Balkan peninsula, culminating in a treaty with Turkey which guaranteed Turkish neutrality. In both the Mediterranean and the Atlantic British naval strength was heavily taxed, especially by German air-strength directed against Malta and Gibraltar and by submarine and mining attacks on transatlantic shipping. In March 1941 the strain was eased by the United States 'Lend-Lease' Act, authorizing President F. D. Roosevelt to put American resources at the disposal of any State whose defence he regarded as necessary for the security of the United States. This kept steady the flow of supplies to Britain, regardless of her ability to pay for them in dollars. But by the end of 1941 some 9 million tons of allied and neutral merchant shipping had been sunk.

Although the year meant relentless defensive efforts by Britain, the prospect was transformed in June, when Hitler launched his attack on the Soviet Union, and yet again in December, when the Japanese bombed the United States base at Pearl Harbor. With the world's two greatest neutral Powers brought into the struggle within six months, the European war in which Britain had hitherto been mainly engaged was dramatically converted into a truly World War. The preponderance of global power was now thrown on to her side. The combined resources of the Americas, Russia, and the Commonwealth would in the end – if wisely mobilized and deployed – be bound to overwhelm the disjointed efforts of Germany, Italy, and Japan. But the Axis had Europe under its heel, Japan had gained immense short-term naval advantages, and the aggressive dictators enjoyed their usual benefits of initiative, surprise, and better preparedness. Their only hope of ultimate triumph lay in immediate and decisive gains. Hence the fury of Hitler's onslaught on Russia, which carried German armies some 600 miles into Russian territory. Hence, too, the speed and savagery of the Japanese attacks on French Indochina, Singapore, Malaya, Burma, and Hong Kong, as well as on many strategic Pacific Islands. *Blitzkrieg* was the essence of their policy no less than their strategy.

By the end of 1941 the Russians still held the key cities of Leningrad, Moscow, Sebastopol, and Stalingrad, and the worst winter in living memory descended on the German invaders. The American people were united by the Japanese attack as nothing else could have united them in an all-out war effort. Britain and the Dominions declared war on Japan; Germany and Italy declared themselves at war with the United States. The Soviet Union, however, remained at peace with Japan, and did not declare war until August 1945. From Britain's point of view the transformation of European war into World War brought severe losses and fresh strains in the Far East, but also formidable reinforcement of strength in Europe. With Germany deeply committed in the east, and United States naval and mercantile help available in the Atlantic, the balance of advantages tipped sharply in Britain's favour. She found herself the pivot of a new Atlantic Alliance, linking the United States with the Commonwealth and the exiled Governments of Western Europe.

As the war entered its fourth phase Britain and the United States concerted policy and unified their military efforts. They agreed to give the war in Europe priority over the war in the Far East. They created the machinery of unified effort, including the necessary joint boards and committees, economic as well as military. Churchill and Roosevelt agreed a common programme. But the tale of reverses was not yet done. In North Africa Erwin Rommel, the new German commander, captured Tobruk, advanced to El Alamein, and made ready to capture Egypt. To mount an effective counter-attack meant that Britain and the United States had to postpone any frontal attack in Western Europe. Germany was still spared that 'Second Front' for which the Soviet leaders were already clamouring. The decisive battle of the desert war was fought in October 1942, at El Alamein. General Montgomery, commander of the

British Eighth Army, routed Rommel's *Afrika Korps* in a mighty combined operation, depriving the enemy of some 60,000 men, 1,000 guns, and 500 tanks. Churchill regarded the victory as a turning-point of the whole war for Great Britain. 'Up to Alamein,' he said, 'we survived. After Alamein we conquered.'

In rapid succession to this victory Anglo-American forces landed in Morocco and Algeria, forcing the Vichy French authorities there to abandon their neutrality and Hitler to occupy the hitherto 'unoccupied zone' of southern France. The landings demonstrated Allied supremacy at sea and their local air superiority. But Allied land forces still faced strong counter-attacks from Tunisia, where German troops had gathered in strength. The final battle of Tunisia, won by joint operation of Montgomery's forces from Libya and combined Anglo-American-French forces under General Alexander in Algeria, was a triumph of combined operations by land, sea, and air. More than 250,000 Germans and Italians were taken prisoner. The completion of the campaign by May 1943 ensured communications in the Mediterranean and exposed what Churchill called 'the soft under-belly of the Axis' – Italy and the Balkans. Even this successful and valuable operation did little, however, to relieve the tremendous German pressure on Russia where, after August 1942, General Paulus and his Sixth Army of 300,000 men stood at the gates of Stalingrad. The cry for a 'Second Front' grew louder. The battle of Stalingrad in the winter of 1942 was the turning of the tide in the east. The Sixth Army was destroyed or captured. It was a momentous contribution to the eventual defeat of Germany.

The war entered its fifth phase in the early summer of 1943. Britain engaged in two kinds of operation against the Axis, short of opening a 'Second Front'. She struck at German communications and industrial centres by air-attack. On 30 May the Royal Air Force made its first thousand-bomber attack on Cologne, then concentrated on the Ruhr as a centre of steel production, on the docks of Hamburg, and on Berlin itself. American night-bombers, based on Britain, went at high altitude by day, the British by night. They left many German cities half in ruins, though later evidence suggested that neither morale nor production suffered as drastically as was expected. It was characteristic of modern warfare that air-power was most effective when functionally coordinated in its purpose with other fighting services: as in the war in North Africa, or in Japan's bid for naval superiority in the Pacific. Air attacks on submarine bases at Lorient and Saint-Nazaire in France, or air reconnaissance against enemy submarines at sea, scored specific gains. Massive bombing of enemy cities yielded doubtful results. As London showed under repeated bombardment, civilian morale could be stiffened rather than broken by savagery.

The attack on Italy began in July 1943. The American Seventh and the British Eighth Armies landed on the coast of Sicily. Though reinforced by German troops, the Italians were ready enough to quit the war. On 25 July Mussolini was deposed by the Fascist Grand Council. Marshal Badoglio, commissioned by the King to form a new Government, continued the war as Germany's ally until he was compelled to make peace and, on 16 September, to turn his forces against the Germans. Thereafter the campaign settled down to a long tough struggle, until Rome fell to the allies in June, Florence in mid-August 1944.

Meanwhile, however, the war had entered its sixth and penultimate phase with the long-awaited 'Second Front'. On 6 June 1944 a mighty armada of 4,000 ships converged from British ports upon the beaches of Normandy: the very beaches from which, in 1066, William of Normandy had set sail for his invasion of England. 'Operation Overlord', aimed at the final defeat of Germany, was commanded by

General Dwight D. Eisenhower, later to become President of the United States. A million and a half American troops had been trained and transported to Britain ready for 'D-Day'. In preparation for the landings German coastal defences, radar installations, and interior communications had been smashed from the air or by local sabotage. The convoys of landing craft were preceded by mine-sweepers and followed by complete prefabricated 'Mulberry' harbours towed across the Channel. British assault divisions landed between Caen and Bayeux. By the sixth day Eisenhower had successfully landed 326,000 men on a bridgehead some fifty miles wide. By 2 July nearly a million men were in France and only 9,000 had been killed, though there were some 61,000 casualties. On 15 August yet another American army under General Patch, with strong French reinforcements, landed in the south of France and advanced up the Rhône valley. By the end of the month the allies had 2 million men in France. Against them Germany had mustered a quarter of her whole army, led by Field Marshal Karl von Rundstedt: and despite stubborn fighting, especially in isolated pockets, they were driven back to the old Siegfried Line in the Rhineland. By the end of 1944 France and Belgium were almost completely liberated.

This phase brought a fresh ordeal to the civilian population of Britain, especially within the London area. Soon after D-Day the Germans used the first of their secret V-1 weapons, unpiloted aircraft-bombs which fell after flying a fixed distance from their launching-sites in the Pas-de-Calais. Even aimed at random within the densely crowded area of the capital, these 'buzzbombs' caused considerable damage and discomfort to the civil population. They had no specific military objective. In August they were succeeded by larger V-2 weapons, rocket-bombs of greater speed and destructive power. The only counter-measure was the effective one of capturing their launching-sites, which was done in the spring of 1945. But a momentous weapon of modern warfare had made its début.

The desperate resistance of the Germans brought further tough battles on land: notably the 'Battle of the Bulge', which began in mid-December with a powerful German counter-offensive in the Ardennes. By late January, when Eisenhower's forces (one-quarter of them British, one-quarter French, the rest American) had pushed the Germans back out of the bulge made in the Allied lines, the Russians had moved deep into eastern Germany. In February Churchill, Roosevelt, and Stalin met at Yalta, in the Crimea, to decide the future of Europe. In March the Allied forces crossed the Rhine; in April the 8th Army swept up into Austria. On 8 May 1945 the war in Europe officially ended.

The crescendo of events between May and September 1945 places these few months among the most crucial in modern times. Already, in April, a conference of the Allied and associated States met at San Francisco to draft the Charter of the United Nations as a permanent and general international organization. Harry S. Truman became President of the United States on the death (12 April) of Franklin D. Roosevelt. At Yalta the Soviet Union, not yet at war with Japan, secretly agreed to enter the war in return for extensive territorial gains in the Far East at Japan's expense. From May until the general elections in July, Churchill led a 'caretaker government'. After them, C. R. Attlee, at the head of a large Labour Party majority, succeeded Churchill as Prime Minister. Thus the last crucial phase of the war, between the surrender of Germany and the surrender of Japan, brought important changes of leadership, of diplomatic alignments, and of prospect.

In the Pacific the tide of Allied defeat had begun to turn in May 1942 with United States naval and air victories in the Coral Sea and off Midway, which cost Japan the loss of five aircraft carriers. By August that year American troops had gained beachheads at Guadalcanal and elsewhere in the Solomons, and Australian and American troops advanced in New Guinea, capturing it by the end of 1943 and thus ensuring Australian security. While United States forces undertook the major campaign against Japan itself, British forces combined with Indian, Chinese, and African forces, within a new South-East Asia Command led by Admiral Lord Louis Mountbatten, to clear Burma. In an intolerable climate and amid almost impassable mountains these forces eventually drove the Japanese from northern Burma and saved India from invasion. By January 1945 the Burma road to China was declared open, and in May Rangoon was retaken. Plans to free Malaya and Singapore were never needed, because Japan was forced to surrender before they could be carried out.

The circumstances of Japanese surrender had the most momentous consequences of all for the future of the world. On 6 August an atomic bomb was dropped on Hiroshima in Japan. It destroyed more than half the city and caused some 80,000 deaths. Two days later the Soviet Union declared war on Japan and invaded Manchuria. On 9 August a second atomic bomb of different type was dropped on the naval base of Nagasaki. Five days later the Japanese Cabinet, on the intervention of the Emperor Hirohito, accepted 'unconditional surrender'. On 2 September Japanese representatives signed the instrument of surrender, and within the following month local Japanese forces everywhere in the Pacific surrendered. Stalin, taken by surprise by the collapse of Japan and alarmed by United States possession of the atomic bomb, began a feverish and suspicious quest for satellites and security. At Yalta Churchill and Roosevelt had paid a price for Russian entry to the war which they need not have paid. If in Europe the Western Powers reaped some of the gains of the Soviet Union's long and exhausting struggle against Germany, in the Far East the tables were turned. There Russia, with minimal effort and loss, harvested all the territories lost after the Russo-Japanese War of 1904-5.

Each of the war's seven phases had left its special impress on the fortunes and outlook of the British people. They had ranged, in experience, from the unrealities of the 'twilight war' and the desperation of Dunkirk to the grim 'Britain can take it' mood of 1941 and the mounting exultations of the final struggles. Overnight, potential and actual enemies had become allies, allies potential enemies. Englishmen had trained or fought in nearly every part of the world. The British Isles had become a refuge for exiles from many European countries, a base for the greatest invading force in all history. The Commonwealth alone had remained a fully belligerent Power from the very beginning to the very end of hostilities. Though parts of it had known enemy occupation, such as Burma and Malaya, and others had known the imminent threat of invasion, as had the United Kingdom, Australia, and India, no part of it was left in enemy hands at the peace. So far as war had been fought by the British peoples to force enemy hands off Commonwealth soil, it completely succeeded.

BRITAIN'S BALANCE-SHEET

Although the Second World War lasted half as long again as the First, British casualties in it were considerably less. Her armed forces lost 303,000 killed, the rest of the Commonwealth lost 109,000. Some 60,000 civilians were killed in air-raids, 30,000 members of the Merchant Navy lost their lives. Compared with Russian, German, or Japanese losses, these were relatively small.

The severest material loss was financial – the expenditure of vast overseas assets and the incurring of large foreign debts; and commercial loss of shipping and of trade. External debts had increased by more than £3,350 million, and Britain had sold £1,118 million of her overseas investments. Of the 18 million tons of shipping lost, only two-thirds had been replaced. When Lend-Lease was abruptly ended in 1945, Lord Keynes negotiated from the United States a loan of 3,750 million dollars. In return Britain had to undertake to restore the convertibility of sterling: a promise which, when fulfilled in 1947, brought a financial crisis. The devices of Cash-and-Carry and Lend-Lease, adopted by President Roosevelt to alleviate British dependence on United States supplies and aid, had to be replaced in 1947 by Marshall Aid to Europe. Britain could neither deny nor escape greater economic dependence on the United States in the post-war world.

The severities and sacrifices of war-time had, however, important effects on national spirit and outlook. Morale, in the services and among civilians as a whole, was always high. Whether in conscription for the services or in voluntary organizations, such as the Home Guard and Air Raid Precaution (A.R.P.), the mass of ordinary citizens gave essential services willingly and with solidarity. Taxes were high, rationing often severe, dislocation of life by evacuation or air raids widespread. Mobilization of man-power was more complete in Britain than in most other belligerent countries. In December 1941 even conscription of women was authorized. By D-Day it was estimated that of every nine members of the total labour force, two were in the armed forces and three were engaged in war production. Any lingering shame for pre-war policies was abundantly wiped out by the whole-heartedness of Britain's contribution to the Allied war-effort. Not only did morale remain stolidly immune to enemy propaganda, even in times of gravest disaster, but as the home of exiled Governments and of such movements as the Free French, led by General de

Gaulle, the British Isles became a place of hope for the occupied countries of Europe. From London, by radio, came the news suppressed by tyrants and the voices of former rulers and present patriots, offering encouragement to internal resistance movements and – latterly – giving instructions in code for activities which would assist Allied armies of liberation.

For all these reasons British prestige and influence in Europe rose during the war. It was untainted by such calamities as the armistice made by the French Government at Vichy, or by the political somersaults executed by the Soviet Union first in the Nazi–Soviet Pact of 1939 and the Finnish War, then after the German attack of June 1941, then again after the Japanese surrender. The war in its course made strange bedfellows, none stranger than the alliance between Stalin and Churchill. In domestic policies from May 1940 until the end it was a time of party political truce. Not only were the bitter recriminations and suspicions of the thirties overlaid and buried by immediate emergencies, but Labour ministers assumed leading positions under Churchill and the trade unions lent solid and strenuous support to the Government in the war-effort.

Chamberlain's War Cabinet of 1939 consisted of nine members, their average age being – as Churchill wryly noted – 64, 'only one year short of the Old Age Pension!' It had included Churchill and Eden, but political reconciliation did not yet extend outside Conservative ranks. When Churchill became Premier in May 1940 he set up a small War Cabinet of only five, including, besides himself, Chamberlain, Halifax, Attlee, and Arthur Greenwood. By September he had enlarged it to seven, taking in Lord Beaverbrook, the Minister of Aircraft Production, and Ernest Bevin, the Minister of Labour and National Service. Their inclusion reflected the priorities given, that winter, to supply of aircraft and of man-power. As Minister of Defence

Churchill kept general supervision of the fighting forces. The political width of the Government was extended by including the Liberal leader, Sir Archibald Sinclair, as Secretary of State for Air, and L. S. Amery, as Secretary of State for India. When Chamberlain retired in September Churchill was elected leader of the Conservative Party. He replaced Chamberlain by Sir John Anderson, who, as Lord President of the Council, became the guiding hand for several Cabinet committees dealing with home affairs. Under Churchill's lead party animosities evaporated, and the Coalition was more authentically 'National' in spirit than any of its predecessors.

Churchill drew strength from the width of the Coalition which left him with no regular opposition in the House or in the country. He drew it also from his own rich experience of the First World War, from his prescience of the inter-war years as regards German rearmament and national defence needs, from the spontaneous acknowledgement of the people that he could be a superb war-leader, and from his own gifts for oratory in Parliament and, even more significantly, by radio. As the King had found in peace, so Churchill quickly learned in war, broadcasting enabled a national leader to project his personality into every home in the land.

The Defence Committee of the Cabinet and the Chiefs of Staffs Committee, over both of which Churchill presided, did not include the Service Ministers, who ceased to play any big part in framing military plans or in conduct of operations. The Defence Committee met frequently in the earlier years (seventy-six times in 1941), but much less often in later years (ten times in 1944). Although the War Cabinet, rising to as many as eleven members, most of them with departmental duties, was the hub of affairs, including home affairs as well as war policies, the Lord President's Committee, over which Attlee presided for most of the time, acted as a sub-Cabinet. The strings of foreign policy were held in the Prime Minister's own hands, for he dealt with Roosevelt and even Stalin by direct correspondence. The carefully contrived machinery succeeded in minimizing those frictions between politicians and soldiers, as well as between allies, which had so unhappily prevailed during the First World War.

As is usual in war-time, the size, powers, and activities of the central Government increased enormously. New departments of government were set up – in 1939 for Supply, Economic Warfare, Information, Food, Shipping, and Home Security; eventually also for Aircraft Production, Civil Aviation, Town and Country Planning, Production, and Reconstruction. New ministries were created out of formerly more limited departments: as were the Ministries of Labour and National Service, Fuel and Power, Works and Buildings. Although some of the new creations disappeared or were merged together after the war, most remained, and to them were added other new post-war creations. As compared with the expansions of 1914–18 'the tide rose higher and it receded less'.

The powers of the central Government were inevitably almost limitless in war-time conditions. The Emergency Powers (Defence) Acts of 1939 and 1940 preserved Parliament's right to annul regulations, but conferred on the Government very wide powers to conduct the war with efficiency, preserve public safety and order, and even to detain persons 'whose detention appears to the Secretary of State to be expedient in the interests of public safety or the defence of the realm'. Arrests carried out by authority of regulations made under these Acts gave rise to considerable popular debate and judicial resentment. The most remarkable feature of war-time Britain was the tolerance and the leniency shown towards individual rights, as compared with the reactions of other modern States in comparable emergencies. One result of recurrent anxieties lest over-drastic powers were being delegated to officials at the expense of individual rights was that in June 1944 the House of Commons set up a 'Scrutiny Committee' to consider every rule or order made by ministries and to draw attention of the House to any deemed objectionable. This effective device remained an important new piece of parliamentary machinery. Despite a few hard cases and a few notorious blunders, even in immediate danger Britain showed itself admirably tender of private conscience and individual rights. In 1943 even Sir Oswald Mosley was released.

Socially the war was a mighty crucible, melting many pre-war contrasts and softening (though not always removing) old rigidities. Experience of evacuation, of mutual aid in air-raids, of great collective sacrifice and service, of stringent rationing and controls in the cause of 'equal shares', all helped to strengthen a tide of egalitarian sentiment that had been generated before war began. Common humanity began to seem more important than distinctions of wealth or birth. Participation in so great a common effort made the pre-war years of insecurity and social hardship seem in retrospect grossly unjust. A new resolve was born to build, from the sacrifices of war, a better society wherein none should be deprived of the necessities of life, and where the opportunity to work and live in decent surroundings should be opened to all citizens. This dream of a more just society was not new. It had appeared from time to time to visionaries of the nineteenth century. Much of the appeal of the pre-war Left had been to those who shared it. The sense of national purpose, rediscovered in war, began to be transferred to this goal. Victory could serve the ends of social justice.

It is growth of this mood which helps to explain the reception accorded to Sir William Beveridge's *Report on Social Insurance and Allied Services* of November 1942. Concerned with proposals for unifying and extending the existing measures for social security, it attracted international attention as a wider statement of practical methods of social reorganization. It set out the concept of comprehensive public protection for all individuals and for the family 'from the cradle to the grave' against sickness, poverty, unemployment, squalor, and ignorance, by provision of minimal social services of public health and free medical aid, pensions and family allowances, insurance against unemployment, improved housing, and public education. Although its specific concern was with the evil of 'want', it presented want as merely one important cause of social insecurity and individual unhappiness. It became the charter of the ideals of 'the Welfare State'. That Britain, only two years after Dunkirk, should debate such ideals caught the imagination of the world.

Necessities, as well as sociological ideals, pointed to new tasks of reconstruction and planning. Britain's economy had become, in effect, highly planned. Keynesian economic theories, given such scant respect in official policy before 1939, now became Treasury orthodoxy. Several special committees studied these problems and proposed courses of action. The Scott Report of 1942 urged state control of rural development. The Uthwatt Report, also of 1942, proposed nationalization of land values and control over the siting of new factories. They bore some fruit in the Town and Country Planning Act of 1944, though it needed considerable subsequent amendment. A White Paper on Employment Policy, of 1944, reflected Keynes's influence and pledged the Government to a policy of ensuring full employment by financial measures. Mr R. A. Butler's Education Act of the same year provided for raising the school-leaving age to fifteen, and for part-time schooling to the age of eighteen. In 1944, also, Lord Woolton as Minister of Reconstruction produced a White Paper on Social

Insurance. It accepted some, but by no means all of Beveridge's proposals, and a Family Allowances Act of 1945 introduced one important part of the scheme.

These measures, passed by Churchill's Coalition Government before the end of the war, were later used by the Conservative Party as evidence that it had fully sponsored the Welfare State, whose basic principles at other moments it condemned. Their adoption did, indeed, represent a changed spirit within the Conservative Party as compared with pre-war attitudes. But these piecemeal measures were passed by the Coalition as a whole, and under increasing pressure from not only the Labour and tiny Liberal Parties but also from the new Common Wealth Party founded in 1942 by Sir Richard Acland. It won by-elections in April 1943 and January 1944. In the forces and in the civilian population there was a mounting demand for a Welfare State, as guarantee against any relapse to pre-war conditions. This mood impinged on all political parties, but less on the Conservatives than on others: which is why the general election of July 1945 reduced the Conservatives and their allies to 213 seats, while returning 393 Labour members and an assortment of small groups.

In retrospect it seems that this trend dates continuously from 1941, when the urgent needs of war drove the country to more systematic planning:

The year 1941 was certainly a watershed in the conduct of the war, producing firm policies of taxation, of free and forced saving, of price control, of rationing and control of civilian supplies, together with exhaustive discussions of wages policy. In 1941, too, these problems were considered as parts of one another. The whole economic situation was illuminated in that year by the new statistical analysis contained in the first white paper on national income and expenditure.[1]

1. W. K. Hancock and M. M. Gowing, *British War Economy* (1949), p. 152.

The instruments of post-war economic planning were thus the direct products of war-time necessities.

Nor, despite the immense losses of capital investment, shipping, and plant destroyed by bombing, was the balance-sheet of war without some material gains. The clearest example of a basic industry given a new direction and fresh impetus to growth by war-time measures was agriculture itself. As a result of the Government's policy of encouraging tillage at the expense of animal husbandry, there were some 5 million more acres of land in tillage at the end of the war. Apart from dairy cattle, which increased in number, stock were fewer. Yield per acre, too, was greatly increased by the use of fertilizers and mechanization. Mechanical horse-power rose from less than 2 millions to nearly 5 millions between 1939 and 1946. County War Agricultural Committees were the main agencies of direction and control, and generous subsidies were given towards capital investment in improvements and towards maintaining guaranteed prices. After the war complaints were often heard that British farmers had been 'feather-bedded', and continued subsidies certainly sheltered them against some of the rigours which other industries endured. But, on balance, farming was modernized, reinvigorated, and made much more productive as a direct consequence of the war.

WAR AIMS AND PEACE AIMS

On the September Sunday morning when Neville Chamberlain broadcast the news that Britain was at war with Germany he remarked: 'It is evil things we shall be fighting against, brute force, bad faith, injustice, oppression, and persecution.' This was, indeed, the original war-aim of Britain and France: to resist, reluctantly but resolutely, Germany's course of conquest. Even Chamberlain – bearer of nothing more warlike than a rolled umbrella – was at last convinced that it was impossible to set limits to the expansion and tyranny of Hitlerism except by destroying it. Britain's aim was to destroy Hitlerism in Germany and in Europe. In this sense her initial purpose seemed to be eventually fulfilled.

During the year between June 1940 and June 1941, when the British Commonwealth alone waged war against the Rome–Berlin Axis Powers, notions of war-aims developed little. The war, for both sides, remained a war for the same issues as in 1939. The resistance movements within the occupied countries had not yet taken coherent form. Communists still condemned the war as one of rival imperialisms. Thereafter, with the German attack on the Soviet Union and the passage of Lend-Lease (March 1941), the entry of larger forces widened the scope as well as the area of the war. The first formal statement of war and peace aims was issued jointly by belligerent Britain and neutral America in the form of the Atlantic Charter of 14 August 1941.

The statement had mixed origins. It contained clear echoes of Woodrow Wilson's 'Fourteen Points', and it repeated ideas which President Roosevelt had enunciated in January 1941 as the 'Four Freedoms'. They had been defined as freedom of speech and expression, freedom of worship, freedom from fear, and freedom from want. To these American formulations were added others predominantly British, such as emphasis on the need for economic development and greater social security. Attlee, acting Prime Minister during Churchill's absence, called a Cabinet meeting at three o'clock in the morning and sent the Cabinet's approval to Churchill 'with a new clause on social security which we wanted among the Allied aims'. Thus were Roosevelt and Churchill, meeting on the battleship *Prince of Wales* in Placentia Bay, Newfoundland, enabled to produce the composite document which was eventually adhered to by all the Allied Governments. It became the ideological cement of the United Nations as an alliance, and was re-endorsed in the Anglo-Soviet Treaty of May 1942.

When the United States became a belligerent in December 1941 no new statement of principles was needed. But concrete cooperation between Britain and the United States as full Allies led to new concepts. Thus the Mutual-Aid Agreement of February 1942 governing conditions under which the two Allies exchanged 'defence articles, defence services, and defence information', spoke of 'benefits' as the criterion of repayment, not merely of money or goods, in the settlement of Lend-Lease arrangements. So, too, the Joint Declaration issued from the Moscow Conference of Britain, the United States, and the Soviet Union in October 1943 stated the need to set up 'a general international organization, based on the principle of the sovereign equality of all peace-loving States . . . for the maintenance of international peace and security'. In November 1943 was set up the first functional United Nations organization, designed to deal systematically with the terrible problems of relief and first-aid which would confront the victors after German defeat: the United Nations Relief and Rehabilitation Administration (U.N.R.R.A.). Financed and recruited internationally and avowedly temporary in purpose, it began its work in the field in the spring of 1944 and came to an end by the autumn of 1948. It saved millions of Europeans from famine and disease; and when it was disbanded its work was taken over by the International Refugee Organization (I.R.O.), the World Health Organization (W.H.O.), the Food and Agriculture Organization (F.A.O.), and the United Nations International Children's Emergency Fund (U.N.I.C.E.F.). It begot these important functional bodies, and in it as in all of them Britain took a leading and formative share, though the bulk of the cost and the supply inevitably came from the United States. These bodies set a new pattern for cooperation in the post-war world.

The aim foreshadowed by the Moscow Conference, of setting up a general international organization to provide security and to replace the old League of Nations, was fulfilled at the San Francisco Conference of 1945 which drafted the United Nations Charter. The pattern of political relationships envisaged therein, especially in the Security Council, was a projection into the post-war world of the sort of 'Grand Alliance' which won the war against Germany and Japan. It consisted of the group of Big Powers (the United States, the Soviet Union, Britain, France, and China) accorded permanent seats and a power of veto, and also a group of secondary Powers. For such a body to work smoothly there had to be an overriding common purpose such as had been provided by agreement to 'win the war'. When no equivalent unified purpose prevailed it was likely to run into great difficulties. A certain inherent dilemma was built into the new structure.

But these formal and organizational peace aims were neither the only, nor necessarily the most important, peace aims that developed during the war as a consequence of the course of events. Britain, as already shown, evolved the concept of a 'Welfare State' which was crystallized by the Beveridge Report of 1942. In the occupied countries the resistance movements, which had gained greatly in coherence and influence by the time of liberation in 1944-5, evolved their own distinctive visions of the sort of society they wanted to create after regaining their freedom. Epitome of these was the French 'Resistance Charter', drafted in March 1944, and adopted by all major political parties in the French elections of October 1945. It was a whole programme of political, economic, and social reforms strongly tinged with the ideas of nationalization, economic planning, social security, and a 'more social democracy'. In the British overseas territories liberated from Japanese occupation, notably Burma and Malaya, strong forces of nationalism demanding complete self-determination and independence had been generated. The currents of opinion in Britain which favoured the Welfare State, and in British oversea territories which favoured independence, were alike parts of a world-wide phenomenon, a tidal wave of sentiment and ideas that inundated the pre-war order. Its long-term revolutionary impetus must be emphasized if events after 1945 are to be understood. The Beveridge Plan was Britain's 'Resistance Charter'. A Commonwealth which for more than a generation had accepted ideals of colonial trusteeship was unlikely to resist the aims now stated, in the United Nations Charter, as the aims of trusteeship in future: 'to develop self-government, to take due account of the political aspirations of the peoples, and to assist them in the progressive development of their free political institutions . . .'.

PART III

FROM WELFARE STATE TO AFFLUENT SOCIETY
(1946–63)

CHAPTER EIGHT

Labour Government and Reconstruction, 1946–51

RECONSTRUCTION

IT is never simple to assess how far the problems that beset a country after a great war were created by the war. As has been seen, Britain was heading for a major domestic crisis anyhow in 1914, and if war had not come many of the problems of 1919 would have arisen, nevertheless, in some form. Likewise, if war had been avoided in 1939, Britain would have had to face tasks of economic overhaul and social reconstruction resembling those which confronted the Government in 1945.

The problems of post-war Britain were to a large extent the endemic problems of twentieth-century Britain – of old and famous industries struggling for survival in unfavourable conditions, of new industries demanding urgent adjustments of capital, skills, and markets, of a commercial nation, still convalescent from war, compelled to trade in a world of crowding competition and rapid, bewildering change. What was the special legacy of war?

It is uncertain, even, whether on balance the experience and effects of the Second World War eased or impeded British attempts to solve these intractable problems. Public acceptance of the disciplines and expenditures needed to institute a national system of social security was greatly facilitated by memories of pre-war unemployment and experience of war-time ordeals; on the other hand, some difficulties, sucn as recurrent unbalance of payments and impediments to exports, were much aggravated by the effects of the war. Post-war problems of reconstruction were of a different order, though they were by no means all different in kind, from the familiar problems of the inter-war years.

What was undoubtedly new, however, was the change of national outlook and of popular resolve: and the spirit of the Labour Party Government, rocketed to power in the summer of 1945, chimed with this new mood. The war had not only accustomed everyone to the spectacle of Labour leaders in ministerial power: it had given the leaders themselves abundant experience of power and the sense of responsibility which comes from such experience. Whereas the Conservatives still bore the brunt of blame for what had not been done at home or abroad in the thirties, Labour shared in the credit for efficient war-time administration, especially as regards organization of man-power, home security, and economic planning. The national mood was in many ways the very opposite to the mood of 1918. Then there had been a prevailing desire to get back to 'the good old days', to rediscover a more secure world such as the pre-1914 world seemed to have been. Now the pre-war world of the thirties seemed so insecure and blameworthy that there was little nostalgia for the past. To look back at all was to look back in anger – and in grief. So men looked forward, damning the recent past perhaps too completely, and shunning so vehemently the errors of the past that they were apt to commit an entirely new set of errors of their own. Uppermost in their minds was the desire for fuller social justice, a lessening of class differences, and greater security and peace. The mood did not favour, as in 1918, continuance of the war-time Coalition, immense though its services to the nation had been. It favoured wholeheartedly a Labour Government.

Churchill misjudged the popular mood, and reverted too fast to pre-war political idiom, when during his electioneering speeches in 1945 he tried to evoke fears of 'a Labour

Party Gestapo'. The Zinoviev letter was not forgotten, nor the fact that Conservative Governments throughout the thirties had kept Churchill in the political wilderness.

The election campaign of 1945 was distinguished alike by the contrasting strategy by which the two chief parties appealed to the electorate, and the strange manner of its decision. The Labour party presented a compact, fully developed programme supported by a powerfully coordinated team of leaders. The Conservative party presented Mr Churchill, and the blessings of his Four-Year Plan. Mr Churchill laid before the electors his manifold experience, and asked for a renewal of their confidence, saying little or nothing of the Conservative party.[1]

Churchill had broadcast the outline of his Four-Year Plan as early as March 1943. Its most concrete achievement to date was the Butler Education Act of 1944; but the rest of its measures remained somewhat vague as compared with Labour's Five-Year Plan. Labour came to power with a clear popular commission to carry out its plan of social and economic reconstruction.[2]

Mr Attlee, in 1937, had outlined his ideas of how to reconstruct the Cabinet so as to avoid excessive centralization in the Prime Minister while ensuring efficient coordination of the main sectors of policy. Now, following both his own precepts and the lessons of war-time, he increasingly introduced a pyramid-shaped structure. Under him he arranged three senior functional Ministers: Ernest Bevin the Foreign Secretary, Sir Stafford Cripps the Chancellor of the Exchequer (from 1947), and Herbert Morrison the Lord President of the Council. Beneath them again were five coordinating Ministers: the Minister of Defence, Lord Privy

1. R. B. McCallum and A. Readman, *The British General Election of 1945* (1947), p. 128.
2. On the genesis of the Conservative Plan see Earl of Woolton, *Memoirs* (1959), Chapters XVII and XVIII; and for Labour's see F. Williams, *A Prime Minister Remembers* (1961), and *The Triple Challenge* (1948).

Seal, Lord Chancellor, Home Secretary, and Chancellor of the Duchy of Lancaster. Beneath them ranked the eight senior Departmental Ministers who were also members of the Cabinet; and beyond them again twelve Heads of Departments not members of the Cabinet. Attlee thus reduced the size of the Cabinet to seventeen, and entrusted to his three immediate lieutenants a large share of the work of coordination. Bevin looked after the whole field of oversea policy including the Commonwealth; Cripps the vast field of economic and financial policy; Morrison domestic social policy and legislative activity. Yet the four key men did not constitute an 'inner cabinet' in the old sense, for general policy decisions remained the task of the Cabinet as a whole. The central machinery was finely geared to the heavy labours of reconstruction, though more of its power had to be devoted to countering crises than anyone foresaw in 1945.[1]

The first part of the programme was nationalization of credit, power, and transport. This fell into two parts: the mainly formal and the substantially novel. The first included the Bank of England Act, the Cable and Wireless Act, and the Civil Aviation Act (all of 1946). The second was accomplished in five major legislative measures: the Coal Industry Nationalization Act (1946), Electricity Act (1947), Transport Act (1947), Gas Act (1947), and the Iron and Steel Act (1949). Even these 'commanding heights' of the economy had already been brought partially under national control, or were run by public corporations or local authorities. The Labour measures were in the long pre-war tradition of State responsibilities and public-service corporations rather than new bases for revolutionary change. The last and most controversial, the Iron and Steel Act, was delayed by the Lords and left the main firms intact for the Conservatives to denationalize steel after 1951. The diversi-

1. See C. R. Attlee, *The Labour Party in Perspective* (1937) and Herbert Morrison, *Government and Parliament* (1954).

fication of the organizations set up to run the industries suggests no doctrinaire uniformity. The National Coal Board and the British Transport Commission were very different kinds of body.

What nationalization could accomplish proved limited. Some 80 per cent of the country's industry was still in private hands, and nationalization of the remaining 20 per cent secured no effective 'commanding heights'. Managements and executives remained very much the same people, workers gained little or no more control than before, and not even wasteful competition was eliminated (e.g. as between gas and electricity). In the next decade the nationalized industries became much more utterly the servants than the masters of private industry. Conditions of employment were often improved (notably in the mines), but employees acquired little of the expected sense of 'participation' or 'partnership', still less of 'ownership'. The changes wrought little transformation in English society, and once again the exaggerated hopes of both enthusiastic supporters and terrified opponents proved equally false.

The second part of the programme – reforms in education and the other social services, and the construction of a 'Welfare State' – became correspondingly more important for satisfying the demands of Labour's supporters. The Butler Act of 1944, raising the school-leaving age to 15, was partly implemented in 1947. It set about ensuring secondary education for all according to age, ability, and aptitude, and for the first time constructed a full national system of education. Other prospects in the Act – notably the extension of higher education to many more young people – were postponed because of shortages of money and staff. Other social reforms needed new legislation. James Griffiths's National Insurance Act (1946) consolidated and extended existing provision in the Beveridge manner. Another Welshman, Aneurin Bevan, as Minister of Health, was responsible both

for the Housing Acts (1946 and 1949) which encouraged
council-house building and for the controversial National
Health Service Act (1946). The latter set out to provide free
medical service for all and took over responsibility for the
voluntary hospitals, now placed under regional boards.
Drugs, medicine, spectacles, and false teeth were provided,
at first free but later for relatively small charges. Strong
opposition came from the medical profession, as it had come
in 1911; and as then it was soon overcome.

In addition to these major measures a host of others were
passed during this spell of intensive legislative activity. The
State gained powers to plan new towns, to develop atomic
energy for peaceful purposes, to pay family allowances. The
extent to which actions by public authorities could inti-
mately affect the daily lives of the ordinary citizen was
greatly enlarged, for good or ill. Two measures were intended to make the State more formally 'democratic': the
Representation of the People Act of 1948, which abolished
special university representation and the double vote for
graduates and owners of business premises; and the Parliament Act of 1949, which was a sequel to that of 1911 in that
it reduced from three sessions to two the time by which the
House of Lords could delay legislation. In 1946 the Trades
Disputes Act of 1927 was repealed, so implementing the
long-standing Labour promise to reverse Baldwin's step
against trade unions after the General Strike. Trade unions
could again affiliate to the Labour Party on a 'contracting-
out' basis.[1]

The most significant changes of all, in these years of reconstruction, came not from legislation but from policy:
especially from the financial policies of Dalton and Cripps,
which kept the very high war-time levels of direct taxation,
and from the policy of ensuring 'full employment', to which
the Government was fully committed. Cripps, when he

1. See above, p. 115.

succeeded Hugh Dalton in 1947, added his own special policy of 'austerity', dictated more by immediate exigencies than by any freely chosen Socialistic policy. The combination of these three policies provided the essential basis for all that the Labour Government was able to achieve in solid recovery and reconstruction, and indeed for the permanent growth of the 'Welfare State' in Britain.

LABOUR POLICIES

The Government's fiscal and financial policies were inevitably conditioned by the emergency situation existing after six years of war. The problem of the 'dollar gap' or the 'balance of payments' remained, for Britain as for other countries, one of the most intractable of financial difficulties. The negotiation of the American loan, to replace the benefits of Lend-Lease, has already been mentioned.[1] By obliging Britain in 1947 to restore the convertibility of sterling its eventual effect was to precipitate a new financial crisis. By that date Britain was still in desperate need of goods and services which could be got only in the dollar area – for dollars – and this inevitably depleted dangerously the sterling area's 'dollar pool'. The Government was compelled to keep controls on currency and to provide financial incentives to export to dollar countries. The year of crisis, 1947, was preceded by an exceptionally severe winter, bringing a fuel shortage that dislocated production and transport, and greatly hampered the drive for exports. Not only was rationing continued, but some foodstuffs (bread and potatoes) were now rationed for the first time. Western Europe as a whole suffered from the same dollar shortage, as well as from the same severe winter. In Britain Sir Stafford Cripps, who had been at the Board of Trade, succeeded Dr Hugh Dalton at the Treasury.

1. See p. 202.

Cripps's prim and puritanical personality matched well the policy of austerity with which he was publicly identified. He was a vegetarian, devoted to a spartan mode of life. Of brilliant intellect, with claim to be both a chemist and a highly successful barrister, he was the son of Lord Parmoor and nephew of Beatrice Webb. For his ultra-Leftist views he had been expelled from the Labour Party in 1939, but he won political eminence as ambassador to Moscow (1940), leader of the 'Cripps Mission' to India (1942), and latterly (1942) Lord Beaverbrook's successor as Minister of Aircraft Production. In 1947 Attlee set up a new Ministry of Economic Affairs with a special economic planning staff to assist it. Cripps took the staff with him to the Treasury, and made the budget his main instrument of control and direction in his fight against inflation. Again, many countries suffered from inflation in these years – some even more so than Britain. The high price of imports, in an economy such as Britain's, combined with the steady pressure for higher wages. Cripps restricted the latter, and enjoyed the immense moral triumph of persuading the trade unions to impose a voluntary wage-freeze. He did not stop inflation – no post-war Government succeeded in that. But he slowed it down to a pace compatible with full employment and with socialistic aims.[1]

The Government's policy of ensuring full employment – of capital resources no less than of labour – was almost completely successful. Conditions favoured it, save for the fuel crisis of the early months of 1947. The post-war boom in basic industries and in building, caused by war-time lags and shortages, was prolonged. Unemployment rarely rose above 2 per cent (400,000 insured workers) and there was no hard core of long-term unemployment. With new equipment both productivity and production rose while the average working week shortened. Yet consumption was

1. See p. 265.

kept down by 'austerity', and the high level of taxation
scarcely encouraged enterprise. Demobilization and reabsorption of servicemen into the economy was accomplished smoothly and without serious dislocation. Industry
was converted to peace-time production. In all these respects
the lessons, hard learned in the twenties, were remembered
and applied with advantage. New industries, such as man-
made fibres and plastics, developed rapidly and created
fresh employment: others that developed more slowly –
notably television – reached significant dimensions after
1950. New methods of organization, including much more
'automation', economized on man-power.

It became increasingly apparent, however, that lack of
balance between the economies of the old world and the
new, persistently manifest in the 'dollar gap', was not
merely an after-effect of the war. The gap had existed since
the thirties, but in the early forties several circumstances
had concealed or narrowed it. These no longer existed. Raw
materials from oversea colonial territories (either British or
European) had provided exports to America, and pre-war
terms of trade had been favourable. On 5 June 1947
George C. Marshall, United States Secretary of State, made
a historic speech at Harvard which stated the need simply
and sympathetically:

Europe's requirements for the next three or four years of foreign
food and other essential products – principally from America – are
so much greater than her present ability to pay that she must have
substantial additional help or face economic, social, and political
deterioration of a very grave character.

This was equally true of Britain, and when the 'Marshall Plan' led to the creation of a special organization –
the Organization for European Economic Cooperation
(O.E.E.C.) – to administer American financial aid Britain
played a leading part in it. Her trade balance improved
considerably. Even so, in September 1949 the pound sterling

was devalued from four dollars and three cents to two dollars and eighty cents: a very drastic measure that opened the door to more inflation and marked the failure of this aspect of the Government's economic policy.

What saved the economy was the immense vigour and success of the exports drive and the maintenance of full employment. The growth of productivity combined with restriction of home consumption made for greater exports. This combination, in turn, was made possible only by public discipline and morale. It was a grim period, coming so soon after the rigours of war. The mood of 'Britain can take it' revived. It may be doubted whether it would have revived under leaders held in less esteem than Attlee, Bevin, or Cripps, or without the assurance that the power of the State would be used to equalize economic sacrifices and promote fuller social justice. One problem that historians must eventually settle is whether the existence of the Welfare State, far from being a source of the economic crisis in that it overburdened the economy and sapped enterprise, was one major reason why Britain overcame the crisis so quickly, in that it ensured public solidarity in sacrifice and effort.

One factor in this process was Labour's readiness to keep or to reimpose controls even when they were very unpopular. Its Supplies and Services Bill of 1947 met with fierce opposition and roused many anxieties. Its extension of the period of national service was unpopular, but accepted. Main foodstuffs were still rationed even in 1950. Severe restrictions remained on hire-purchase agreements, tourists' currency allowances, building licences, and much else. Food subsidies were reduced by Cripps, but in 1950 they still had an upper limit of £410 million. This means of keeping food at prices within reach of the poor was often denounced as a burden on taxes which lowered incentives for enterprise. But the charge against Labour's affection for controls is less that they aimed at integrated 'economic planning' than that they were used piecemeal and only as need dictated. Conservative nightmares of doctrinaire planning and limitless 'socialization' proved ill-founded. What Labour seriously aimed at, no less than what Labour in fact accomplished, during its first period of real power, fits easily into the tolerant, parliamentary, genial traditions of British political life. Its greatest failures, such as the wasteful Tanganyika groundnuts scheme, arose from over-optimism, but brought it great discredit.

In February 1950 general elections registered the decline in Labour's popularity after nearly five years in power. There was a 3 per cent turnover of votes from Labour to Conservatives. This reduced Labour seats to 315 and increased the seats of Conservatives and their allies to 298. Liberals and Independents were almost eliminated. Labour resumed office faced by a much more formidable Opposition and unable to put through more controversial legislation. The election reached a new pitch of efficiency and central organization in electioneering. Each major party fought the elections fully prepared, and put into the field an army of highly trained professional constituency agents. Smaller parties were forced to the wall. Radio electioneering played a rather less important part than in 1945, and television broadcasts had not yet begun. The rival leaders loomed larger in popular choice than the local candidates, but after experience of Labour rule the contrast of programmes was also clearer. Public-opinion polls were held on a scale not hitherto known in Britain, and raised questions of how far forecasts might themselves influence the eventual results.

The outbreak of war in Korea, in July 1950,[1] involving United States forces on a large scale, brought about another economic crisis in Britain and occasioned rearmament at a level which forced up both taxes and prices. It revived, in an acute form, the old pre-war dilemma of

1. See p. 238.

'guns or butter'. In October Hugh Gaitskell succeeded Cripps at the Exchequer and economized on the National Health Service costs by charging 50 per cent of the cost of spectacles and dentures to the recipients. Aneurin Bevan and Harold Wilson, treating this change as an abandonment of principle, resigned in April 1951. The Government was haunted by ill-health. Bevin, Cripps, and Attlee himself fell ill. The narrow majority it enjoyed in the Commons and the Opposition's harassing tactics, imposing all-night sittings, put great strain on ministers. The position was totally different from that of the 1945 Government. The impetus had been spent: it was probable that the next election – which could not long be postponed – would bring further decline.

The dissolution came in September 1951, and the electoral campaign was unsensational. A further 1 per cent of the votes swung against Labour: enough to tip the balance of seats in favour of the Conservatives, with 321 against Labour's 295 – an almost exact reversal of the position eighteen months earlier. Labour's prestige as a party had dropped meantime, if Conservative prestige had not very greatly grown. The Liberals dropped, even more catastrophically, from nine members to six.

Developments in colonial and foreign policy during the Labour administration include such momentous events as the grant of independence to India, Pakistan, Ceylon, and Burma, and the formation of the North Atlantic Treaty Organization (N.A.T.O.). These aspects will be considered below.[1] Taken together with Labour's domestic legislation, social reforms, and economic policies, they make the years 1945–51 a time of great historical significance. The essential change is not aptly described, as many tried to describe it at the time, as a 'social revolution'. Politically, it marked a climax of Labour Party achievement after a decade

1. See pp. 236–41.

of continuous Conservative rule (and indeed of one single Parliament); but it can now be seen as an important interlude in a continuing Conservative Government, with little divergence between the two in most issues of national policy. Labour could build on the domestic legislation of Neville Chamberlain.[1] In this sense Labour's tenure of power, far from involving a social revolution, marked the establishment of Labour as the regular parliamentary alternative to Conservatism. It accepted fully – and was seen to accept – British parliamentary patterns. In the same sense, Labour's profoundest achievement in these years was perhaps its most silent and unnoticed. It made impossible any sense of alienation from the community on the part of the workers. The British State was now 'theirs' as much as anybody else's – dedicated to the interests and welfare of every citizen, however humble. Of this the 'Festival of Britain' in 1951, fostered mainly by Herbert Morrison, was in some ways a symbol: a national folk-festival in modern idiom.

The real revolution was a psychological one, marking reaction against the inter-war class strife. Attlee achieved in peace what Churchill had magnificently achieved in war: a spirit of national solidarity and sense of community, able to transcend the strong fissiparous forces of modern life. That so self-effacing a man was able to do this was due partly to his own shining integrity of character which none could question, and partly to the combination of able lieutenants whom he gathered around him. To the final result the sturdy loyalty and robust energy of Ernest Bevin contributed more than most. Bevin captured the ears and hearts of the mass of ordinary Englishmen as no other but Churchill could. Attlee's corresponding achievement in Commonwealth affairs – settlement in India – was equally due to his ability to discover good men and put them in the

1. See above, p. 100.

right places at the right time. His choice of Lord Mountbatten as Viceroy could not have been bettered. Though
lacking the flair for public relations and the colourful
character of Churchill, Attlee revealed high qualities in
judgement of men and wisdom of measures. Though no
orator, he could be an effective parliamentary debater. Like
his contemporary, President Harry S. Truman of the United
States, he had the qualities of toughness, pertinacity, and
sagacity which count for much in political leadership.

EVOLVING THE COMMONWEALTH

The new post-war Britain had to rethink its own relations
with the world on which it depended for survival: it had
also to reshape relations with a new world, itself transformed
by the war and presenting a bewildering kaleidoscope of
patterns old and new. In this sense Commonwealth and
foreign relations became inseparable, virtually inter-
changeable aspects of British relations with the whole of the
rest of the world. The traditional claim, to have specially
privileged connexions with Dominions and Colonies of a
kind that would not be equally acceptable to those countries
if they were foreign sovereign States, would soon have to
end. An invincible spirit of national autonomy and equality
was abroad.

Here, too, was the culmination of a pre-war process,
accelerated and intensified by the circumstances of the war.
In 1942 Sir Stafford Cripps had led a mission to India, seeking India's full cooperation in the war against Japan in return for the promise of an Indian-made constitution,
Dominion status, and government by Indians in everything
except defence. The mission failed, in that the Congress
Party rejected the offer. Attlee had himself served on the
Simon Commission of 1928,[1] and kept a lively personal

1. See p. 105.

interest in Indian affairs. He was convinced that Britain must leave India, but must do so in the manner least disruptive to India and least harmful to Britain.

Separation had to be arranged, and none could have arranged it more delicately than Attlee. Mr Jinnah and the Moslem League had gained in strength, and bitter communal dissensions between Hindu and Moslem bedevilled the prospect as much as ever. Attlee sent out Lord Mountbatten as Viceroy, to replace Lord Wavell and to end the British Raj. By force of personality he got Gandhi, Nehru, and Jinnah all discussing together how to take over power without chaos: and Attlee announced in February 1947 that whatever happened Britain would leave India not later than 1 June 1948. Britain proposed partition and the creation of a separate Moslem State of Pakistan as the only way of preserving peace. Congress leaders greatly disliked the idea – there was the usual complaint of 'divide and rule' – but this time there was an inexorable necessity for Indians to agree before Britain abandoned them. 'I'd come to the conclusion,' said Attlee later in his casual way, 'that there was a great deal of happiness for them in asking for everything, and putting down everything that was wrong in India to British rule, and then sitting pretty. . . . I concluded the thing to do was to bring them right up against it and make them see they'd got to face the situation themselves.' The device involved both courage and calculated risks. But it worked.

On 15 August 1947 two Dominions – India and Pakistan (the latter itself divided into two parts) – were instituted. Riots and considerable bloodshed ensued. Grave loss of life, as well as partition, were the price of independence. But the Indian Independence Act of July 1947 opened a new era in the long story of Anglo-Indian relations. Some 400 million people – one-sixth of all mankind – gained political independence overnight. That they were capable of receiving it without greater detriment was due to the progressive measures of semi-independence granted since 1919. Britain won a fund of goodwill that was to benefit her relations with all the coloured peoples of the world.

In the same year Ceylon and Burma gained independence. The Union of Burma came into being in January 1948, as further proof of Britain's sincerity of purpose: and when, unlike India and Pakistan, Burma decided to leave the Commonwealth, Britain did nothing to prevent it. 'We want,' said Attlee, 'no unwilling partners in the British Commonwealth.' From February 1948 the former Colony of Ceylon was accepted as a fully self-governing Dominion within the Commonwealth. The precise status of the new Dominions of India, Pakistan, and Ceylon took some years to define. Clearly they were different in kind from the old settled Dominions. They were also new in form, because in January 1950 India, and in 1956 Pakistan, became Republics. That even Republics could be comprised within the new elasticized Commonwealth was due to the work of the Commonwealth Prime Ministers Conference of April 1949.[1]

The device of fixing a date for withdrawal was adopted also in the mandated territory of Palestine, where Zionism and Arab nationalism were challenging British administration and continually clashing with one another. It was decided to withdraw all British forces by May 1948, after United Nations intervention failed and after the United States had refused to be associated with British efforts to keep the peace. The result was open war between Jews and Arabs and the eventual establishment, in 1948, of the independent sovereign State of Israel. The defeat by Israel of the Arab forces, drawn from her four neighbouring States and from Iraq, won for the new State more territory than the United Nations award of November 1947 would have given

1. See p. 234.

it. The rest of Palestine was combined with Transjordan to form the new Hashemite Kingdom of Jordan under King Abdullah. The lesson of the whole episode, quickly noted in the Middle East, was that intransigence could pay.

In other parts of the Commonwealth Britain at first made no attempt to accelerate independence. In Malaya, another region of South-East Asia greatly influenced by Japanese conquests, a single nationalist movement was prevented by the co-existence of several national groups. By 1948 Communist guerrilla bands operated from the jungle and British troops faced very difficult problems of preserving order. It was 1956 before agreements were reached at the London Conference which set up a new Federation of Malaya. In August 1957 it became the eleventh member State of the Commonwealth.

In Africa the Gold Coast set the pace towards independence, partly by reason of its internal cohesion and partly because of its expanding economy. There were riots in 1947, but the Convention People's Party led by Dr Kwame Nkrumah gained enough in prestige to take over power from Britain. He became Prime Minister in 1951, and by March 1957 the State of Ghana came into being by combination of the Gold Coast with the trusteeship territory of Togoland. It attained Dominion status within the Commonwealth, with the Queen as Sovereign. Thus was started the complex process of accelerated independence in Africa which reached a climax in the sixties. By setting the pattern and the pace for African development, Ghana assumed a special importance within the new Commonwealth and helped to keep it truly multi-racial. There has been no other span of six years within which so much happened to shape anew its whole development.

The monarchy retained much of its former function as the symbol of unity and the focus of common loyalties, notwithstanding the choice of republican constitutions. That it should have done so under a Labour Government is testimony to the reconciliation of socialism with nationalism which had so completely occurred in Britain by mid century. The redefinition of the Commonwealth which made the evolution possible was achieved at the conference of Commonwealth Prime Ministers held in London in April 1949 to determine the future status of India. It has rightly been likened to the Balfour definition of 1926 and the Statute of Westminster as an important landmark in British history.

Like all successful conferences it had been most carefully prepared. Since May 1947 the Cabinet Committee on Commonwealth Relations, with Attlee as its Chairman, had devoted much thought to the problem. Emissaries had visited the other Dominions to discover their views. Various possible arrangements were explored and discarded. Mr Nehru was cooperative. Within a week the seven Prime Ministers (and Mr Lester Pearson representing the Prime Minister of Canada) reached complete agreement. On 27 April 1949 they accepted India's continuing membership as a sovereign independent Republic on the basis of India's 'acceptance of the King as the symbol of the free association of its independent member nations and as such the Head of the Commonwealth'. They accordingly declared that 'they remain united as free and equal members of the Commonwealth of Nations, freely cooperating in the pursuit of peace, liberty, and progress'.

The work of the Conference was an even greater piece of statesmanship than the grant of independence to India. By remarkably skilful adaptation to changes in environment the Commonwealth survived with renewed vigour into the age of colonial revolutions. The formula whereby Republics could be also Dominions shaped the new Commonwealth of the later twentieth century. Even at this hour the past proved obdurate. The Conference was the first to meet without a representative of Eire. In November 1948 the *Dáil* had passed the Republic of Ireland Act. On 18 April (Easter Monday) 1949 the new Republic was nostalgically proclaimed at the General Post Office in Dublin. It was only three days before the London Conference met – enough to exclude Ireland from it. The formula it eventually adopted was substantially the arrangement of 'external association' which Mr De Valera had first propounded to Lloyd George in 1921. It might have served to keep Ireland within the Commonwealth, had she not left it so short a time before. Fortunately the break was softened by traditional illogicality. It was mutually agreed that the citizens of Ireland and of Commonwealth countries should not be regarded as foreigners, and in London Anglo-Irish relations went on being handled by the Commonwealth Relations Office. Actual relations expanded and improved, despite the tangled absurdities of the formal breach.

WORLD RELATIONS

Until his resignation because of ill health in March 1951, Ernest Bevin was Labour's Foreign Secretary. Though identified until 1945 with his work at the Ministry of Labour during Churchill's war-time Coalition Government, and with trade-union affairs rather than foreign, he had long experience of international conferences and their techniques. Collective bargaining, moreover, had taught him shrewdness and realism in negotiations. He proved himself a great Foreign Minister.

British policy in these years falls broadly into three successive phases, each embracing a wide complex of problems. In texture Britain's external relations could be seen as a series of overlapping circles: her relations with Europe, particularly her western neighbours; with the two new giant Powers, the United States and the Soviet Union; with her partners of all kinds in the new general international bodies, especially the United Nations; and with the countries of the Commonwealth. The last of these 'circles' has already been described. The intersections of the others produced the main issues with which Ernest Bevin and his advisers had to wrestle between 1945 and 1951. The three phases divide at roughly the end of 1947 and the summer of 1949.

The first, from the Potsdam Conference in July 1945 to the Conference of Foreign Ministers at the end of 1947, was distinguished by efforts on Britain's part – efforts which increasingly became more hopeless – to fulfil the intentions of the war-time conferences and prolong into peace the alliance of the United Nations. Bevin offered to extend the Anglo-Soviet Alliance (1942) for a period of fifty years. Though already distrustful of Russian policy as he had witnessed it at Potsdam, at the Paris peace negotiations of 1946, and in the United Nations, he tried for as long as possible to reach an understanding with the Kremlin. But its policy of blatant expansion and domination in eastern Europe, and of obstruction in wider world relationships, blocked any such hopes. He turned to western Europe and to the United States.

In March 1947, at Dunkirk, Bevin signed with the French Foreign Minister, M. Georges Bidault, a 'Treaty of Alliance and Mutual Assistance'. Greece, plunged into civil war in the autumn of 1946, was helped by Britain until in March 1947 President Truman enunciated his famous 'doctrine', promising American aid to both Greece and Turkey. Even so, fighting went on for two more years before Communism was checked in Greece. In June 1947 Secretary Marshall launched the proposal for extensive American economic aid to Europe which evolved into the Marshall Plan. Bevin saw that Britain's future must lie in close cooperation with western Europe and in the 'Atlantic Alliance'. It has been claimed that the final redirection of British policy came after a particularly vitriolic attack by the Soviet Foreign Minister, Molotov, at the Conference of Foreign Ministers in London at the end of 1947. Bevin's patience snapped: 'Now 'e's gone too bloody far,' he remarked to his advisers.

Bevin took a vigorous initiative in assembling the international conference which accepted and arranged to adminster Marshall Aid. He set about drawing closer together the peoples of western Europe. The second phase began, in March 1948, when the Pact of Brussels was signed by representatives of Britain, France, Belgium, the Netherlands, and Luxembourg. At the end of February a Communist *coup* in Prague added Czechoslovakia to the countries pulled behind the 'iron curtain' that now descended between east and west in Europe. In June the Soviet authorities of occupation in Germany blockaded the western sector of Berlin. The image of a concert of major Powers (the United States, Soviet Union, Britain, and France) collectively administering an occupied Germany now collapsed into a dual division between the western half (made by a fusion of the three western zones) and the eastern half. Each was administered separately. The Soviet attempt to make the West's position in Berlin untenable by blockade evoked the astonishing Anglo-American airlift which, night and day for 323 days, flew supplies into the city. The Russians admitted defeat by lifting the blockade in May 1949.

Bevin's policy towards defeated Germany was the characteristic one of loyally striving to carry out the undertakings given by the Allies at the end of the war. Frustrated in this by Soviet obstruction and aggression, and ever mindful of Britain's need for economic recovery and growth no less than for national security, he was ready to take a full part in any organization, regional or general, which would serve these ends. Accordingly, he took a leading part, also, in the formation of the North Atlantic Treaty Organization, set up in April 1949. It comprised Britain's partners in the Brussels

Pact and the Dominion of Canada, as well as the United States, Denmark, Norway, Iceland, and Portugal. In May a Federal German Government came into being at Bonn, to govern the three western zones of occupation. An occupation Statute reduced and defined the responsibilities of the occupying authorities.

This second phase of Labour policy, identified with the policy often called 'containment' of Communism, rested on the notion of defensive alliances aimed at preserving a balance of power in the world likely to deter further Communist expansion. It entered a totally new phase in September 1949, when it was known and announced that an atomic explosion had occurred in the Soviet Union. The equalization of appalling destructive power, and the new crop of mutual fears it engendered, inaugurated the period of 'cold war' – of open schism in the world, of apparently irreconcilable ideological conflict between Communism and democracy, and the looming mushroom cloud of nuclear war. By the end of 1949 the two giant Powers were exerting strong polarizing influences on all world relationships.

At the same moment, however, a new factor began to operate. In China the Communist Party led by Mao Tsetung and Chou En-lai set up the People's Republic of China. Driving the remnant of the old Kuomintang off the mainland on to the island of Formosa (where it survived with United States backing), the new Chinese Communist Government set about a vigorous regeneration of that vast country.

The third phase of policy in these years was marked, therefore, by a hardening of world relationships along the lines of ideological schism and the 'cold war'; but also by a frightening tendency for open warfare to flare up along the disputed borderlands. In June 1950 war broke out in Korea, where – after the expulsion of the Japanese – the northern part had been occupied by the Soviet Union, the southern by the United States. Now northern troops struck south. In support of a United Nations demand for withdrawal of the northern forces behind the old borderline of the 38th parallel, the United States sent strong forces to the south. Communist China backed the north Koreans, and other members of the United Nations (including Britain) backed the Americans. Only great restraint on each side kept the war limited, and it relapsed into stalemate during 1951. An armistice was signed in July 1953. The incident made Britain aware of the perils of commitment to one side in the 'cold war', for British opinion did not fully support the more aggressive strategies of some American generals. It also made Britain more aware of the new factor of a Communist China.

The Labour Government disliked and distrusted several features of United States policy. It disliked the witch-hunt of 'subversives' by Senator McCarthy, for many he dubbed 'reds' would count as socialists or even liberals in Britain. It also distrusted the movement for closer European integration which American policy seemed over-eager to sponsor. The movement was suspected because it was favoured so unanimously by Catholic Democratic parties in France, Germany, and Italy, and by big-scale capitalism in both Europe and the United States. The Coal and Steel Community projected in western Europe in 1950 was criticized as likely to lead to cartels or to technocracy, neither attractive to Socialism. By the time Herbert Morrison took over the Foreign Office from Bevin in March 1951, for the last eight months of the Labour Government, Britain's concern was to avoid too binding a commitment to support policies motivated primarily by anti-Communism. This implied no sympathy at all for Communism. Morrison's term at the Foreign Office was anyhow brief and inglorious: it was not his natural *milieu*.

Hugh Gaitskell's defence budget of 1951 in effect opened

old wounds within the Labour Party. The British rearmament programme contemplated spending £1,500 million a
year, and the budget proposed making certain charges
under the National Health Service. Faced with the dilemma
of 'guns or butter' – national or social security – the Party
divided according to its bias of mind as regards American
policies and how best to resist the spread of Communism.
To alleviate poverty in the underdeveloped countries, it
could be argued, would do more to check the spread of
Communism than ruinous expenditure on armaments.
Aneurin Bevan and Harold Wilson resigned. 'We have
allowed ourselves,' protested Bevan, 'to be dragged too far
behind the wheels of American diplomacy.' In the absence
of the massive cohesive influence of Ernest Bevin, who died
in April, the old geological fault within the party again
mattered. Popular confidence declined fast, and the return
of the Conservatives to power gave Eden the chance to lead
British policy back to a more traditional mode of action.
Ernest Bevin had followed so much in Eden's footsteps that
he had been accused of realizing 'the importance of being
Anthony'. Eden's return meant, broadly, continuity in the
foreign policy Bevin would have pursued: with the crucial
exception of his Suez exploit in 1956.[1]

In world relations the years 1945–51 brought one of the
most rapid and tragic reversals in modern history. The
hopes of a concert of major Powers collaborating to aid
recovery and build peace never materialized. From an early
moment strong forces of aversion between east and west
began to operate until the world seemed doomed to split
into two bitterly hostile camps, each wielding the terrifying
threat of nuclear destruction. In economic reconstruction
and revival, even in political settlement, most parts of the
globe achieved much by 1951. But in the crucial fields of
conciliation and international security deterioration had

1. See p. 252.

been sharp. Confronted with this world situation Britain had to adapt its policies to it. The Government faced a series of profound dilemmas: to lean towards the Atlantic alliance and especially the United States, or to the new evolving Commonwealth, with its large neutralist Dominions now led by India; to join closely with western Europe, whose prosperity and security were so plainly a British interest, or to hold aloof, lest continental ties be too close; or, in the end, to hold to all these courses 'to some extent', hoping to make them compatible and restrain extremists of all kinds, at the risk of shouldering inconsistent commitments? For the following decade British policy continued to waver between variant versions of these courses of action.

CHAPTER NINE

Revival and Reversion, 1951–6

THE RETURN OF CHURCHILL

WHEN his great Coalition broke up in May 1945 Winston Churchill had formed a 'Caretaker Government' pending the election of a new Parliament. It is remarkable that, apart from that two-months' interim ministry, the first Conservative Government Churchill ever formed (and the first of any kind in peace-time) was that which he formed in October 1951. From the outset it suffered from certain anomalies. Although it had the slender majority of twenty-six seats over Labour, the Conservative Party had received 231,000 votes fewer than Labour. Committed as it was to extensive undoing of the work of its predecessor, it found this position embarrassing. Churchill, aged seventy-six, composed his ministry partly of senior and experienced party men (many of whom were now in the Lords), partly of younger men to whom he opened the doors of a ministerial career. The mainstays of the ministry were Sir Anthony Eden, Lord Salisbury, and Mr R. A. Butler. Churchill also attempted an experiment, which proved so unhappy that it had to be abandoned, of appointing 'coordinators' for the three important sectors of activity: food and agriculture, fuel and power and transport, and research and development. As the individuals chosen were, respectively, Lords Woolton, Leathers, and Cherwell, they were dubbed 'Overlords' and were resented because they could not be questioned in the Commons. Churchill, as Minister of Defence, worked closely with Eden at the Foreign Office.

The administration was haunted, too, by several misfortunes. King George VI, having partially recovered from a grave illness, unexpectedly died in February 1952. Although the accession of the young Queen Elizabeth II, and her coronation in 1953, prompted much talk of the beginning of a 'new Elizabethan age', the live issues of domestic, Commonwealth, and international affairs recalled more strongly an all too familiar recent past. Nor did Churchill himself enjoy good health, and early in 1953 he had a serious stroke. Increasingly Eden, as acting Prime Minister, assumed a larger share of guidance and control, but he, too, was ill in 1953. With its slender majority, and its own record of harassing tactics in the previous Parliament, the Conservative Party now suffered from even more vigorous parliamentary harassing at the hands of the Opposition. It was, moreover, saddled with a burden of its own making, as the Chairman of the Party himself ruefully pointed out later.

We had also a heavy load of promises. We had said we would 'set the people free'; we had declared our firm intention – against all the usual practice of incoming governments – of revoking much previous legislation. ... The Churchill Government was pledged in its election manifesto to undo much of the Socialist legislation of the preceding six years, which involved the nationalized industries. ... Repealing legislation with a majority of sixteen (*sic*) is an unwelcome process. ... [1]

While financial stringency forbade too hasty a removal of controls and regulations, good sense and lack of political support forbade any wholesale denationalization. Churchill, by his own speeches as a Liberal in 1906, was committed to nationalizing the railways. It was much too dangerous to tamper with the mines, which the Sankey Commission of 1919 had wanted to nationalize. In effect, controls and subsidies were eased as occasion arose, and only road transport and steel were seriously scheduled for denationalization.

1. Earl of Woolton, *Memoirs*, pp. 366–78.

The legislation setting up the Welfare State was not only preserved but in some details (such as family allowances) it was improved. The Government was haunted by a curious air of unreality, arising from the disparity between the Churchillian ferocity of its utterances and the tepidity of its deeds, dictated by its inherent limitations. Nor, it seems, were Cabinet meetings always conducted with great efficiency. Lord Woolton records that 'not infrequently the entire time of the meeting had gone before he arrived at the first item on the agenda', adding that 'the Cabinet under Mr Churchill was often reminiscent of bygone times'.

Churchill's Government survived, with a few changes, until April 1955, when he retired at the age of eighty. Despite the electoral exaggerations of difference in policy, in home affairs it was faced with much the same problems as its predecessor, and responded to them in closely similar ways. Whereas Mr Gaitskell as Labour Chancellor had found money for guns by imposing charges on patients under the Health Service, Mr Butler as Conservative Chancellor found it by cutting food subsidies: a lack of fundamental difference which made people talk about 'Butskellism' – a continuity in fiscal policy parallel with the continuity currently regarded as very desirable in foreign policy.[1] A fresh balance-of-payments crisis occurred in 1951, but the exports drive succeeded well enough to keep it within bounds. The Government's greatest economic windfall was the drop in world prices of raw materials, which immediately improved the balance-of-payments position. As between the wars, so now, economic recovery was as likely to come from general improvements in the world's economy as from any measure of national policy. Inflation crept on, encouraged by the cuts in food subsidies which inevitably raised the cost of

1. Compare the hero in Edward Hyams's novel *Gentian Violet* (1953), who was elected to Parliament as *both* Conservative and Socialist, without being found out.

living. But the standard of living was, in general, rising too, and by contrast with the grim years of austerity, these were years of increasing plenty. A mood of prosperity began to grow, encouraged by the outstanding success of Mr Macmillan as Minister of Housing and by Mr Butler's budget of 1955 which, for a second time, took sixpence off the standard rate of income tax.

Politically, too, the Government enjoyed a windfall in the form of divisions within the Labour Party, which tended to widen now that it was in opposition. The 'old guard', led by Attlee and Morrison and supported by moderates like Gaitskell and by the mass vote of the larger trade unions, were opposed by the 'Bevanites'. The eloquent, vehement, and colourful Aneurin Bevan, having resigned from the last Labour Government, attracted considerable backing in the constituency organizations of the Party and among the younger generation of Socialists. Doubly freed from responsibility, the Bevanites (including Harold Wilson) could appeal to the pure idealistic doctrines of Socialism and condemn the concessions and compromises made to meet realities. Roused to fury by the Government's avowed aims of denationalization and its cuts in food subsidies, the Bevanites fought to save the Labour Party from what they regarded as cowardly surrenders. But the spectacle of prolonged schism did not persuade a majority of voters to support the Party in the general elections of 1955.

The schism tended to become a feud between the two personalities, Gaitskell and Bevan, which reached its climax when Attlee accepted an earldom and resigned the leadership in 1955. Gaitskell was elected leader by a large majority over Bevan, and proceeded to unite the Party on a moderate and yet positive party programme. The Bevanites continued, however, to try to sway the Party's policy towards further nationalization and unilateral disarmament. Some reconciliation came when Bevan became Labour's

'Shadow' Foreign Secretary (1956) and in opposing unilateral renunciation by Britain of the hydrogen bomb (1957)
even ceased to be a 'Bevanite'. He died in 1960, genuinely
lamented and missed by many who had been his fiercest
political opponents, for he had generous gifts and elements
of greatness.

THE INTERLUDE OF EDEN

Winston Churchill decided to resign and retire from active
political life, though not from membership of Parliament.
Since 1940 he had regarded Eden as his successor. In 1951
he had even recommended Eden to the King as Secretary of
State for Foreign Affairs and 'Deputy Prime Minister' – a
title which George VI deleted on the grounds that no such
office existed constitutionally, and indeed by appearing to
pre-determine the succession could fetter the Sovereign's
future choice. But, as Eden remarked, the position of 'crown
prince' was 'not necessarily enviable in politics'. When
Eden formed his new ministry in April 1955 it was inevitably
regarded as a continuation, under new management, of the
former firm. He decided to ask the Queen to dissolve Parliament, and general elections were held at the end of May.
This enabled him to leave existing ministers unchanged
until June, save for such inevitable changes as putting
Harold Macmillan at the Foreign Office, and Selwyn Lloyd
to replace Macmillan at the Ministry of Defence. The calculations which, on balance, determined him to go to the
country, apart from the general desirability of doing so after
Churchill's retirement, were significant: 'In 1955 employment was at a very high level, the balance of payments for
once was giving no trouble, and electorally, so far as one
could judge, the tide appeared to be with us.'

The elections had the result he desired: a Conservative
majority of sixty, and very nearly half the total votes cast.

Eden did not significantly reconstitute his ministry until the end of the year. Butler left the Treasury to be Lord Privy Seal and Leader of the House. Macmillan succeeded him at the Treasury, and was himself replaced at the Foreign Office by Selwyn Lloyd. Lord Monckton became Minister of Defence, and was succeeded at the Ministry of Labour by Iain Macleod. It was a reshuffle of the same pack, which produced a balanced and able team with moderate men in the key positions.

The economic situation facing the new Government was better than any since the war. Housing, as after 1918, had been a grave social problem. It had been tackled with impressive energy and success by Harold Macmillan, who, from 1951 to 1954, had been Minister of Housing. He exceeded the promised target of getting 300,000 houses built in a year, and when Eden became Premier the Conservative Party could boast of having equipped the country with more than 1 million new houses, as well as much public building. The prestige and popularity so gained made Macmillan the strongest candidate for the Exchequer in 1955, and thereafter put him in line for leadership of the party when Eden retired.

Eden's domestic policy was to promote 'a property-owning democracy' and 'partnership in industry'. In the latter, as he explained, he included 'joint consultation, the giving of full information to employees about the affairs of the companies in which they work and also profit sharing in a number of forms, particularly when it offers opportunities for employees to hold shares, and so acquire a real stake in the enterprises in which they work'. It was an appeal aptly geared to the realities of the changing social structure of Britain. Britain from 1947 onwards was becoming a nation with a very large intermediate income-range of lower middle class and well-paid working class. The Hulton Readership Survey for 1955 showed that since

1947 these two groups had risen from 75 to 81 per cent of the whole. However contestable the figures, they reflect one consequence of the Welfare State and of a spell of full employment. The statistics of small savings and building-society deposits tell the same story. The centre of gravity of Britain, whether for the commercial advertisers utilizing the Hulton Survey or for political party headquarters contemplating electioneering appeals, was the well-to-do working class and the lower middle class. There were to be found both the domestic consuming power and the electoral voting power. The centre of gravity shifted upwards a little with the coming of the affluent society. But to depict the attractions of an extensive 'property-owning democracy' was highly astute political leadership in the fifties.

The better balance-of-payments position, combined with the boom (much encouraged by the building and rearmaments programmes) and the absence of unemployment, made prospects favourable. On the other hand, there were several large strikes, mostly unofficial, affecting the newspapers, railways, and docks. Relations between employers and workers (even between trade unions and workers) could be much improved. The new Chancellor, Harold Macmillan, shifted the emphasis on to saving. He cut government expenditure by £100 million and set out to stabilize prices and wages. He issued more profitable defence bonds and savings certificates and, in an appeal to the gambling instincts of even the small saver, introduced the novelty of 'premium bonds', using the interest as stake in a lottery. There was a mood of growing prosperity, despite distressing industrial stoppages.

In colonial and foreign affairs, however, these years of reinvigorated Conservatism brought pressing problems enveloped in violent controversy. They were mostly current versions of old problems; but they created a gathering sense of disquiet. Two of the worst situations arose in Cyprus and in Kenya. The agitation of Greek Cypriots for *enosis*, or union with Greece, had simmered since 1950, but in 1955 resulted in fresh terrorism. Field-Marshal Sir John Harding became governor in September, banned the terrorist organization E.O.K.A., and declared a state of emergency. The leader of the movement for *enosis*, Archbishop Makarios, had launched a campaign of passive resistance, and talks with him broke down. Britain continued to value the island as a military and naval base in the Mediterranean. In March 1956 Makarios was deported to the Seychelles and terrorism was suppressed with severity. When he was released a year later and allowed to go to Athens (but not to Cyprus) the terrorist activity came to an end, and British relations with Greece improved. No settlement was forthcoming until 1960.[1] Even that proved temporary.

Kenya was beset by the rise of tribal nationalism among the Kikuyu, the most numerous African people in the country. There arose the secret terrorist and guerrilla movement of Mau Mau which, from the autumn of 1952 until the end of 1956, engaged large numbers of British troops in an effort to protect both Europeans and defenceless Kikuyu. The nationalist leader, Jomo Kenyatta, was regarded as the Mau Mau chief, though he denied responsibility: a Kenya African Congress party, led by the younger Tom Mboya, demanded greater self-government. Here, as in Cyprus, Britain's resolve to remain in control led her into measures of repression that were uncongenial and unpopular, and were only too easily misrepresented and denounced in the underdeveloped countries as well as in the United States and the Soviet Union.

In world affairs as a whole Britain's position and policy were overshadowed, however, by even more momentous

1. See below, pp. 280–1.

issues. One was the persistent but unavailing effort to reach a *détente* between the two sides in the 'cold war', whether by meetings of Foreign Ministers or 'summit meetings' or through the machinery of the United Nations. The other was a growing preoccupation with the affairs of Egypt and the Middle East, which cut across this wider concern and reached a climax in the Franco-British Suez expedition of October 1956.

World tensions were automatically eased for a time by the death of Stalin in March 1953, and by the complex jostlings for survival and power among his successors which lasted throughout the next two years. The emergence of Mr Khrushchev, with a policy of easing relations abroad and of 'de-Stalinization' at home, at first contributed to a relaxation of tensions. There was less talk of 'containment', more of 'peaceful co-existence'. The change on both sides was not unconnected with the growing power of Communist China, nor with the fact that in 1953 the United States and the Soviet Union almost simultaneously produced the even more alarmingly destructive hydrogen bomb. Armistice in Korea was signed in July 1953. The Foreign Ministers of the United States, the Soviet Union, Britain, and France met at Berlin early in 1954; the summit meeting of the four heads of State took place at Geneva in July 1955. Neither meeting yielded very substantial results. Nor did the visit of Mr Khrushchev and Marshal Bulganin to Britain in April 1956.

Eden's greatest personal triumph in diplomacy was the Paris Agreements of 1954. The western allies (France, Italy, West Germany, and the Benelux countries) had signed a treaty in 1952 to set up a European Defence Community (E.D.C.), of which the main feature was an integrated European army. Its implementation was blocked by the reluctance of the French Parliament to ratify the treaty. In August 1954 France's Premier, Pierre Mendès France, decided to end the uncertainty: he allowed Parliament to kill the project of E.D.C. All the Powers were now anxious to find some form of cooperation to put in its place. At this point Eden took the initiative. He called a meeting in London of the E.D.C. Powers, along with Britain, Canada, and the United States. The outcome was the Paris Agreements, which were ratified by all six Powers by April 1955. They included an agreement to admit West Germany and Italy to a new Western European Union, to allow German rearmament, and to bring West Germany into the North Atlantic Treaty Organization. Britain undertook to maintain on the Continent four divisions and the Tactical Air Force. The agreements began a process of Franco-German *rapprochement* which was to reach its height nine years later.

These agreements contributed to a general pacification of Europe, marred as ever by the barrier of the 'iron curtain' and the partition of Germany. But the divisions of Europe were coming to be accepted as part of those world problems men must learn to live with. Equilibrium in Europe was unstable, but at least there was equilibrium. The adjacent area of the Middle East was in a gravely different condition. It was by involvement there, in the historic feud between Arab and Jew, that Eden's policy was to meet its greatest challenge; and by misjudgement of world reactions, to run into temporary ruin.[1]

THE SUEZ CRISIS

Britain's withdrawal from Palestine in 1948, already described, the creation by the Jews of the new State of Israel, and after 1952 the emergence of Egypt under Colonel Nasser as the leading Arab state, transformed the whole situation

1. For Eden's own account of both the European agreements of 1954 and the Suez Crisis of 1956, see *The Memoirs of Sir Anthony Eden: Full Circle* (1960). For a factual account of the Suez affair see *Survey of International Affairs, 1956–1958* (Ed. G. Barraclough) (1962), Part I.

of the Middle East. Reminiscent of the nineteenth-century
'Eastern Question', the new situation was such as to invite
intervention – by Communist infiltration or supply of arms,
or by Western Powers anxious for the safety of strategic bases
and communications. Until the crisis of 1956 British relations with Egypt seemed to be taking a turn for the better.
The two countries signed an agreement in October 1954
whereby Britain undertook to evacuate troops from the Suez
Canal base which, for seventy years, had been the keystone
of Britain's defence system in the East. Their withdrawal
released fresh hostilities between Israelis and Egyptians
along the border. It also paved the way for an agreement,
in September 1955, for Egypt to get arms from Czechoslovakia in return for Egyptian cotton and rice. It seemed
quite likely that, as Britain moved out, influences of the
Soviet *bloc* would move in. Moreover, Britain was moving
her base from Suez to Cyprus – when conditions inspired
little confidence that it would long survive there, either. The
end of 1955 brought a general Soviet diplomatic offensive to
gain influence throughout the Middle East, economic and
technical no less than political and military. Russian trade
with Egypt increased greatly, and there were reports of
offers of assistance from the Communist States to build the
Aswan high dam, a project dear to Nasser's heart.

At the end of 1955 the United States offered 56 million
dollars, Britain a further 14 million dollars, to help finance
the project. After some wavering Nasser accepted the
Western offer. Then the American State Department
abruptly withdrew its offer. When Britain followed suit,
Nasser retorted with a drastic measure. On the fourth anni-
versary of the revolution which brought him to power
(26 July 1956) he proclaimed the nationalization of the Suez
Canal Company. It was a violent breach of agreements, but
it should not have been so surprisingly unexpected as it was
in London or Washington. Egyptian nationalistic and anti-

Western feeling was so strong that no rebuff, such as Nasser received over the Aswan dam, could be accepted without administering an equally dramatic rebuff. It is plain from his own *Memoirs*, as it was clear at the time, that henceforth Eden was obsessed by the image of Nasser as a second Hitler, breaking agreements with impunity and threatening the whole fabric of Western security against the aggressions of Communism. 'A man with Colonel Nasser's record,' wrote Eden, 'could not be allowed "to have his thumb on our windpipe".' He adds that: 'The Chiefs of Staff were instructed to get ready a plan and a time-table for an operation designed to occupy and secure the canal, should other methods fail.'

The first of the 'other methods' amounted to summoning in London a conference of twenty-two maritime Powers, including Australia, New Zealand, India and Ceylon. When the Australian Premier, Robert Menzies, had failed to win Nasser's agreement to the proposals made by a majority of the conference, the American Secretary of State, John Foster Dulles, produced the idea of forming a 'Canal Users' Association' to organize navigation, hire pilots, and manage the canal. The scheme failed because the Egyptians themselves, contrary to expectations, succeeded in maintaining traffic through the canal without breakdown.

The next 'other method' was recourse to the United Nations. The Security Council opened its hearing on 5 October and moved some way towards mediating the dispute, but ran into the Soviet veto of proposals to secure guarantees for the Western Powers in their use of the canal. On 16 October Eden and Selwyn Lloyd met their French counterparts, M. Mollet and M. Pineau, in a private session in Paris. What was then agreed is not known precisely, but it is probable that there was some collusion in the projected Israeli attack on Egypt. This was launched on 29 October, and Israeli troops quickly occupied the whole of the Sinai peninsula and the Gaza strip. Next day France and Britain served a joint ultimatum on both sides, demanding the withdrawal of their forces ten miles from the canal. When Nasser rejected it the Franco-British attack was launched on 31 October to end the conflict and safeguard the canal.

The campaign lasted only until 6 November, and in that week the Anglo-French forces captured Port Said and a strip of the canal. The United Nations was stirred into action, as was the Parliamentary Opposition in Britain. The action of Israel, France, and Britain was generally regarded as aggression, and the General Assembly called for a cease-fire. Apart from Australia and Belgium, few lent support to Britain and France. The United States vehemently condemned their action, as did most Dominions other than Australia. At home two junior ministers – Mr Anthony Nutting and Sir Edward Boyle – resigned and others, it seems, threatened to resign in protest. Gaitskell, for Labour, attacked the ultimatum to Egypt as 'a positive assault upon the three principles which have governed British foreign policy for, at any rate, the last ten years – solidarity with the Commonwealth, the Anglo-American alliance, and adherence to the Charter of the United Nations'. The Press was very critical. Taken aback by the vehemence and extent of the reaction, the British and French Governments halted the operation on 6 November and agreed to withdraw their forces on the arrival of an international task force assembled by the United Nations to police the area. Meanwhile, however, the canal had been blocked and made unusable by any shipping, the oil pipe-line in Syria had been cut, and Britain's gold and dollar reserves fell sharply by 84 million dollars in October and another 279 million dollars in November. This last act, according to Eden, weighed heavy in the decision to bow to United Nations requests.

The operation, so dramatically launched, was thus halted half-way, before its full military objectives had been attained. Nasser's military humiliation by Israel was converted into a diplomatic victory over Britain and France. The canal was put out of action for a long time, yet supplies of oil – for which free use of the canal had been thought so vital – were not lacking. Whatever the purposes of the expedition, judged by its results it was a diplomatic blunder of the highest order. Relations with both Commonwealth and America were strained, and (because of the abrupt halt) even with France as well. Nasser was invested with a new prestige, despite his defeat. The Arab world remained one of deep unrest, in which the influences of east and west would again often clash. Opinion at home had been bitterly divided and left greatly perturbed. The Suez canal remained in Egyptian hands.

Sir Anthony Eden claimed, later, important long-term gains. 'Our intervention at least closed the chapter of complacency about the situation in the Middle East. It led to the Eisenhower doctrine and from that to Anglo-American intervention in the following summer in Jordan and the Lebanon. It helped to show that the West was not prepared to leave the area wide open for infiltration and subversion by others. But these were only partial gains. The uneasy equipoise still continues.' It might be added that the example of submission, by two major Powers, to the will of the United Nations, and the precedent of an international police-force, were positive if unlooked-for gains from the whole adventure. But it might also be added that the Soviet Union's brutal crushing of Hungary, which occurred at the same time with impunity whilst the Western Powers were preoccupied with Suez, was an even greater blow to international justice and peace. Such balancing of long-term gains and losses is always very difficult: within a few years of the event it is impossible to determine the final balance.

In the history of parliamentary government in Britain the Suez episode may hold an important place. It stretched to the uttermost the doctrine of collective ministerial responsibility, while demonstrating the remarkable power, in modern conditions, of the Prime Minister personally. On the other hand, it revealed how thin the sovereignty of Parliament, and even its ability to control government in major decisions of policy, had become in mid-twentieth-century Britain. Eden's reversal of policy did not lead to the fall of the Conservative Party from office. On the other hand, Eden's behaviour over Suez 'is not different in any important respect from the way in which Neville Chamberlain and his close associates planned and executed British policy in the late summer of 1938, the Cabinet being told about the visit to Hitler only after this had been arranged'.[1] The domestic importance of the Suez crisis must not be over-dramatized. The Rent Act, given its second reading while Eden was Premier but enacted only in June 1957, under his successor, aimed at the progressive abolition of rent controls. It was greatly amended under pressure from several directions, and in its long-term effects on political issues was probably more important than Suez.

At the end of the year Eden's former illness recurred and the physical strain of remaining in office became too heavy to bear with efficiency. It was probable, too, that both party and country would now gain from a change of leadership. Events had split the party and weakened its hold on Parliament and on public esteem. Those not antagonized by the Suez operation were apt to be alienated by its cessation. The Prime Minister accordingly resigned on 9 January 1957, and on the next day the Queen asked Harold Macmillan to form a new Government.

The Suez crisis left him with two severe disadvantages in domestic politics. Conservative Party popularity, as mea-

1. J. P. Mackintosh, *The British Cabinet* (1962), p. 436.

sured by the thirteen by-election results of the following six months, showed a decline by 4·5 per cent. At the same time Labour had found new unity in its attack on the Suez exploit. It took much of the rest of the year for the new Prime Minister to restore confidence. Despite the few 'Suez rebels', the Conservative majority in the Commons remained large, and Macmillan's poise and acumen were such as to ensure nearly another three years of Conservative rule before the existing Parliament was dissolved in September 1959. The party's resilience surprised its critics and even many of its friends. Nevertheless, the era of Conservative government since 1951 – amid much economic improvement and widespread prosperity – had been an unhappy time in many respects. It was a time of troubled national conscience and moral doubts: doubts about industrial strife at home, colonial repression, nuclear power, and finally Suez. Was Britain now reaching a plateau not only, as it was hoped, in levels of wages and prices, but also in modes of colonial government and 'decolonization' and of international cooperation? This was the hope as Harold Macmillan began, rather inauspiciously, his leadership of Britain in 1957: a year which brought the highest number ever recorded (2,859) of stoppages of work due to industrial disputes, involving loss of 8,412,000 working days.

CHAPTER TEN

The Affluent Society,
1957–64

'THE BEST PRIME MINISTER WE HAVE'

HAROLD MACMILLAN brought to his delicate and exacting task a strong combination of intellectual ability, imperturbable temperament, and reputation for efficiency. As a successful publisher he was shrewd and business-like, and not unaware of the need to project a favourable public image of himself and his party. His three main ministerial assignments had been accomplished with success: as Minister Resident in North Africa from 1942 onwards, as Minister of Housing between 1951 and 1954, and as Chancellor of the Exchequer from 1955 to 1957. R. A. Butler, by dint of long experience and distinguished ministerial record, might have been expected to succeed Eden. But in the peculiar circumstances of Eden's sudden retirement, and on the advice of Lord Salisbury and Churchill, it was Macmillan whom the Queen first approached. His more infectious optimism and buoyant confidence, his greater flair for personal publicity, made him at that moment what Butler had ruefully called Eden -- 'the best Prime Minister we have'. The next seven years were the era of Macmillan.

His first ministry was a wide but judicious combination of different political wings and of old and new faces. Several key ministers kept their posts. Butler took the Home Office, but remained leader of the House of Commons. Peter Thorneycroft went to the Treasury, Duncan Sandys to the Ministry of Defence. A new Ministry of Power was set up with an industrialist, Sir Percy Mills, at its head. The ministry was modified in September, when Lord Hailsham left the Ministry of Education to become Lord President of the Council (and also Chairman of the Conservative Party). When the general elections came in October 1959 they registered Macmillan's success in making people forget Suez. The Conservatives returned with an enhanced majority of more than 100, and with 49·4 per cent of the actual votes. He presided over a phase of material prosperity that earned for prevailing conditions, both material and psychological, the label of 'the affluent society'.

The eminent American economist, J. K. Galbraith, whose widely read book of 1958 popularized the phrase, summed up his argument in its final paragraph as follows:

To furnish a barren room is one thing. To continue to crowd in furniture until the foundation buckles is quite another. To have failed to solve the problem of producing goods would have been to continue man in his oldest and most grievous misfortune. But to fail to see that we have solved it and to fail to proceed thence to the next task would be fully as tragic.[1]

The 'next task' he held to be 'investment in men' rather than in things. Twenty years earlier Harold Macmillan had also published a book about economic attitudes and social policies in contemporary society. He had written:

The fixing of a minimum standard of life must not be regarded as merely humanitarian. It is closely related to the whole question of economic stability. There is a clear relationship between the purchasing power in the hands of the people and the demand for consumers' goods. There is an obvious relationship between the demand for consumers' goods and the level of employment among workers engaged in producing those goods.[2]

Both books were concerned with the economics of the Welfare State, but also with appropriate adjustments of political

1. J. K. Galbraith, *The Affluent Society* (1958), p. 277.
2. Harold Macmillan, *The Middle Way* (1938), p. 188.

outlook and principle. Macmillan argued for keeping private enterprise in sectors of the economy that were rapidly expanding, but he equally favoured 'the Socialist remedy' wherever 'private enterprise had exhausted its social usefulness, or where the general welfare of the economy requires that certain basic industries and services need now to be conducted in the light of broader social considerations than the profit motive will supply'. Both books were, in essence, applications of the economic teaching of Lord Keynes (whose books had been published by Messrs Macmillan); they were attacks on the traditional capitalist view of the autonomy of economic activities, and were efforts to relate production and economic growth to social and political purposes instead of regarding them in nineteenth-century fashion as ends in themselves.

What happened during the fifties, though it may not be what Macmillan or his colleagues or, indeed, anyone else expressly intended, was the arrival of the British version of 'the affluent society'. British society now presupposed full employment, economic growth, mass consumption, and therefore mass advertising of the self-perpetuating kind described by Professor Galbraith. Unlike the Welfare State, it cared little about inequalities of wealth. It was not averse to encouraging enterprises with rich rewards, nor to viewing successful gambles with complete equanimity. Its symptomatic phrases were Macmillan's own, 'You've never had it so good', and the workers' own, 'I'm all right, Jack'. Its ethos was that of a competitive, thrusting, yet liberal-minded business society, placing high values upon material success and comfort while remaining humanitarian and tolerant in spirit. Its significant innovations were commercially sponsored television (the Independent Television Authority was created in 1954), betting shops, and the craze for 'Bingo' which for a time filled otherwise superfluous cinemas. Even more significant, when so many millions of pounds were spent on mass-consumption of gadgets and on gambling, liquor, tobacco, and entertainments, was what was not done. The equipment needed and expected by the Welfare State was not provided: it 'could not be afforded'. The public sector did not keep pace with the private, and the neglected classes of old-age pensioners and the sick were left behind in the race for affluence and status. One sociologist saw the fifties in this jaundiced way:

Alongside this was the evident belief of the Government that the country could not *afford* to build a single new hospital – or prison: none were built during the decade. There was the lag in subsidized housing; the inadequate provision for old-age pensioners; the relative slowness in replacing antiquated school buildings, in providing youth clubs and playing fields. . . . There was the persistent shortage of nurses (what would have happened but for girls from overseas?) of teachers in state schools, of policemen, penal officers, midwives, youth workers (or for that matter of clergymen).[1]

The Treasury, and the economists who advised it, had learned carefully the lessons taught by Keynes: that economic depression can be controlled by judicious manipulations of credit and the flow of investment. The business world had learned the even more welcome lesson, that thrift is not in all circumstances a social virtue, nor seeking personal advantage a social ill. What troubled successive Chancellors of the Exchequer in Macmillan's Cabinets was how to keep within bounds the strong inflationary pressures natural to such a society. 'Expansion without inflation' became the aim, though they differed greatly about the appropriate means. For the first year Peter Thorneycroft tried to restrict governmental expenditures. In September he raised the bank rate abruptly from 5 to 7 per cent (its highest level since 1920). He also budgeted for a large surplus as a deflationary device. The trade figures for November 1957

1. T. R. Fyvel, *The Insecure Offenders* (1961), p. 121 of Pelican edition (1963).

were the best for seven years. Britain's gold and dollar reserves had risen fairly steadily. The Chancellor's objection
to any increase of expenditure in 1958 led to his resignation
in January of that year. Enoch Powell and Nigel Birch, two
secretaries to the Treasury, resigned with him. He was
succeeded by D. Heathcoat Amory, whose budget in April
raised expenditure by £155 million.

The new Chancellor, who held office until July 1960, progressively lowered the bank rate to 4 per cent by November
1958. There it stayed until after the general election, but by
June 1960 it was up to 6 per cent again. The balance-of-
payments situation worsened in these years, as British exports encountered severe competition from other countries
in the world's markets. A new export drive followed in
1960-1. The 'credit squeeze' of 1959 was unpopular: the
'pay pause' of Heathcoat Amory's successor, Selwyn Lloyd,
proved even more unpopular. In his first budget (1961) he
made concessions to surtax-payers which the Opposition
vigorously denounced. Compelled to reimpose restrictions
in July, he had to admit, later, that he had miscalculated
trends. The earlier phase of rapid economic growth and
fairly stable prices was now followed by one of slow growth
and rising prices. The balance of payments deteriorated
further. The 'affluent society' seemed unable to stabilize
itself in affluence, despite the variety of fiscal prescriptions
and tonics. The Conservative defeat by a Liberal candidate
in March 1962 in the strongly middle-class constituency of
Orpington seemed a danger signal.

These discouraging events prompted thoughts of more
long-term economic planning, whether for industrial growth
or for wider national ends. Mr Lloyd met with disappointing
reactions from the Trades Union Congress when he invited
its cooperation with the Treasury in such planning: his 'pay
pause' was accused of keeping down wages but not profits.
But the Government devised two new instruments of

planning: a National Economic Development Council to make plans for systematic economic growth, and a permanent National Incomes Commission, to help shape an 'incomes policy'. Dr Beeching's drastic plans to reorganize British Railways were a further effort to streamline the economy.

Selwyn Lloyd was the most eminent victim of Macmillan's major reconstruction of his Government in July 1962. In the so-called 'purge' seven Cabinet Ministers lost their places – all of them original members of the first Macmillan Government of 1957. Reginald Maudling replaced Selwyn Lloyd. By now, however, the most clamorous national problem was the growth of unemployment, especially in those areas of traditional industrial depression – parts of Scotland, North Ireland, North-East England, and South Wales. Nothing could more quickly arouse political anxieties. It was a threat the Government had to take very seriously. By October 1962 the number of unemployed in Great Britain passed the 500,000 mark. By January 1963 it exceeded 810,000, though much of the increase was seasonal and improved with the weather.

That the Treasury changed hands four times in five years was an indication of the importance of financial direction and economic planning, but also of the lack of any one agreed set of principles for shaping such policies. The differences between the Chancellors, as between the political parties, were mainly variations of emphasis and choice of devices, rather than any avowed clash of purposes. Macmillan's domestic policy was, characteristically, one of trial and error, of moderate measures varying empirically according to personalities and conditions. It was not self-evident, in the uncertainty and fluidity of the world economy and the world political scene, that these unheroic measures were necessarily bad: and by 1963 there were signs that a more concerted effort to shape an incomes policy and a system of economic planning was emerging. 'Butskellism' was not dead. The only serious Labour criticism of Maudling's budget of 1963 was that its encouragement to expand did not go far enough.

In the meantime, however, Mr Macmillan's position was beginning to crumble. The wholesale reconstruction of his Cabinet, which he subsequently admitted was a mistake, had already dented the image of 'unflappability' which he had so carefully cultivated since becoming Prime Minister. Then, in January 1963, President de Gaulle vetoed Britain's entry into the European Economic Community (E.E.C. or Common Market). Apart from its foreign policy implications,[1] this had important consequences in the field of domestic politics, as a senior Conservative Party official later explained:

Europe was to be our *deus ex machina*; it was to create a new, contemporary political argument with insular Socialism; dish the Liberals by stealing their clothes; give us something *new* after 12-13 years; act as the catalyst of modernization; give us a new place in the international sun. It was Macmillan's ace, and de Gaulle trumped it. The Conservatives never really recovered.[2]

The hapless Macmillan was next confronted by a scandal within his own Government when his Secretary of State for War, Mr John Profumo, was compelled to resign in June 1963 after lying to his colleagues and to the House of Commons about his liaison with a call-girl. Although the Opposition concentrated on the security aspects of the case – one of the girl's other lovers was an attaché at the Soviet embassy – press and public proceeded to indulge in an orgy of prurient speculation concerning the sexual habits of the country's rulers. As Mr Macmillan recorded at the time, '. . . a kind of Titus Oates atmosphere prevailed, with the wildest rumour and innuendo against the most respectable

1. See pp. 273-4.
2. D. E. Butler and Anthony King, *The British General Election of 1964* (1965), p. 75.

Ministers. Altogether . . . more than half the Cabinet were being accused of perversion, homosexuality and the like.'[1]

A judicial enquiry scotched the rumours and acquitted the Government of any breach of security, but the affair was a further blow to the Prime Minister's prestige and there were increasingly vocal demands that he should stand down. By his own account, he had resolved to fight on when, like Eden before him, he was struck down by illness and forced to resign in October 1963. The struggle for the succession, which was more heated than usual, resulted in a surprising victory by the Foreign Secretary, Lord Home, over several other contenders including the unfortunate Mr Butler, who, having lost to Mr Macmillan in 1957, now saw himself passed over a second time. Renouncing his peerage so that he could become Prime Minister,[2] Lord Home entered the House of Commons as Sir Alec Douglas-Home. Although he appears to have been chosen largely because it was felt he would divide the Conservative Party least, two of the younger members of Mr Macmillan's Cabinet, Mr Iain Macleod and Mr Enoch Powell, refused to serve under him. The key figure, Mr Butler, agreed to do so, however, and took over from Home himself as Foreign Secretary.

The new Prime Minister did not have an easy task. Not only did he have to reunite his party, he had to do it quickly, for an election was due in a year's time at the latest. His expertise, moreover, was almost entirely in the field of foreign affairs, whereas the election was likely to be fought on domestic issues. His aristocratic background did not help him and critics claimed that he was more at home on the grouse moors of his native Scotland than in piloting his country through the increasingly complex problems of

1. Harold Macmillan, *At the End of the Day* (1973), pp. 443–4.
2. Ironically, the legislation permitting peers to renounce their titles had only recently been passed, largely as a result of the campaign organized by the reluctant Labour peer, Viscount Stansgate, better known as Tony Benn.

modern society, a charge which gained some credence from his own candid admission that he used matchsticks to help him understand economics. Finally, he was hampered by that most besetting difficulty for a modern politician: he did not come over well on television. He himself wistfully recalls how a young television make-up girl told him that there was nothing that could be done about this as he had a face like a skull.

Nevertheless, his Government was not without achievements. Mr Maudling, who continued as Chancellor of the Exchequer, stuck to his policy of expansion and soon brought down the level of unemployment. His colleague at the Board of Trade and erstwhile rival for the party leadership, Mr Edward Heath, sought to attack inflation and introduce more competition into the retail trade by abolishing retail price maintenance, a measure which gave rise to considerable opposition among Conservative back-benchers mindful of the votes of small shopkeepers who feared that they would be driven out of business by price cutting on the part of the big retailers. The Government also approved the expansion of higher education as recommended by the Robbins Committee, and increased expenditure on roads, especially motorways, both decisions being presented as part of a strategy to improve the infrastructure of a modernizing Britain.

When the general election took place on 15 October 1964, however, the Labour Party won it, albeit by a wafer-thin majority of four seats. Paradoxically, this was something of a triumph for Sir Alec Douglas-Home, for few would have predicted anything but a substantial Labour victory after the Conservative misfortunes of 1962 and 1963. In a longer perspective, however, it was the Labour revival which was the more remarkable phenomenon. The party's defeat at the hands of Mr Macmillan in 1959 had been a staggering blow and there were those who thought it would never recover, a prediction which seemed to be borne out by the way in which the party tore itself apart, first over Clause Four of its constitution (which committed it, in theory at any rate, to wholesale nationalization), and then over unilateral nuclear disarmament. A resolution in favour of the latter was carried at the party's Scarborough conference in 1960 against the wishes of its leader, Mr Hugh Gaitskell, who pledged himself to 'fight and fight and fight again' to reverse the decision. He succeeded in doing so and was slowly leading the party back to the middle ground which he felt it must occupy if it were to stand any chance of electoral success when he died suddenly in January 1963. His successor, Mr Harold Wilson, might have seemed at first sight to be unlikely to continue on this path. After joining the Attlee Cabinet at the remarkably early age of thirty-one in 1947, he resigned with Aneurin Bevan three-and-a-half years later and was widely regarded as a left-winger throughout the 1950s and in 1960, when he un-successfully challenged Gaitskell for the leadership of the party after the Scarborough conference. Mr Wilson's prime concern, however, was always party unity rather than ideology, as he was to demonstrate during his thirteen years as Labour's leader. A skilled debater, he delighted his supporters by the way in which he savaged successive Conservative leaders; a born conciliator, he was much more successful at smoothing the ruffled feathers of outraged members of his own party than the abrasive, somewhat self-righteous Gaitskell had been. Some regarded him unfairly as devious, and he was perhaps not always wise in his choice of friends and advisers, but he came close to achieving his ambition, which was to make Labour rather than the Conservatives the natural governing party in Britain.

Mr Wilson's main theme in the 1964 election campaign was the need for purposive change, which he contrasted with the stagnation and drift that had allegedly prevailed under the Conservatives. The Labour Party's manifesto called for

A New Britain – mobilizing the resources of technology under a national plan; harnessing our national wealth in brains, our genius for scientific innovation and medical discovery; reversing the decline of the thirteen wasted years; affording a new opportunity to equal, and if possible surpass, the roaring progress of other western powers while Tory Britain has moved sideways, backwards but seldom forward.

All that had to be done now was to translate these brave words into deeds.

'OF MUCH MORE IMPORTANCE THAN OPULENCE'

Adam Smith justified the Navigation Acts, as an exception to the case for free trade, on the grounds that 'defence is of much more importance than opulence'. Britain's dilemma both in defence preparations and in foreign policy in the second half of the twentieth century is that defence has become so costly, warfare so destructive, that no modern State can contemplate adequate measures of self-defence without overstraining its resources in peace-time and incurring devastation in war. The paradox of 'the affluent society' is that lavish public expenditure on armaments and defence measures is a built-in part of its economy, and one of the mainstays of full employment. Up to a point defence is a *source* of opulence. Yet beyond a certain point it is also a competitor with the social services and a challenge to the growth of the Welfare State. During the Macmillan Governments not even the most thrifty Chancellor of the Exchequer could economize on defence expenditures, although lavish expense repeatedly failed to purchase adequate defences. For this reason Ministers of Defence changed with nearly the same frequency as Chancellors.

Mr Sandys succeeded Mr Head in 1957, to be replaced by Mr Watkinson in 1959, and he, in turn, by Mr Thorneycroft in 1962. The policy of seeking to provide an independent nuclear deterrent (that is, one capable of being delivered by Britain without United States help) led to expenditure and research on developing the 'Blue Streak' missile. In April 1960 the project was abandoned. Two months later Watkinson announced that agreement had been reached with the United States about production of 'Skybolt', a missile that could be launched from modified bombers and was therefore less vulnerable than 'Blue Streak', which needed fixed launching-pads. Before long, however, 'Polaris' missiles launched from submarines began to seem superior, and at the end of 1962 the Americans proposed that further work on 'Skybolt' should be ended. The danger that Britain would thus be left without an independent deterrent was discussed by President Kennedy and Mr Macmillan at their meeting at Nassau in the Bahamas in December, as part of a wider discussion of other outstanding allied problems. It was agreed that 'Skybolt' should be abandoned, but that Polaris missiles would be made available for British submarines as a move towards a multilateral N.A.T.O. nuclear force. Britain's defence estimates for 1963 exceeded £1,837 million (the actual figure for the previous year having been £1,777 million).

The three major technological developments which had revolutionized defence during the previous decade had been atomic and hydrogen bombs, the evolution of intercontinental ballistic missiles of great range and accuracy, and rapid advances in space research. Coupled with the continuance and – at times – the intensification of competition between the United States and the Soviet Union, these three developments elevated national defence to a level of grand strategy. It became possible for the two super-Powers to hurl missiles at one another without intermediate bases or allies. What guarantee, then, unless these allies had such capabilities too, had they that consultation would take place before action, or – still more important – that the help of the major ally would be forthcoming in conflicts in which only lesser allies were involved? What especially fostered such fears in Britain was the Cuban crisis of October 1962.

It brought the world closer to the brink of nuclear war than any previous international crisis. On 22 October President Kennedy disclosed that Soviet missile sites existed in Cuba capable of delivering nuclear warheads to large areas of the United States and Central America. He imposed a quarantine on shipping to Cuba and called on Khrushchev to remove this threat to world peace. He also asked for an emergency meeting of the Security Council. Each Power made war preparations, as tension rose fast. The United Nations Secretary-General, U Thant, appealed to both sides to avoid 'confrontation' in the Caribbean. Khrushchev and Kennedy exchanged letters. On 28 October Khrushchev agreed to dismantle the Soviet missile bases on Cuba (previously described as purely defensive weapons) under international supervision. The crisis receded. Afterwards it came to be realized how close had been collapse – how little other states could have done to prevent it had either major power been bent on war, or merely foolish in its reactions. One happy result was the nuclear test-ban agreement signed in Moscow in July 1963. The British Prime Minister talked of partnership and interdependence. The problem remained how to ensure real interdependence in action, when survival itself might be at stake. War had become a push-button war. 'Whose finger on the button?' became the apt journalistic phrase for the main dilemma of defence in the nuclear age.

In modern conditions not only is defence a source of opulence, in the sense of being a mainstay of full employment: it is also a consequence of opulence, in the sense that only a large and vigorously growing economy can sustain the full burden of non-obsolete modern armaments. Only the United States and the Soviet Union could afford to undertake the massive research required in the space-race, and by 1963 even Khrushchev announced he would no longer compete for the moon. Their competition, however, had made the year 1961 a landmark in world history, for in April the Soviet airman, Major Yuri Gagarin, orbited the earth in a spaceship and returned safely; and in May the American, Commander Alan Shepard, travelled 115 miles into space and returned safely. These events were the culmination of nearly four years of intense competition, starting with the Soviet's first artificial earth satellite (*sputnik*) in 1957. Although Commonwealth, French, and Italian space research made important contributions, the developments that could yield maximum prestige and power were the Russian and American. America won the race to the moon by July 1969. Mastery of space assumed the appearance of rivalry in power: and here, too, other states could play only subordinate roles. Just as the quest of individuals in the affluent society was for status, so the quest of states in the atomic age was for stature: the stature of a nuclear Power.

Considerations of stature, among others, had helped to draw together the nations of Western Europe into a series of close-linked combinations, including the European Economic Community (E.E.C. or 'Common Market') and 'Euratom', both of which were set up by the Treaties of Rome in March 1957. They were avowedly intended as steps towards political unification, in the belief that only a Western Europe forged into unity could act as any sort of effective counterpoise to the two giant Powers. Britain, distrustful of political unification which would conflict with both British sovereignty and Commonwealth ties, yet unable to ignore the growth of the Common Market among countries with whom she had one-sixth of her trade, proposed a looser Free Trade Association. Long negotiations for reconciliation between the two schemes failed, and at Stockholm, in January 1960, Britain joined with Austria, Denmark, Norway, Portugal, Sweden, and Switzerland to set up the European Free Trade Association (E.F.T.A.). The seven now confronted 'the six' (France, Western Germany, Italy, and the three 'Benelux' partners) who had formed the E.E.C., and the prospect of two rival Western European trading *blocs* was dismal. In Britain both major parties, like public opinion itself, were divided about the issue.

During the year 1961 the British Government moved towards a decision to apply for membership of the E.E.C., subject to adequate arrangements being agreed to meet the interests of Commonwealth countries, Britain's partners in E.F.T.A., and British agriculture. It was assumed that entry into the Common Market would mean entry, also, into 'Euratom' and the European Coal and Steel Community. Only application could reveal how acceptable would be the conditions. The ultimate consideration was indicated clearly enough by Mr Edward Heath, who became the chief British negotiator: 'We now see opposite to us on the mainland of Europe a large group comparable in size only to the United States and the Soviet Union, and as its economic power increases, so will its political influence.' Negotiations went on, with considerable success, throughout the year 1962. In January 1963 General de Gaulle abruptly demanded they should end. The long, patient discussions came to nothing, despite protests from the other five signatories of the Rome Treaties that they would prefer to see Britain a member of the Common Market. The way in which the Common Market talks were brought to an end, by France imposing its will on all participants with consequent tensions between Britain and France, made the year

1963 a turning-point in British foreign policy: and near-coincidence in time with the Cuban crisis and the Nassau meeting suggested that Britain had come to the end of one phase without offering any clear indication of the shape of the next.

The struggle for international stature, however, was conditioned by the joint pressure of the two giant Powers – by the sheer economic weight and the speed of scientific advance, no less than by the conscious policies, of the 'international Joneses'. This unwelcome but unavoidable truth was borne in upon Britain from several directions during the fifties and early sixties. The fact that both the United States and the Soviet Union were by traditional bias strongly anti-colonial helped to bring them together. The Suez crisis saw them voting together on several occasions at the United Nations in opposition to Britain and France. In economic affairs both were providentially immune to difficulties of dollar gaps and balance of payments which persistently haunted the Governments of Western Europe. The Cuban crisis made manifest that their intercontinental missiles rendered them both nuclear overlords, able to disregard the rights of smaller Powers in a manner in which no smaller Power could disregard theirs. Their persistence in nuclear tests despite protests from other nations, their neck-and-neck rivalry in the space-race which left all other competitors far behind, alike reinforced the realization that America and Russia had very much greater freedom of decision and effective independence of action than any lesser Power. The mounting sense of subordination reached a climax when Britain's attempt to join the European Economic Community, into which she had been propelled by the joint but contrary pressures of Russian and American policies in Europe, was humiliatingly frustrated by the intransigence of France. Was British foreign policy to remain at the mercy of others' policies and acts of defiance?

'LIFE, LIBERTY, AND THE PURSUIT
OF HAPPINESS'

Superficially, at least, the most apparent forms of American pressure on British life were those affecting popular culture and public taste. They operated at almost all social levels. The business world increasingly resorted to mass advertising and used as its media newspapers, glossy magazines, and television. Britain's educational system, especially at the level of technical colleges and universities, was repeatedly compared disadvantageously with the American system. The middle classes, followed closely by the newly well-to-do working classes, spent more of their money on cars, television sets, washing machines, refrigerators, vacuum cleaners, and a wide range of other electrical gadgets. Teenagers spent their new-found wealth (the consequences of full employment and the well-paid youthful labour force it produced) on long-playing records of 'pop' singers, on transistor radio sets, scooters, and cosmetics, and created for themselves a phantasy world of juke-box delights confined within the realities of late-night cafés. The kingdoms (and the fortunes) built up by mass publicity and the blare of advertisement existed in Britain on a pattern very closely assimilated to those of the United States. Cultural bulldozers were at work.

This generalization was subject to two reservations. One was that so far as these social and cultural changes were due to American influences they were the outcome of a very protracted process. It had continued throughout the whole of the twentieth century and rested on the basis of an 'Atlantic community' created during the nineteenth century. The mass migrations to North America, and the strong bonds of language, culture, and ideals which had been forged, made possible a constant interplay between America and Britain in the twentieth century. It was inevitable, as the size, wealth, and power of the United States surpassed that of all other countries, that it should exert increasing impact on British life. That British wealth and power were sharply depleted in two world wars only made this impact more dramatic. It was not *caused* by the wars. The second reservation was that many of these social and cultural changes attributed to Americanization were due more to wider technological and economic forces, which having first shaped American life then went on, in due time, to shape life elsewhere: not in Britain alone but also in the Soviet Union, Western Europe, and even in lands as remote as Australasia and Japan. The growth throughout the world of an urban, industrial, scientific civilization based on such patterns was a consequence less of Americanization (which itself was only a particular and advanced specimen of this civilization) than of westernization in general.

The most important cultural and intellectual phenomenon of the years after 1945 was the upheaval (and extensive abandonment) of traditional values, and the quest for new values felt to be more appropriate to life in a rapidly changing, materialistic, and scientific civilization. This could be described in various ways. The novelist, C. P. Snow, described it as a gulf between 'the two cultures', scientific and literary. Moralists pointed to the affinities between an economic system wherein take-over bids, golden handshakes, and lavish expense-accounts had become a regular feature of business life, and a social system wherein new-found affluence was spent on striptease clubs, alcohol (£1,000 million), tobacco (despite medical evidence that smoking helped to cause cancer, £1,200 million), betting and gambling (£762 million). Criminologists indicated, in turn, the possible links between a society of this kind and the alarming increase in juvenile offenders, illegitimacy, and prostitution.

Sexual ethics, especially, underwent a rapid and drastic change, just as views on what constituted 'public decency' changed as regards literature, stage, and television.

The key events here were the Obscene Publications Act of 1959 and the court decision in the same year to allow Penguin Books to publish the unexpurgated version of D. H. Lawrence's novel, *Lady Chatterley's Lover*. Homosexuality also came to be more openly discussed and more commonly regarded as an affliction. A Home Office committee under Sir John Wolfenden even recommended in 1957 that homosexual acts between consenting male adults in private should no longer be subject to criminal prosecution, but this reform had to await the more permissive climate of the late 1960s.

To all who, before the war, had held the materialist view that crime was caused largely by slums, poverty, and bad economic conditions, it was disconcerting to discover that the Welfare State brought a steep rise in crime. Moreover, it was precisely among teenagers, whose incomes had risen most spectacularly, that there appeared gang warfare, vice, and the propensity to commit violent crime. Of 182,217 indictable offences in England and Wales in 1961, 64,284 were committed by youngsters under the age of seventeen. A governmental report in 1959 remarked:

It is a disquieting feature of our society that, in the years since the war, rising standards in material prosperity, education, and social welfare have brought no decrease in the high rate of crime during the war: on the contrary, crime has increased and is still increasing.[1]

The conclusion seemed to be that crime is determined not by material conditions alone, but by the whole social environment, including such intangible factors as the ethical standards and values prevalent in society as a whole, the

1. *Penal Practice in a Changing Society* (Cmnd. 645, 1959, p. 1).

personal and collective anxieties to which men were subjected, and even the effectiveness of humanistic or religious teaching about human relationships. That 'a community gets the criminals it deserves' was truer, perhaps, than the original makers of the phrase had known. That so much current literature and reflective writing was devoted to problems of human relationships suggested fresh awareness of ethics, as distinct from mere hedonistic interests, as a foundation, for the good society. In this, many felt, the Churches had given too little guidance.

The place of the Churches, and still more of religion as such, in the lives of British people after 1945 was peculiarly difficult to assess.[1] The intellectual, cultural, and spiritual atmosphere of the time was not obviously religious, nor was it unusually anti-religious. There was widespread indifference; but when, in modern times, was there not? The number of buildings registered as meeting-places for religious worship in England and Wales was greater in 1950 than in 1920, by more than 6,000; but does that signify much? Broadly, the largest religious bodies in the fifties were the Church of England and the Church in Wales (some 3 million members), the Roman Catholic Church (about 2 million), the Methodist Church ($\frac{3}{4}$ million). The decline in churchgoing – though fluctuations in time and place make even this generalization dubious – was not necessarily accompanied by any decline in activities with a spiritual basis, or in a profound concern for spiritual values. The intense interest aroused by the Bishop of Woolwich's book, *Honest to God* (1963), showed that there was no lack of public concern for theological issues. The popularity of religious broadcasting modified even the image of an indifferent non-worshipping community. The influence of Archbishop

1. For discussion of these issues see B. S. Rowntree and G. R. Lavers, *English Life and Leisure* (1951), chap. XIII; A. M. Carr-Saunders and others, *A Survey of Social Conditions in England and Wales* (1958 ed.), chap. 18. But in no field is sociology more drearily crude and inadequate.

William Temple in the thirties found no sequel in the fifties, though Bishop Mervyn Stockwood and Canon John Collins attracted devoted followers.

It was tempting to depict Britain of the sixties as a money-lusting, sordid, decadent society. The outright pursuit of happiness led straight to much unhappiness. But in no society have moralists found it difficult to discover vice and omens of decadence, especially among a generation younger than their own; it is always easy to confuse the silly with the sinful, the merely trivial with the vicious. A generation which had known extermination camps like Auschwitz, the devastation of Hiroshima, the highest scientific intellects devoted to destruction, could hardly avoid some nihilism. Dilemmas so absolute did not evoke orthodox reactions. The young supporters of the Committee for Nuclear Disarmament who marched from Aldermaston at Easter, or the pacifists (led by the aged Earl Russell) who sat down in Trafalgar Square, were heirs of the Peace Pledge Union of the thirties. Their actions, however strange, suggested no spirit of indifference to the deepest spiritual problems of the age.

From contemporary literature – from the plays of Samuel Beckett or John Osborne, the novels of John Wain or Kingsley Amis – they heard only similar blind protests. Kitchen sinks and angry young men offered little inspiration. Spiritual guides failed them, for only a few turned to the Churches and to established faith. But the generation which sustained the Third Programme (from 1946 on), the Edinburgh Festival of Music and Drama (from 1947 on), and the many successful exhibitions of painting was not culturally bankrupt or spiritually indifferent. In Voluntary Services Overseas, in generous response to human needs in time of great disasters such as floods, famines, and earthquakes, in a general quickening of human sympathies, the British people revealed strong impulses of self-sacrifice and

service. Too many critics kept one eye closed when survey-
ing the social scene.

The United Kingdom of the sixties comprised some 10
million more people than that of 1914; it had passed the
50 million mark in 1950.[1] Some of this increase came from
immigration, though immigrants were at times more than
offset by emigrants, and the most important reasons were a
low infant death-rate and a rising birth-rate. Many young
families, including skilled scientists and technologists,
migrated to the United States and the Dominions. Considerable numbers of Commonwealth citizens – from the West
Indies, India, Pakistan – and immigrants from Ireland and
Europe came into Britain. The flow of West Indians began
on an important scale in 1952, and by 1961 reached the
figure of 50,000 in a year. With roughly a quarter of a million
West Indians making homes and livings in Britain,
especially in certain concentrated areas in London and some
Midlands towns, there arose acute problems of housing,
education, and work. Small Fascist organizations exploited
the situation, and there were outbursts of local disturbance.
The Commonwealth Immigrants Act of 1962 stipulated
that immigrants must have a job to come to or must possess
some 'special skill' useful in Britain, and that criminal
offenders could be deported. This departure from uncon-
trolled entry of Commonwealth citizens was condemned as
making possible a 'colour bar', but it reflected both official
and public concern lest an increase in unemployment
should cause yet greater troubles.

Although the annual number of deaths in England and
Wales remained astonishingly constant from 1870 onwards,
at something around 500,000, this happened within an ever-
larger population, and the causes of death changed greatly.

The main causes of death in 1951 were, as we should expect,
cancers and heart diseases, which are the killers of middle-aged
1. See above, p. 19.

and elderly people, so that it seems as though the diseases which killed young and old alike in the nineteenth century have by now been replaced by diseases which attack and kill mainly the middle-aged and elderly.[1]

From the twenties the death-rate continued at around 12 per thousand, while the birth-rate rose sharply in the later forties, and again in the later fifties. Britain, like the United States, disproved the old belief that rising standards of living and comfort check rises in birth-rates. Contrary to expectation, the birth-rate rose from 16 per thousand in 1956 to 17·7 per thousand in 1961. People married younger, had children earlier, and had longer to have more children; the average family went up from two children to three or more; and the infant death-rate halved between 1945 and 1956. Britain, once expecting to have an ageing population, found itself with an unusually young population: even when penicillin and new sulpha-drugs kept many older people alive for longer.

Besides being more numerous, children of the new Britain were undoubtedly of better physique, more healthy, better fed, clothed, and housed, and more intelligently educated to a higher level, than the children of any previous generation. More of them went to grammar schools, technical colleges, and universities. The expansion of secondary and higher education was the biggest cultural accomplishment of the half-century since 1914. The number of pupils attending English and Welsh grant-aided secondary schools was 160,600 in 1910, but 683,700 in 1950.[2] The percentage of

1. David C. Marsh, *The Changing Social Structure of England and Wales, 1871-1951* (1958), p. 232.
2. *Education 1900-1950* (Cmd. 8244), p. 247. This report of the Ministry of Education contains valuable historical assessments. The Newsom Report, *Half Our Future* (1963), showed, however, how much more remained to be done for the education of 'pupils aged thirteen to sixteen of average and less than average ability'.

children aged fifteen to eighteen at such schools doubled between 1938 and 1956. Here was the real 'social revolution'. The connexions between warfare and welfare are subtle and many. All the great Education Acts of the century were passed at the end of wars: in 1902, 1918, 1944.

The people as a whole enjoyed a higher standard of living, better housing, longer holidays and shorter working-hours, more foreign travel, wider facilities for leisure and recreation, than the British people had ever enjoyed before. In 1963, as compared with 1914, its age structure was different, more lived in towns or suburbs, occupations were more varied and there was less inequality in distribution of wealth and of educational opportunity. 'Despite inflation,' says Professor David Marsh, 'it is probable that even in real terms the mass of the population in the 1950's have a higher material standard of living than ever before.'[1]

The improvement was not only material. More read books and had access to good music, serious drama, intelligent discussion. The decline of the cinema in favour of television was not necessarily a cultural loss, and the publication, sales, and library provision of books continued to increase. The 'paper-back revolution' kept good books within reach of all, and more new books were published annually in Britain than in the United States. There were not only new towns and new schools, but new universities and even new cathedrals (at Guildford and Coventry), affording unprecedented opportunities for architects. If the individualistic arts of poetry and painting were not at their most flourishing, the public 'collective' arts of architecture, ballet, opera, and orchestral work enlisted much creative activity. In scientific research and technology Britain kept some pre-eminence: in radiophysics, biology, medicine, and in engineering there were fine records of accomplish-

1. op. cit., p. 226.

ment.[1] The country which contributed to technology the jet engine, the hovercraft, nuclear power stations, and much of value in electronics, could not be said to lack inventive originality. If the receipt of Nobel Prizes be any index of comparisons, in the whole record of awards since 1901 Britain came second only to the United States in Physics and Physiology and Medicine, and second only to France in Literature. She ranked no lower than third in any field. All these facts hardly betoken a demoralized or decadent society.

The more rounded image of Britain in the sixties, half a century after the Great War began, was of a vigorous, growing nation, with a high proportion of young people and an expanding economy, struggling with partial success to adjust itself to the novel and ever-shifting conditions of the twentieth-century world. In less than one man's lifetime it had produced leaders of human thought and action of the eminence of Rutherford and Fleming, Shaw and Russell, Beveridge and Keynes, Lloyd George and Winston Churchill. It had endured much, shown great courage, contributed to the progress of mankind, and had influenced every continent of the globe, not least Asia, where dwelt more than half mankind. What, in wider world perspective, was the remaining challenge of the twentieth century?

'THE WIND OF CHANGE'

Agreements to give greater self-government and independence to former colonial territories were often depicted as 'retreats' of British imperialism. By the fifties and sixties they could more properly be seen as quests for new relationships with underdeveloped countries. But not all sections of

1. As, indeed, in such activities as motor and speed-boat racing, in which Donald Campbell proved a worthy successor to his father, Sir Malcolm, in breaking speed records, and Jim Clark won world eminence in 1962-3.

opinion adjusted themselves fast enough to this focus. Accordingly, the history of British 'decolonization' in these years fell into two main phases: one of reluctant and sporadic repression (already described in Chapter 9) under Churchill and Eden; and one of almost eager emancipation under Macmillan. Some Mediterranean islands valued chiefly as bases and some African territories had been ill-prepared for sweeping grants of self-government and autonomy. The problems of Cyprus, Malta, and Kenya belonged to these categories of especially intractable issues.

When Archbishop Makarios, leader of the Greek Cypriot movement for *enosis*, was released in March 1957, Lord Salisbury resigned in protest against what he regarded as weakness in face of terrorism. Intricate negotiations went on throughout 1958 and 1959. It was the autumn of 1960 before projects both of *enosis* (union with Greece), as the Greeks wanted, and of partition, as the Turks wanted, were formally dropped in favour of autonomy and independence for the island as a whole. A conference in London of representatives of Greece, Turkey, and the United Kingdom agreed a settlement. By the Cyprus Act (1960) the island became an independent sovereign Republic, with a Greek Cypriot President and a Turkish Cypriot Vice-President. In February 1961 it was accepted as a member of the Commonwealth, but its future remained troubled by civil strife.

Malta, which had enjoyed a measure of self-government since 1947, in 1957 contemplated political integration with the United Kingdom. In the deadlock that followed breakdown of this proposal a state of emergency had to be declared, and in 1959 an interim Constitution gave wide powers to the Governor. A new Constitution set up the 'State of Malta' (March 1962), though it had to be modified later. The Maltese Government asked for independence within the Commonwealth.

Other former colonial territories followed a similar

course. Ghana, which adopted a new constitution in 1957, became a Republic within the Commonwealth in July 1960. In 1957 the Federation of Malaya became an independent country within the Commonwealth, and began to canvass a project for a larger 'Federation of Malaysia', including Malaya, Singapore, North Borneo, Sarawak, and Brunei. This met with opposition from Indonesia and produced revolts in the last-named three territories at the end of 1962. Singapore had gained internal self-government in June 1959. The pattern of a multi-racial Commonwealth proved very flexible.

By the sixties it was in Africa that the wind of change blew strongest. Former French African colonies were transformed into independent members of the new *Communauté*, no less liberal in its structure and spirit than the new Commonwealth. The former Belgian Congo became an independent State in June 1960; but its people had been so little prepared for independence, and the Belgians quitted it so abruptly, that chaos soon ensued. United Nations forces, called in to keep the peace, remained heavily embroiled in the violent and erratic politics of new native leaders. The Congo was important in British history as a warning and a reminder of the intense difficulties of 'decolonization' and the dangers of letting the 'cold war' assume colonial forms. So was the long French struggle in Algeria, which ended only in March 1962. Against this lurid and tragic background of African development most British changes were relatively smooth and happy.

The commonest pattern, especially for a large territory, was federation and progressive measures of representative self-government, combined with some safeguards or reservations for British defence bases and facilities, and eventual independent membership of the Commonwealth. The large territory of Nigeria followed this course during 1958–60. It achieved full independence as the Federation of

Nigeria in October 1960, continuing as a member of the Commonwealth. Sierra Leone, Tanganyika, Somaliland, and Uganda trod the same path by the end of 1962. It was happily a fairly smooth path. Tanganyika and Uganda avoided some of the material disadvantages of independence by sharing, with Kenya, the new East African Common Services Organization which undertook to administer, under the control of a central assembly, services such as communications, finance, commercial and industrial co-ordination, and social services.

Formal constitutional and political independence was of great psychological importance, given the surge of nationalist sentiment throughout the world. It was an irony of history that just as European States were groping towards supra-national organizations which would limit their political autonomy, the peoples of Asia and Africa were asserting their separateness and autonomy. Amid so much political fragmentation it was of material importance that financial, commercial, and technological cooperation should be extended between the developed and underdeveloped countries. Britain took a full share in promoting this, though inevitably the United States led the world in finance and aid. In 1962 the old Colonial Development Corporation was rechristened the Commonwealth Development Corporation, extending its work to include independent members of the Commonwealth. By that stage more than £250 million had been provided, since 1946, under the Colonial Development and Welfare Act. Both constitutionally and economically the new Commonwealth recognized and rested upon the material need of such new States to remain in relations of cooperation and interdependence even after winning formal independence. In most of them universities were set up or expanded with direct help, especially in staffing, from British graduates. Moreover, most members of the Commonwealth, on gaining sovereign autonomy, applied for and became members of the United Nations. They thereby acquired a right to share in the many functional agencies and services of world organization, and helped to double United Nations membership as compared with 1946.

The whole process of 'decolonization' mattered for Britain in two main respects: in so far as it raised issues that split public opinion at home or raised moral dilemmas – about the rights of white settlers in Kenya or Rhodesia, or the degree of tolerance to be extended to terrorist leaders; and in so far as it interacted with foreign affairs – such as in the safeguarding of naval and air bases overseas or opening doors to Communist intrusions. During the post-war years as a whole both types of issue had recurred. The problems, desires, and needs of underdeveloped countries had never before impinged so directly on British politics nor received so much attention from British politicians. Events happened fast, and the climate of British opinion (as of world opinion) was so favourable to colonial emancipation that little resistance was offered to each new claim for larger self-government or for sovereign independence. The essential problems – whether self-government would lead to boss-rule or military dictatorship, sovereign independence to economic detriment or social injustice – were too seldom discussed. The values of nationalism were assumed to be absolute, their righteousness taken as self-evident.

Yet historical experience has often shown that the principle of national self-determination, carried to extremes, makes for fragmentation little short of chaos and for the tyranny of demagogues or generals. So now the former British West Indies, grouped hopefully into one Federation in 1958 and given powers of self-government, disintegrated in May 1962. In August the largest island, Jamaica, became independent within the Commonwealth, to be followed by Trinidad and Tobago. The remaining eight territories were formed into a new, contracted West Indies Federation centred on Barbados. So, too, the Federation of Rhodesia and Nyasaland, created in 1953, was broken in 1963 by the claims of Nyasaland and Northern Rhodesia to secede, and the inclination of all three partners to claim independence. The changing winds of the sixties still blew fitfully. In 1961 the Union of South Africa followed Burma and left the Commonwealth.

Between 1945 and 1960 some 500 million people in former British dependencies became completely self-governing. 'This,' says Lord Strang, 'is a major event in world history.' But the problems remaining in Kenya and Southern Rhodesia were related to a more intricate issue:

Will it be possible to evolve in British territories the multi-racial community based on partnership, in accordance with the principle of British colonial policy, enunciated as early as 1923, that wherever the interests of natives and of European settlers appeared to conflict, those of the natives would not be subordinated to those of the Europeans?[1]

What most complicated the process of colonial emancipation by the sixties was the new force of Pan-Africanism now greatly exacerbated by the racialist policies pursued by the South African Government. The omens of a general clash in Africa on purely racial grounds, though inflamed by the intrusions of cold-war calculations and ideological conflicts, were among the most sinister in the international scene of the sixties. Liable still to be entangled, by reason of a Katanga lobby, as in the Congo disaster, or by former responsibilities, as in Southern Rhodesia or Kenya, British policy could not ignore the mighty ferment in Africa. But if she could not ignore it, neither could she do very much to control it. It was symptomatic of the whole new status of Britain that some of the most vital aspects of her position in the world were substantially beyond her own control.

1. Lord Strang, *Britain in World Affairs* (1961), p. 363.

PART IV

FROM AFFLUENCE TO UNCERTAINTY
(1964–79)

CHAPTER ELEVEN

The Labour Government, 1964–70

THE TYRANNY OF ECONOMICS: AT HOME

THE fruits of thirteen years in opposition were such that, apart from the Prime Minister himself, only two members of the 1964 Labour Government had held Cabinet office before.[1] There were, however, some interesting features about the new team. Mr Frank Cousins had been persuaded to take temporary leave from his post as General Secretary of the powerful Transport and General Workers' Union to become Minister of Technology, a move which was widely interpreted as an attempt to gain trade union support for the Government's economic policy. The latter, moreover, was now in the hands of two senior ministers of equal rank: Mr James Callaghan, the Chancellor of the Exchequer, and Mr George Brown, the Secretary of State in charge of the newly created Department of Economic Affairs (D.E.A.). The avuncular Callaghan, who seemed to epitomize solid common sense, was a perfect foil to the mercurial Brown, but the contrast went deeper than personality. Conservative economic policy had never seemed able to escape from the cycle of 'stop–go', in which any attempt to expand the economy seemed inexorably to result in inflation and a balance of payments crisis, which necessitated the imposition of controls which in turn brought the growth to a halt. The Labour Government was determined to break out of this vicious circle; indicative planning, which had appeared to work so well for some of Britain's conti-

1. Mr Patrick Gordon Walker and Mr James Griffiths.

nental competitors, was to be the instrument; and the D.E.A., free of the old orthodoxies which were thought to prevail inside the Treasury, was to be the Government department to shape and use it. The unresolved question, however, was the extent to which the Treasury would be prepared to cede its traditional primacy in the formulation of economic policy to this newcomer.

A decision taken during the early days of the new Government was to have a crucial bearing upon the answer to this question. Mr Maudling's policy of growth, like that of his predecessors, had produced a balance of payments deficit which the Treasury – somewhat inaccurately as it later turned out – estimated at about £800 million for 1964 as a whole. It was imperative to take action to cope with this situation, but what sort of action was it to be? Most experts now argue, although few did so at the time, that immediate devaluation would have been the best solution, but Mr Wilson and his senior colleagues ruled this out. They did not want the Labour Party, which had been forced to devalue in 1949,[1] to become tagged as the devaluation party. Mr Wilson, moreover, believed that devaluation was a soft option: it would do nothing to bring about the structural changes in British industry which were needed to make it more competitive, but would merely cushion it against the need to make such changes for a few more years. The Government therefore decided to act directly on imports by imposing a temporary surcharge of 15 per cent upon their value. Unfortunately, the revelation of the deficit, coupled with Mr Callaghan's first budget on 11 November which increased expenditure on the social services in line with Labour's election promises, upset the financial community and led to a run on the pound. On 23 November the Chancellor had to resort to the time-honoured deflationary

1. See pp. 225-6.

expedient of increasing Bank Rate, and an international credit of $3,000 million was hastily arranged to prop up the currency. 'Stop–go', it seemed, had returned, and as long as the Government's policy was dominated by the Treasury's short-term aim of maintaining the parity of sterling, the D.E.A.'s long-term aim of securing sustained economic growth was bound to suffer.

A more hopeful sign for the future was the announcement on 16 December 1964 of a 'Joint Statement of Intent on Productivity, Prices and Incomes' signed by representatives of the Government, industry and the trade unions. An important condition for the success of a policy of economic growth is that money incomes do not increase more rapidly than productivity, or inflation will result. The Conservatives had sought to implement an incomes policy, but the trade-union movement, deprecating their emphasis upon wages as opposed to prices and profits, boycotted their National Incomes Commission. Thanks to its links with the unions, the new Government was more successful. It replaced the National Incomes Commission by a National Board for Prices and Incomes,[1] which, as its title indicates, had a wider remit. It soon became clear, however, that a voluntary policy of the kind agreed upon would not be enough.

Sterling once more came under heavy pressure in the summer of 1965 and the Government was forced to introduce another series of deflationary measures in July. Since wage settlements had been running at about twice the rate envisaged at the time of the 'Statement of Intent', there was pressure for a statutory wage freeze. The Government resisted it, however, and in September 1965 Mr Brown reached agreement with the C.B.I. and the T.U.C. on legislation compelling employers and unions to notify

1. It became better known as the Prices and Incomes Board (P.I.B.).

intended price rises and wage claims in advance so that they could be referred to the P.I.B. for consideration.[1]

By coincidence, the same month also saw the publication of the Government's National Plan for the economy. It envisaged a relatively modest rate of growth of 3·8 per cent per annum in real terms, which would have meant an overall increase of one quarter in national output during the period 1964-70. However, as the Plan's architect subsequently pointed out,

One of the assumptions we made was that the plan would take priority and other policies pursued by the Government would be made to fit its provisions. In the event this was not done ... and as a result the 4 per cent growth rate was made impossible of achievement.[2]

For a short time the situation seemed to get better: confidence in sterling returned, the balance of payments improved, and, despite two bouts of deflation, unemployment fell to a record low level. Always a shrewd tactician, and well aware that the good fortune would not last, Mr Wilson decided that this was the moment to go to the country in order to give his party a decent working majority.

The Conservatives fought the election under a new leader. Sir Alec Douglas-Home had stepped down in July 1965, and in order to avoid a repetition of the bitterness which had characterized his own emergence as leader, he had seen to it that his successor would be chosen, not by means of the old system of informal consultations by the whips and elder statesmen of the party, but by a direct election by Conservative M.P.s. Mr Heath narrowly beat his nearest rival, Mr Maudling, but when it came to the more important election on 31 March 1966 he in turn was thoroughly

1. The legislation was not in fact introduced until July 1966. See below, p. 296.
2. George Brown, *In My Way* (1971), p. 119.

trounced by Mr Wilson. The Labour Government was returned with an overall majority of 97, a result which bore comparison with the landslides of 1906 and 1945, if not with those of 1918 and 1931.

While the election may have made the Government's position in Parliament virtually unassailable, it did not of course solve the country's more fundamental problems. The budget had been postponed because of the election and when the time came to draw it up, it was found that the balance of payments was again giving cause for anxiety and that further restrictions were needed. When the budget was introduced on 3 May, therefore, it contained a proposal for a new Selective Employment Tax (S.E.T.) which, by imposing a pay-roll charge on employers in the service sector, was designed to perform the twin function of taking £250–£300 million out of the economy and of encouraging a shift of resources away from 'unproductive' services into 'productive' industry. There is considerable doubt as to whether it ever achieved the second objective, and while it did achieve the first, it did not do so quickly enough to make any impact upon the looming crisis over the balance of payments.

What undoubtedly precipitated this crisis was a crippling six weeks strike by the country's merchant seamen which began on 16 May. Alarmed at the way in which wage settlements were still failing to come down to a level which it regarded as acceptable, the Government resolved to stand firm against the seamen's pay claim and the Prime Minister publicly castigated 'a tightly knit group of politically motivated men' – by which he meant the Communist Party and its sympathizers – for prolonging the strike as part of their campaign against the Government's prices and incomes policy. The loss of exports occasioned by the strike plunged the balance of payments further into the red and produced a fresh round of speculation against the pound. 'Very soon,' one Cabinet minister recorded in his diary on 3 July, 'we shall be faced with the choice between devaluation or intensive deflation.'[1]

As in 1964 the Government chose deflation. On 20 July Mr Wilson unveiled a series of measures designed to reduce demand by £500 million, including a cut of £150 million in public investment, a 10 per cent surcharge on indirect taxes, and a tightening of hire purchase controls. He also announced that there would be a six months' wage freeze, followed by a further six months of 'severe restraint'.[2] This last measure was to be tacked on to the Prices and Incomes Bill introduced earlier in the month to implement the agreement reached with the C.B.I. and the T.U.C. the previous autumn, a bill which had already led to the resignation from the Government of Mr Cousins, who was opposed to any form of statutory wage control.

The Government nearly lost the services of Mr Brown as well. He was one of a now sizeable minority in the Cabinet who had wanted to consider the alternative of devaluation, and while Mr Wilson had succeeded in buying off most of the opposition by agreeing that the matter could be examined in the context of a possible failure of the deflationary package, the Secretary of State for Economic Affairs was not won over. Indeed, he assures us that he was only dissuaded from resignation by pressing appeals from all sides to stay on and by the realization that he would be unable to disclose the real reasons for his resignation without precipitating yet another run on the pound. After completing the unpalatable task of piloting the revised Prices and Incomes Bill through the House of Commons in the teeth of opposition from both the Conservatives and the left

1. Richard Crossman, *The Diaries of a Cabinet Minister*, vol. 1 (1975), p. 557.
2. Prices were also to be controlled, but not so strictly.

wing of his own party, Mr Brown exchanged Cabinet posts with the Foreign Secretary, Mr Michael Stewart. As he subsequently admitted in his memoirs, he had lost credibility in the economic sphere since everyone knew he was opposed to the Government's deflationary policies, and while the D.E.A. continued to exist for another three years, the July measures and Mr Brown's departure marked not only the defeat of its bid to take over control of the British Economy from the Treasury, but also the demise of the 'National Plan' and the end of the Government's dream of replacing 'stop–go' by sustained economic growth.

Like its predecessor of 1965, the deflation of 1966 proved to be only a temporary palliative. The statutory incomes policy worked reasonably well – during the period from July 1966 to July 1967 wage and price increases remained in step at a modest 2 per cent – but the balance of payments obstinately refused to come right and from May 1967 onwards the pound was once more under pressure. Paradoxically, since it had been taken in part for economic reasons, the Government's decision to apply for membership of the European Economic Community[1] was the principal destabilizing factor. At a Cabinet meeting on 29 April 1967 the President of the Board of Trade, Mr Douglas Jay, presented what one of his colleagues described as a 'massive unanswerable demonstration that entry to the Market would produce a balance-of-payments crisis . . . and one devaluation if not two'.[2] Foreign holders of sterling were, of course, just as aware of this as the Government and they acted accordingly. A further blow was the Arab–Israeli war of June 1967[3] which, by closing the Suez Canal,

1. See below, pp. 309–10.
2. Richard Crossman, *The Diaries of a Cabinet Minister*, vol. 2 (1976), p. 333.
3. See below, p. 304.

added £20 million a month to the balance of payments deficit. It became increasingly clear that the country could not stand a further deflation and on 18 November 1967 the decision was taken to devalue the pound by 14·3 per cent, from $2.80 to $2.40.

If George Brown had been the chief casualty of the July 1966 measures, that unenviable position was undoubtedly filled in November 1967 by his rival, James Callaghan. The Chancellor of the Exchequer had been the last to accept the need for devaluation, later even than the Prime Minister, and less than a fortnight after it had taken place, he exchanged posts with the Home Secretary, Mr Roy Jenkins. But whereas Mr Brown was to resign from the Government in March 1968,[1] lose his seat at the 1970 general election and eventually leave the Labour Party, Mr Callaghan was to make a remarkable come-back in the years that followed.

Devaluation did not obviate the need for further un-palatable measures of the kind which had become common-place over the past few years. Although the new parity for sterling made British exports more competitive, it also made imports more expensive, requiring the export of even more goods to pay for them. If there was any sign that the balance of payments deficit would not be eliminated, the new parity could in turn be undermined by speculation. In a 'letter of intent' to the International Monetary Fund, the Government made clear its determination to get the balance of payments right, even at the cost of private consumption and public expenditure. This determination was at the root of the series of tax increases and spending cuts over the next few years, which involved measures as sensitive to the Labour Party as the reintroduction of prescription charges, the very issue upon which Mr Wilson had resigned from

1. He resigned over what he felt was Mr Wilson's autocratic style of government.

the Attlee Government in 1951.[1] Not for nothing was this period dubbed the 'two years' hard slog'.

From the point of view of its principal objective, the Government's policy was spectacularly successful. As one commentator has pointed out, there was

a substantial shift of resources into the balance of payments at the expense of private consumption and government expenditure. Between 1967 and 1970 the G.D.P. rose by 7·7 per cent, but private consumption rose by only 5·4 per cent and public consumption by less than 1 per cent. The volume of exports, by contrast, grew by 27 per cent, compared with a 17 per cent rise in the volume of imports.[2]

Indeed, in 1970 there was a balance of payments surplus on current account of £735 million. Unfortunately, the policy was highly unpopular. The Government lost by-election after by-election, including some in what were normally solid Labour seats.

Compounding the Government's unpopularity with its own supporters was the continuation of the statutory incomes policy, which seemed to hold down wages at this time of increasing tax burdens. In the autumn of 1968, both the T.U.C. and Labour Party conferences voted for an end to the policy. By the turn of the year, the Prime Minister, Mr Jenkins, and the dynamic Secretary of State for Employment, Mrs Barbara Castle, had decided that a more effective, and much more popular, way of intervening in the economy was to take powers to reform Britain's somewhat antiquated system of industrial relations. In April 1965 the Government had appointed a Royal Commission under Lord Donovan to report on trade unions and employers' organizations. The incidence of unofficial strikes and

1. See above, p. 228. Prescription charges had been abolished by the Government in 1965.

2. Michael Stewart, *Politics and Economic Policy in the U.K. since 1964* (1978), p. 89.

apparently frivolous demarcation disputes was the back-drop to the Commission's appointment and investigations,[1] but while its report of July 1968 recognized the dimensions of the problem, it saw no short-term solution. Mr Wilson and Mrs Castle disagreed. There was, moreover, a powerful political argument in favour of action. As the Prime Minister's personal and political secretary has recorded,

Harold knew the Labour Party must keep the initiative on this so that Edward Heath and the Conservative Party could not make capital from it. As with immigration and crime and violence, they felt that industrial relations provided an area where they could stir up a great deal of feeling in the country.[2]

The outcome was a White Paper, 'In Place of Strife', which was published in January 1969, and an Industrial Relations Bill based upon it, the most controversial provisions of which were for a 'cooling-off' period in the case of unofficial strikes and for fines in the event of non-compliance. The legislation was announced by Mr Jenkins in his budget speech on 15 April 1969, together with the decision to phase out the prices and incomes policy. Whatever the relative popularity of an incomes policy and industrial relations legislation in the country as a whole, however, the Labour Party and the trade unions regarded the latter as even more objectionable than the former. Already on 3 March no less than 55 Labour M.P.s had voted against 'In Place of Strife' in the House of Commons and a further 40 had abstained. The Opposition, moreover, was not confined to the left wing of the party but extended into the highest echelons of the Cabinet. Thus, it was Mr Callaghan who spoke against the first draft of the White Paper when it was presented to the Cabinet and who challenged the doctrine of collective responsibility by voting against the imposition of sanctions

1. In 1964–6 95 per cent of strikes were unofficial and in 1964–7 wage claims formed only 36 per cent of all reasons for disputes.
2. Marcia Williams, *Inside Number 10* (1975), p. 206.

upon trade unions at a meeting of the National Executive of the Labour Party on 26 March. For him, as for many others across the whole spectrum of Labour opinion, the very foundation of the party – the alliance with the trade union movement – was under threat. In the event, Mr Wilson, Mrs Castle and Mr Jenkins found that they were unable to carry their Cabinet colleagues with them, let alone the parliamentary party or the Labour movement in the country. They therefore had to make do with a 'solemn and binding' undertaking by the T.U.C. on 18 June to exert its influence against unofficial strikes and demarcation disputes. Despite his claim that, in accepting such responsibilities, the T.U.C. had 'moved forward forty years in a month', there can be little doubt that the final outcome was a defeat for the Prime Minister. The Conservatives were bitterly critical of his 'surrender' to union power and promised that they would take a more resolute line.

With no statutory incomes policy and no compensating curbs upon the trade unions, Britain experienced a wages explosion in 1969–70, with both weekly wage rates and average earnings increasing by 13 per cent. Since this was not matched by a comparable growth in productivity, the rate of inflation also began to accelerate. At the same time, the Government's deflationary policies had pushed unemployment back up to the high level it had reached in 1963. These inauspicious omens notwithstanding, the Government's electoral fortunes at long last began to show signs of revival in the spring of 1970 and after a good Labour showing in the borough elections in May Mr Wilson called a general election for 18 June. No sooner had he made his announcement than the opinion polls seemed to prove him right, for they showed the Labour Party drawing ahead. Nevertheless, in the only poll which mattered it was the Conservatives who won, securing 46·4 per cent of the vote (compared to Labour's 42·9 per cent) and a comfortable overall majority of 30 seats in the House of Commons. Had it not been for the opinion polls, no one would have been surprised. Devaluation and deflation had left scars that were hard to heal, and it is significant that more than one in four of the electorate – the highest proportion since the war – did not even bother to vote.

The Labour Government of 1964–70 undoubtedly had some substantial achievements to its credit. It bequeathed to its successor one of the largest balance of payments surpluses in British history. It took positive steps to tackle the problems of the country's less favoured regions, with the creation of Development Areas, the Regional Employment Premium and special investment grants. Despite the economic constraints under which it had been forced to operate, it increased Government spending and redistributed it in favour of the social services. It was during the term of this Government that expenditure on education and health and social security first overtook that on defence. Finally, it sponsored a great deal of progressive social legislation.[1] Nevertheless, as a former Cabinet minister and the Labour Party's leading theorist conceded in 1974, 'Nobody disputes the central failure of economic policy. In 1970, unemployment was higher, inflation more rapid and economic growth slower than when the Conservatives left office in 1964.'[2] In view of the fact that Labour had come to power in 1964 proclaiming its intention to revitalize a stagnant economy, this was a crucially damning indictment.

THE TYRANNY OF ECONOMICS: ABROAD

The harsh realities of the economic situation which so blighted the Labour Government's domestic programme

1. See below, p. 352.
2. Anthony Crosland, *Socialism Now* (1974), p. 18.

were no less important in moulding its foreign policy. Despite its election promise to scrap the so-called 'independent nuclear deterrent'[1] – which, incidentally, it never fulfilled – Labour had by no means abandoned the belief that Britain had an important role to play in world politics. 'We are a World Power and a world influence,' Mr Wilson proudly proclaimed on 16 November 1964, 'or we are nothing.' The area in which this influence was primarily to be exerted was 'East of Suez', and for three years the Government fought a long-drawn-out battle against the economic odds and the protests of its left-wing supporters to preserve a military presence in the Persian Gulf, the Indian Ocean and the Far East. To begin with, there was one very good justification for this: in August 1964 the Indonesian dictator, Achmed Sukarno, had launched a policy of 'confrontation' against the newly independent Commonwealth state of Malaysia. The Conservative Government had pledged military support to help the Malaysians combat Indonesian infiltration and its Labour successor felt honour bound to continue the policy. But Sukarno fell from power in 1965 and 'confrontation' was brought to an end by his successors in the summer of the following year. In the meantime, moreover, the economic chickens were coming home to roost. The new Government had instituted a full-scale defence review and, for financial reasons, felt constrained to limit the defence budget to £2,000 million in real terms. Among other things, this involved a decision not to order a new aircraft carrier for the Royal Navy. In February 1966 both the First Sea Lord, Admiral Sir David Luce, and the Minister of Defence for the Navy, Mr Christopher Mayhew, resigned in protest. It was easy to represent this as wounded pride on the part of the navy, but

1. 'So-called' because, since the 'Polaris' deal of December 1962 (see above, p. 269), Britain's nuclear deterrent had in fact been dependent upon the goodwill of the United States.

Mr Mayhew cogently argued in his resignation statement that a new carrier was essential to carry out the 'East of Suez' policy. The problem was the £2,000 million ceiling: 'it is too small if we want to stay east of Suez,' he maintained, 'and much too big if we do not'.

Even this figure proved to be more than Britain's economy could bear. An immediate reduction was made after the financial crisis of July 1966, and by October the Secretary of State for Defence, Mr Denis Healey, was considering further substantial cuts. The crucial events occurred, however, in 1967. First of all, there was the 'Six Day War' between Israel and the Arab states in June of that year. As one Cabinet minister subsequently recalled:

> Our inability to prevent it (which came out starkly in sharp and angry Cabinet debates);[1] to affect its course; or to do anything about the subsequent Arab reprisals against our trade and our supplies of oil – all this greatly strengthened the already growing conviction in the Cabinet that our presence East of Suez was both vain and costly.[2]

Secondly, devaluation in November not only added £50 million to Britain's overseas defence costs, but also compelled a further re-examination of the whole defence budget in the context of the need to reduce public expenditure. The Government bowed to the inevitable. In January 1968 it announced that Britain would withdraw from 'East of Suez' by the end of 1971, and the defence White Paper in February stated unambiguously: 'Britain's defence effort will in future be concentrated mainly in Europe and the North Atlantic.' An era in British history had come to an end.

One of the justifications Mr Wilson had offered for

1. It appears that, at one stage, Mr Wilson and Mr Brown proposed the despatch of a naval task force to break the Egyptian blockade of the Straits of Tiran, but that they were overruled by their Cabinet colleagues.
2. Patrick Gordon Walker, *The Cabinet*, 2nd edn (1972), p. 129.

Britain's presence 'East of Suez' was that, if she withdrew, America would be left to face China 'eyeball to eyeball' in the Far East, and that this was 'the surest prescription for a nuclear holocaust' he could think of.[1] This statement reflected the growing American involvement in the civil war between Communists and anti-Communists in Vietnam, which did indeed pose the threat of an armed confrontation between the United States and China, although both sides took steps to avoid it. Britain had certain residual obligations in Indochina stemming from her co-chairmanship, with the Soviet Union, of the Geneva Conference of 1954, which had brought the First Indochina War between France and the Communist insurgents to an end, and Mr Wilson spent much time and energy in trying to bring about a negotiated settlement of this second conflict. At one point, when the Russian Prime Minister, Mr Kosygin, was on a visit to London in February 1967, it looked as though he might succeed, but in the event neither of the two co-chairmen could, in the ugly jargon of the day, 'deliver' their respective allies: the United States and North Vietnam. The British Prime Minister received little credit for his efforts, either from the Americans or from the left wing of his own party, which continually criticized the Government for its broad support of U.S. policy.[2] As in the rest of the western world in the late 1960s, Vietnam became a symbol around which rebellious British youth rallied in noisy demonstrations against the *status quo*.

Mr Wilson is said to have remarked that his own 'Vietnam' – in the sense of a stubborn foreign problem which sapped the strength of the Government – was to be

1. Speech to a meeting of the Parliamentary Labour Party on 15 June 1966.

2. It is worth noting, however, that the British Government consistently refused American requests to send troops to Vietnam. Both Australia and New Zealand did send them.

found in Rhodesia. After the collapse of the Central African Federation in 1963,[1] the white minority regime in Southern Rhodesia, now under the control of the right-wing Rhodesian Front Party, began to clamour for independence to be granted on the basis of the constitution of 1961, with its restrictive provisions designed to perpetuate white rule. The Conservative Government had refused to concede this, insisting that 'five principles' would have to be fulfilled before the colony could become independent: (1) the constitution would have to be amended to guarantee unimpeded progress towards majority – i.e. African – rule; (2) there would have to be guarantees against any retrogressive amendment of the new constitution; (3) there would have to be an immediate improvement in the political status of the African majority; (4) there must be a firm intention to end racial discrimination; and (5) the new constitution would have to be accepted by the Rhodesian people as a whole. The Rhodesian Front refused to accept these principles, which were endorsed by the incoming Labour Government, and on 11 November 1965, after prolonged but futile negotiations, the Southern Rhodesian Prime Minister, Mr Ian Smith, proclaimed a unilateral declaration of independence (U.D.I.) from Britain. The nub of the Rhodesian problem, as far as the British Government was now concerned, was how to bring this rebellion to an end and reassert its authority over the colony.

Mr Wilson was much criticized by the left in Britain and by some of the black African Commonwealth states for refusing to use force against Mr Smith, a refusal which he had indeed stated publicly even before U.D.I. Apart from the logistical problems involved in intervening against a well-equipped Rhodesian army and air force, what prompted the British Prime Minister to abandon what

1. See above, p. 287.

many believe was his only real chance of bringing the rebels to heel? Political considerations were undoubtedly important. According to one of his Cabinet colleagues, 'he had told me how enormously aware he was of the internal domestic problems involved in U.D.I. – particularly the danger of our getting into a state of war with the British white settlers, which would be ruthlessly exploited by Heath'.[1]

There were also the feelings of the armed forces to be taken into account. Without drawing too close a parallel with the famous 'Curragh mutiny' of 1914, when the British army in Ireland let it be known that it would not coerce Ulstermen to submit to the Liberal Government's plans for Home Rule,[2] it is likely that many officers would have resigned their commissions rather than fight against those they regarded as 'kith and kin' in Southern Rhodesia fifty years later. Finally, there was always the possibility of economic crisis looming in the background. Suez had produced a run on the pound in 1956;[3] might not Rhodesia produce an even more disastrous one in 1965?

Instead of using armed force, therefore, the Government chose to fight the Rhodesian rebellion with economic sanctions, a course of action with which the Conservative opposition reluctantly concurred. At the Lagos meeting of Commonwealth Prime Ministers in January 1966, Mr Wilson rashly predicted that these sanctions 'might well bring the rebellion to an end within a matter of weeks rather than months', but it soon became clear that supplies of many products – including the most vital: oil – were still

1. Richard Crossman, *The Diaries of a Cabinet Minister*, vol. 1 (1975), p. 356. A public opinion poll taken immediately after U.D.I. showed only 27 per cent of voters in favour of sending troops to restore lawful government in Southern Rhodesia and 60 per cent against.

2. See above, p. 32.

3. See above, p. 254.

getting through to Rhodesia, due largely to the connivance of the South African and Portuguese Governments, which were both sympathetic to the Smith regime.[1] Against a background of growing tension within the Commonwealth, Britain tried to reach a negotiated settlement with the rebels and an agreement was actually drawn up by Mr Wilson and Mr Smith when they met off Gibraltar in H.M.S. *Tiger* in December 1966. However, as the British Prime Minister explained to his Cabinet,

This isn't like the French surrendering to the Germans at Compiègne [in 1940]. This is a British Government which has failed to achieve its objectives, painfully accepting the best agreed terms they could get for the voluntary winding-up of the rebellion by the rebels themselves . . .[2]

Even so, Mr Smith and his colleagues rejected the agreement.

At Britain's suggestion, the United Nations imposed increasingly comprehensive mandatory sanctions against Rhodesia in 1967 and 1968, but they too remained largely ineffective thanks to the uncooperative attitude of South Africa and Portugal, together with some other powers. The only answer would have been to extend sanctions to these countries in turn, but in the case of South Africa in particular, this would have imposed an intolerable strain upon the British economy and the Government was not prepared to contemplate it. Indeed, rather than antagonize the South Africans, it was prepared to countenance a 'swap' arrangement whereby South African subsidiaries of British oil companies supplied oil to a French company to compensate the latter for fulfilling the subsidiaries' obligations to Rhodesia under South African law without technically

1. At that time Portugal ruled the colony of Mozambique, which bordered on both Rhodesia and South Africa.

2. Richard Crossman, *The Diaries of a Cabinet Minister*, vol. 2 (1976), p. 147.

breaking the sanctions order forbidding British companies to trade with the rebel regime.[1]

Further shipboard talks took place between Mr Wilson and Mr Smith (aboard H.M.S. *Fearless*) in October 1968, but once again the British Government's terms, although even less stringent than those presented two years earlier and bitterly attacked by a sizeable minority within the Labour Party, were spurned by the Rhodesian rebels. Indeed, their response was to enact a new republican constitution in 1969 which was even more restrictive than its predecessor. The Labour Government's policy towards Rhodesia has been summed up in the formula, 'No sell-out; no force; no confrontation with South Africa'. Unfortunately, the first objective seemed increasingly incompatible with the other two.

Forced to withdraw from 'East of Suez' and thwarted by rebellion in Rhodesia, could Britain recover her former self-confidence in closer association with Western Europe? Following President de Gaulle's veto of British entry into the Common Market in January 1963,[2] the European issue had lain relatively dormant. Since the Labour Party had opposed the original negotiations, moreover, it was not expected that the new Government would seek to revive it. Nevertheless, there were supporters of a new initiative in the Labour Party and the Cabinet, and after the 1966 election, they began increasingly to make their influence felt. Once again, it is clear that economic considerations played an important part, many ministers believing that only membership of the E.E.C. could provide the necessary stimulus to Britain's stagnant economy. The decision to re-apply was announced on 2 May 1967.

3. The details of this transaction are set out in the *Report on the Supply of Petroleum and Petroleum Products to Rhodesia* (the so-called 'Bingham Report'), published by the British Government in 1978.

2. See above, p. 272.

There remained a formidable obstacle in the shape of President de Gaulle. Mr Wilson and Mr Brown had endeavoured to overcome his resistance during the course of a tour of Common Market capitals in January 1967, but despite the British Prime Minister's attempt to appeal to the French·President's anti-Americanism by emphasizing the way in which European technological cooperation could prevent undue subservience to the United States, they had failed to make much impression. Indeed, the main difference between the situation in 1963 and 1967 was that, while the General took only one of his magisterial press conferences to veto the British application on the former occasion, he took two the second time around: 16 May and 27 November 1967. It is true that in 1963 he had cited Britain's overseas ties as his justification, whereas he now stressed her parlous economic condition, but the basic reasons for his opposition to British entry into the E.E.C. remained the same: Britain's close ties with the United States and the threat her membership would pose to the existing balance of power within the Community.[1]

In a conversation with the British Ambassador in Paris, Sir Christopher Soames, on 4 February 1969, President de Gaulle seemed to be shifting his ground. He indicated a growing disillusionment with the E.E.C. and wondered whether its enlargement and transformation into a free trade area would be such a bad thing, provided the new entity was genuinely independent of the United States and was run by a four-power directorate, consisting of France, Britain, West Germany and Italy. He proposed secret,

---

1. On this second point, President de Gaulle had told Mr Brown 'about the impossibility of two cocks living in one farmyard with ten hens. He said that he·had had a lot of trouble getting the five hens to do what France wanted, and he wasn't going to have Britain's coming in and creating trouble all over again, this time with ten.' George Brown, *In My Way* (1971), p. 220.

bilateral talks with Britain to explore this possibility further. According to Mr Wilson, he saw nothing new in these ideas, but the Foreign Office suspected some sinister plot on the part of the French to embroil the British in discussions which could then be used as evidence of their lack of commitment to the E.E.C. as it stood, and insisted upon informing France's Common Market partners of what had transpired. The inevitable leak occurred and Anglo-French relations plummeted to new depths of mutual recrimination in the wake of the so-called 'Soames affair'.

Anti-marketeers in the British Government would undoubtedly have preferred to see the Labour Party go into the 1970 election on a platform of opposition to any further attempt to enter the E.E.C., which would not only have set it apart from the Conservatives under the fanatically pro-European Mr Heath, but would also have coincided with the views of a clear majority of the British people at the time. Mr Wilson and most of his senior colleagues, however, remained convinced that Britain's future lay in Europe and were encouraged by the slightly more flexible attitude of President de Gaulle's successor, M. Georges Pompidou, to believe that the French might abandon their opposition. The Common Market was not therefore an issue in the election, although it was to become one soon afterwards.[1]

CRISIS IN ULSTER

As if problems like the economy, Rhodesia and the Common Market were not enough, the Labour Government also faced the re-emergence of the Irish question which had so plagued British politics in the nineteenth and early twentieth centuries.[2] The partition of 1921 had left the population of Northern Ireland, which remained part of the United

1. See below, p. 325.
2. See above, pp. 32, 55, 70–5.

Kingdom, roughly divided into two unequal religious segments: two-thirds Protestant and one-third Roman Catholic. The former regarded the latter as potentially if not actually subversive, owing its real allegiance to the Republican Government in Dublin, and making use of the extensive devolved powers conferred upon the parliament of Northern Ireland by the 1920 Government of Ireland Act, it established a one-party statelet which deliberately excluded the minority from effective participation in public affairs and subjected it to various forms of discrimination, notably in housing and employment.[1] Successive British Governments, understanding little of Irish politics and caring only for a quiet life, were prepared to tolerate this state of affairs. Although Northern Ireland sent twelve M.P.s to Westminster, all discussion of the province's affairs was discouraged, while the Home Office, which was the Government department charged with the oversight of these matters, did not have a single full-time civil servant concerned with them until 1968.

Given the repressive nature of the regime in Northern Ireland, an explosion would almost certainly have occurred sooner or later. Two factors probably accounted for its taking place in the late 1960s. The first was the cautious reformism of the province's Prime Minister since 1963, Captain Terence O'Neill. As de Tocqueville pointed out more than a century ago, the most dangerous moment for an oppressive government comes when it tries to reform itself, for grievances hitherto patiently endured suddenly become intolerable when there is a prospect of their being removed. O'Neill's attempts to integrate the Catholics

1. Not surprisingly, many Catholics did support reunification with the South, but it is worth noting that, according to a public opinion poll taken in 1968, no less than 33 per cent supported the existing constitution (i.e. partition) and only 13 per cent approved 'any measures' to end it. The latter were the hard-core Republicans.

into Northern Ireland's political life did not go far enough to satisfy them, but were more than sufficient to produce a dangerous backlash among the more extreme members of his own party, who accused him of selling out to Republicanism and Popery. The second factor was the growth throughout the western world in the 1960s of a new style of radical politics. The civil rights movement in the southern states of the U.S.A. and the revolutionary students of Berkeley, Berlin and Paris had their counterparts in Northern Ireland in the Civil Rights Association and the People's Democracy. In late 1968 and early 1969 the agitation of these groups for a more equitable distribution of political power and an end to discrimination against Catholics was relayed to the rest of the United Kingdom – and indeed the world – by television, as was the often violent response of the province's overwhelmingly Protestant police force.

'Any liberal-minded person,' Captain O'Neill subsequently wrote, 'must admit that the Civil Rights movement brought about reforms which would otherwise have taken years to wring from a reluctant Government.'[1] It was helped, too, by pressure from an aroused British Government, and in November 1968 Captain O'Neill announced a package of reforms, including changes in the system of allocating council houses, the appointment of an Ombudsman to investigate complaints against the provincial Government, and the reform of the local government franchise. These policies met with considerable opposition from powerful elements within the ruling Unionist Party. Hemmed in between them on the one hand and the civil rights demonstrators on the other, Captain O'Neill sought to achieve greater room for manoeuvre by calling an election in February 1969, but he failed to win sufficient support for his moderate approach and in April was forced to resign.

1. *The Autobiography of Terence O'Neill* (1972), p. 111.

In August 1969 communal violence between Protestants and Catholics erupted in Northern Ireland's two largest cities, Londonderry and Belfast. It soon reached such a pitch that the police, who were in any case regarded by the Catholics as a hostile force, were quite unable to control it, and Captain O'Neill's successor, Major James Chichester-Clark, appealed to the British Government for troops. The request, which had been anticipated, was granted and British troops moved on to the streets of Londonderry on 14 August and on to those of Belfast on the following day. They were welcomed by the Catholic community, which saw itself in imminent danger of being overwhelmed by Protestant mobs, an attitude which was understandable when one recalls that 8 out of the 10 fatal casualties in the rioting were Catholic and that 83·5 per cent of the houses damaged or destroyed were occupied by Catholics. There was no opposition to the decision to send in the troops, but by doing so the British Government had put itself in an extremely exposed position. As a Cabinet minister recorded,

Callaghan and Healey[1] both reminded us that our whole interest was to work through the Protestant Government. The Protestants are the majority and we can't afford to alienate them as well as the Catholics and find ourselves ruling Northern Ireland directly as a colony. We have also to be on the side of the Catholic minority and try to help and protect them against their persecutors.[2]

Subsequent events were to show that it was difficult, if not impossible, to reconcile these two objectives.

1. The Home Secretary and the Secretary of State for Defence were the two ministers most closely involved apart from the Prime Minister himself.
2. Richard Crossman, *The Diaries of a Cabinet Minister*, vol. 3 (1977), p. 622.

CHAPTER TWELVE

To the Brink and Back?
(1970–79)

SUPERFICIALLY, 1970–79 was a decade of considerable political change. There were four general elections, three changes of Government and four different Prime Ministers. For much of the last five years, moreover, the Government was in a minority in the House of Commons and had to rely upon the support or abstention of minor parties whose growth seemed to herald the approaching end of a two-party system which had dominated British political life for at least forty years. Beneath it all, however, there was an underlying unity, for the problems with which these Governments, Prime Ministers and parties wrestled were depressingly constant: inflation and unemployment, trade-union power, relations with the Common Market, Rhodesia and the unity of the United Kingdom. Despite much proclaimed disagreement, moreover, successive Governments often ended up pursuing depressingly similar policies towards these problems. Finally, it could hardly be said with any confidence that most of these problems were nearer a solution at the end of the decade than they had been at the beginning. Between them they had taken Britain to the brink of disaster and could easily do so again.

THE CONSERVATIVE GOVERNMENT, 1970–74

Mr Heath's senior Cabinet colleagues in June 1970 formed a strong and experienced team: Sir Alec Douglas-Home as Foreign Secretary, Mr Iain Macleod as Chancellor of the

Exchequer, and Mr Reginald Maudling as Home Secretary. It was a misfortune that this team did not survive intact throughout the Government's term. Mr Macleod died suddenly on 20 July 1970, barely a month after taking office, and Mr Maudling felt compelled to resign two years later because of past business associations with an architect charged with corruption. The commonsense and moderation of both men were missed, but the loss of Mr Macleod was felt particularly acutely, not only because it occurred so soon, but also because his successor, Mr Anthony Barber, never acquired the same authority.

The new Government's strategy, we are told, 'was no less than an attempt to change the whole attitude of mind of the British people: to create a more dynamic, thrusting, "go-getting" economy on the American or German model ...'[1] Its most immediate problems, however, were unemployment – a legacy of its predecessor's deflationary policies – and inflation, which was partly the result of the wages explosion that followed the end of incomes policy in 1969. Unemployment rose steadily throughout 1970 and 1971, reaching what was then a post-war peak of 967,000 in the first quarter of 1972. This led the Government to reverse one of the main components of its economic policy: the reduction of public expenditure. The financial rescue operations mounted in early 1971 to save the bankrupt firms of Upper Clyde Shipbuilders and Rolls-Royce, both examples of the kind of 'lame duck' which Government spokesmen had earlier stated would be allowed to go to the wall, showed which way the wind was blowing, and in the second half of the year a more systematic and widespread retreat from the Government's commitment to cut its own spending began. Indeed, public expenditure actually

1. Brendon Sewill, 'In Place of Strikes', in *British Economic Policy 1970–74: Two Views* (1975), p. 30. Mr Sewill was Special Assistant to Mr Barber.

increased by more than 8 per cent in real terms between 1970 and 1972, and while this certainly helped to reduce the level of unemployment, the fact that it was not offset by any general increase in taxation[1] led to a huge increase in Government borrowing, thereby adding fuel to the fires of inflation.

These were already burning brightly as a result of the Government's failure to control wages. Having abolished the Prices and Incomes Board as a superfluous example of Socialist bureaucracy, it sought to limit wage increases by means of a gradual reduction in the level of pay settlements in the public sector where it was the employer. Such a discriminatory policy was bound to antagonize the public sector trade unions and in January and February 1972 one of the most powerful of the latter, the National Union of Mineworkers (N.U.M.), smashed its way through the Government's guidelines with its first official national strike since 1926, securing an average wage increase for its members of 30 per cent as opposed to the Coal Board's original offer of $7\frac{1}{2}$ per cent. The miners' strike of 1972, with its aggressive picketing of power stations, brought the question of trade union power to the forefront of post-war British politics by demonstrating the ability of a strong and determined group of workers to bring the country to a halt. As one senior adviser to the Government wrote later,

At the time many of those in positions of influence looked into the abyss and saw only a few days away the possibility of the country being plunged into a state of chaos not so very far removed from that which might prevail after a minor nuclear attack. If that sounds melodramatic I need only say that – with the prospect of the breakdown of power supplies, sewerage, communications, effective government and law and order – it was the analogy that was being used at the time.[2]

1. Taxation was in fact reduced to provide further incentives for expansion.
2. Brendon Sewill, op. cit., p. 50,

Trade union power was also the issue in the conflict over the Government's legislation on industrial relations. Contemptuous of what they saw as the Labour Government's surrender to trade union pressure in 1969,[1] the Conservatives had promised that they would not be deterred from reforming the unions if they were returned to power. The main feature of their Industrial Relations Bill, which went far beyond that abandoned by the Labour Government, was to make collective agreements between employers and unions legally enforceable unless both parties agreed otherwise. A new hierarchy of courts, headed by a National Industrial Relations Court (N.I.R.C.), was set up to adjudicate upon disputes arising under the new law. The N.I.R.C. also had the power to order, at the request of the Government minister responsible, a 'cooling-off' period and/or a compulsory ballot of all union members before a strike.

As if to purge its soul of the last traces of its own flirtation with statutory reform of the trade unions, the Labour Party fought the Government's proposals tooth and nail in Parliament, but the most effective opposition came from the trade unions themselves after the Bill had finally become law in August 1971. They simply boycotted the machinery set up by the Act and unions which registered under it were expelled from the T.U.C. The flashpoint came in July 1972 when the N.I.R.C. committed five dockers' shop-stewards to prison for refusing to obey one of its injunctions. Against a background of widespread industrial action in support of the stewards and a threatened one-day general strike called by the T.U.C., the House of Lords set aside the N.I.R.C.'s judgment and a potentially explosive situation was avoided. This episode, however, dealt the Industrial Relations Act a blow from which it never recovered, especially since its

1. See above, p. 301.

provisions for a 'cooling-off' period and a strike ballot had already failed to prevent a rail strike earlier in the year. Far from improving industrial relations, the new Act had only succeeded in making them worse, a point which was conceded by the Chairman of the C.B.I. in 1974.

Faced with the collapse of his Government's industrial relations policy and with inflation still rising, Mr Heath turned to the path of conciliation. In tripartite talks with the T.U.C. and the C.B.I. he tried to hammer out a voluntary agreement to restrain wages and prices, but the unions were now so mistrustful of the Government that the negotiations broke down on 2 November 1972. Four days later the Government carried out another spectacular reversal of its previous policies and announced the statutory control of wages and prices. While the first two stages of this policy – which ran from November 1972 to October 1973 – were reasonably successful, the third – and with it the Government itself – was destroyed by two factors: the phenomenal rise in world commodity prices which took place in 1973, and trade union action, spearheaded once more by the N.U.M.

Even before the rise in oil prices which followed the Yom Kippur War between the Arab states and Israel in October 1973, commodity price rises had added £2,000 million to Britain's import bill and the balance of payments, which had been healthily in the black since the Labour Government had achieved a surplus in 1969, was plunging back into the red. Fearful of jeopardizing its policy of expansion by imposing tax increases or public expenditure cuts, the Government pinned its hopes on the expectation that commodity prices would level off and that the decision in July 1972 to float the pound instead of trying to maintain a fixed parity would restrain imports and encourage exports. When the Yom Kippur War led to the quadrupling of oil prices, however, it became clear that the balance of payments could only get worse. The Government promptly slammed on the brakes: on 17 December 1973 Mr Barber announced cuts in public expenditure totalling £1,200 million, a surtax surcharge and tighter credit and hire purchase restrictions.

In the meantime the rise in commodity prices as reflected in the cost of food was making the trade unions increasingly restive about the third phase of the incomes policy. The oil price rise, moreover, put the miners, as suppliers of the country's principal indigenous fuel, in a very strong bargaining position. After the trauma of 1972 the Government had no wish for a second confrontation with the N.U.M. and sought to buy it off in advance with a special provision in the third phase of the incomes policy for additional payments for working 'unsocial hours'. This concession did not satisfy the miners, however, and they began an overtime ban on 12 November 1973. Power engineers and train drivers also began industrial action in support of their pay claims, and on 13 December Mr Heath announced that industry would have to go over to a three-day week in the New Year to conserve the nation's dwindling energy supplies. As the crisis loomed, the 'Doomsday' atmosphere of 1972 reappeared. 'I said to my wife and children,' one Cabinet minister subsequently recalled, 'that we should have a nice time, because I deeply believed then that it was the last Christmas of its kind that we would enjoy.'[1]

After further unsuccessful negotiations the N.U.M. decided on 5 February 1974 in favour of an all-out strike beginning five days later. Faced with a seemingly insoluble deadlock, a reluctant Mr Heath finally gave in to the

1. Stephen Fay and Hugo Young, *The Fall of Heath* (1976), p. 6. Intemperate statements by some miners' leaders which suggested that their main aim was not industrial, but political – i.e. to bring down the Government – further inflamed an already tense situation.

mounting pressure from colleagues and supporters in the country that it was time to seek a popular mandate to take on the unions. On 7 February he called a general election for the 28th.

It is often said that the British people voted in February 1974 for a quiet life. If this means that they voted for a Labour Government which would give the miners what they wanted and so end the three-day week, it is a very misleading statement. Although the Labour Party was returned as the largest single party in the new House of Commons, its share of the vote was lower than at any election since the debacle of 1931. With the Liberals receiving almost a fifth of the vote – but thanks to the electoral system only one forty-fifth of the seats – and the Nationalist surge in Scotland,[1] the result was more a condemnation of both the major parties than an endorsement of either. Indeed, so convinced was Mr Heath that Labour had not won the election that he attempted to do a deal with the Liberals which would enable him to remain in power. The Liberals would not oblige, however, and so Mr Harold Wilson returned to No. 10 Downing Street as leader of Britain's first minority Government since Ramsay Macdonald in 1929.

Like the Labour Government of 1964–70, the Conservative Government of 1970–74 had failed in its central aim of breaking away from Britain's dismal record of economic stagnation. Indeed, its failure was even more spectacular, culminating as it did in the most bitter class conflict the country had witnessed since the General Strike of 1926. To some extent Mr Heath and his colleagues were unlucky. The increase in world commodity prices was beyond their control, and events in Ulster distracted their attention from developments nearer home during the early stages of both confrontations with the miners in 1972

1. See below, p. 347.

and 1973.[1] Much of the blame for what happened, however, must rest squarely upon their shoulders. As the Prime Minister's Political Secretary at the time has recognized:

> The single-minded pursuit of growth involved acquiescence in the growth of the money supply during 1972 and part of 1973 beyond the limits of likely production. This made it more difficult to cope with the explosion of world prices, and more difficult to restrain wage settlements through incomes policy . . .[2]

Equally if not more important, perhaps, was the Government's style. Another senior political adviser has written that its members

> shared an impatience with the political compromises and shilly-shallying which were thought to have characterized the previous decade. There was a desire to take whatever decisive action was necessary – regardless of short-run political considerations – in order to drag the nation squealing and kicking into the new age. If it had succeeded, this approach would have been widely commended. In the event, however, an abrasive image was projected and antagonisms built up, so that in the end when an appeal had to be made to the people the necessary public support was not forthcoming.[3]

In foreign policy, the Conservative Government of 1970-74 experienced one conspicuous failure and achieved one notable success. The failure was in Rhodesia. Although it was Sir Alec Douglas-Home's Government of 1963-4 which had originally laid down the famous 'five principles' for the settlement of the Rhodesian problem,[4] there was much more sympathy for Mr Ian Smith and the Rhodesian whites within the ranks of the Conservative Party than within those of Labour, and accordingly that much more pressure

---

1. See below, pp. 328-30.
2. Douglas Hurd, *An End to Promises* (1979), p. 141.
3. Brendon Sewill, op. cit., pp. 31-2.
4. See above, p. 306.

upon Mr Heath to concede recognition of the rebel regime's independence. The new Government lost no time in putting out feelers to Salisbury, but serious negotiations were delayed until the Commonwealth Prime Ministers had given their approval at their conference in Singapore in January 1971. After some months of preliminary discussions, the Foreign Secretary, Sir Alec Douglas-Home, told the House of Commons on 9 November 1971 that he would shortly be flying to Salisbury for direct negotiations with Mr Smith. These took place between 15 and 24 November and ended in an agreement which Sir Alec described as 'fair and honourable'.

What seemed 'fair and honourable' to a white minority determined to cling on to its power and privileges and to a British Government desperately anxious to rid itself of what it regarded as an albatross around its neck did not, however, necessarily appear in the same light to the blacks who constituted the vast majority of Rhodesia's population. The basic flaw in the agreement from their point of view, and from that of critics outside the country, was that while it provided in theory for a gradual widening of the franchise leading to eventual majority rule, the structure of Rhodesian society, reinforced by the policies of the Smith regime, made it extremely unlikely in practice that most blacks would qualify for many years, if at all.

Since the Commonwealth Prime Ministers had only agreed to a further attempt at a negotiated settlement on condition that the terms were acceptable to the Rhodesian people as a whole, the British Government sent a special commission headed by an Appeal Court Judge, Lord Pearce, to Rhodesia in January 1972 in order to determine its acceptability. In its report, published on 23 May, the Pearce Commission stated unequivocally:

We are satisfied on our evidence that the proposals are acceptable to the great majority of Europeans. We are equally satisfied, after considering all our evidence including that on intimidation,[1] that the majority of Africans rejected the proposals. In our opinion the people of Rhodesia as a whole do not regard the proposals as acceptable as a basis for independence.[2]

The Government had no alternative but to admit defeat. Sanctions continued, of course, but since they also continued to be ignored by Portugal and South Africa among others, the Rhodesian regime found them no more irksome than before. It was to be a change in the circumstances of Rhodesia's allies, and not any action by the British Government, which was to bring about the next move in the seemingly endless search for a settlement.

The success of the Conservative Government's foreign policy, and no doubt the achievement for which Mr Heath would most like to be remembered, was Britain's entry into the E.E.C. Before the Labour Government's defeat in June 1970, Britain and the Common Market countries had agreed to reopen negotiations for British membership of the Community in Luxembourg at the end of that month. The new Conservative Government, under the leadership of one of the most fervent 'Europeans' in British politics, could scarcely display less enthusiasm than its predecessor and the negotiations duly began at the appointed place and time. The key to their success, however, lay not in Luxembourg, but in Paris. Not until Mr Heath paid a personal visit to President Pompidou in May 1971, when he apparently succeeded in convincing the French leader that Britain was indeed prepared to accept the obligations as well as the privileges of Community membership, was it clear that there would be no third veto. On 7 July the Government published a White Paper outlining the terms of entry and on the

1. Mr Smith and his supporters consistently maintained that the mass of Africans would have accepted the terms of the settlement but for intimidation by extremist elements.

2. Cmnd. 4964, p. 112.

following day the Prime Minister told the nation in a broadcast statement: 'For twenty-five years we have been looking for something to get us going again. Now here it is.'

To the consternation of British 'Europeans', however, the Labour Party now seemed to be turning its back upon the E.E.C. When in opposition, the party often moves to the left, and the Labour Left had always regarded the Common Market with suspicion as a capitalist and conservative bloc. Mr Wilson's principal objective was, as always, to maintain party unity. He therefore sought to appease the Left – and, incidentally, to make a great deal of political capital – by violently attacking the entry terms which the Conservatives had negotiated,[1] while at the same time carefully refraining from committing either himself or the party to opposition to entry at any price. In the long run his tactic worked, although it did little to enhance his reputation as a man of integrity. In the short run, however, even party unity came under strain when 69 Labour 'Europeans' voted in support of the Government's policy on 28 October 1971 in defiance of a three-line whip,[2] and when the leader of those 'Europeans', Mr Roy Jenkins, resigned from the deputy leadership of the party in April 1972.

After a long parliamentary struggle, during which most of the Labour rebels returned to the fold and the Government had to impose the guillotine, the legislation enabling Britain to join the E.E.C. was finally enacted, and on New Year's Day 1973, almost ten years after General de Gaulle's first veto, she finally became a member. The battle was,

1. This was in spite of statements by former Labour ministers responsible for E.E.C. matters to the effect that they would gladly have accepted such terms.

2. Indeed, it was their support which enabled the Government's motion to be carried against the opposition of 39 of its own M.P.s. The Government deliberately allowed a free vote on the Conservative side in the hope of encouraging the Labour rebels to defy their own whips and the gamble paid off.

however, not yet over, for the Labour Party was now pledged to re-negotiate the terms of entry if it were returned to power and to consult the British people on the results of the re-negotiation, either by means of an election or by a strangely Gaullist device, a referendum. In the meantime, the Labour Party and its allies in the trade union movement deliberately boycotted such Community institutions as the European Parliament and the Economic and Social Committee.

Constitutionally speaking, Northern Ireland is part of the United Kingdom and not a foreign country – that, indeed, lies at the root of its problems – but the events which took place in the province between 1970 and 1974 seemed so alien to most British eyes that it is perhaps fitting that they should be dealt with after a discussion of the Conservative Government's foreign policy. The key event in Northern Ireland in 1970 was the breakdown of the initially good relationship between the Catholic minority and the British army. It is true that there had always been Catholics who detested the British and wanted them out of Ireland altogether, and that some of these hard-core Republicans had formed a new para-military organization known as the Provisional I.R.A.[1] at the end of 1969, which was dedicated to armed struggle against the British 'army of occupation'. To begin with, however, they did not enjoy the support or even acquiescence of the vast majority of Ulster's Catholic population. What changed the picture was the way in which the army gradually came to be seen by the latter, not as an impartial guarantor of order, but as

1. The original Irish Republican Army (I.R.A.) of the early 1920s (see above, pp. 71–4) was still in existence, but in the 1960s it seemed to have abandoned some of its former militant nationalism in exchange for a brand of Marxist ideology which put more emphasis on political than military struggle. This upset the more traditionally-minded Republicans, who broke away to form the Provisional I.R.A. – 'Provisional' because they hoped the split would not be final.

an instrument of the Protestant Unionist Party provincial Government which had been oppressing them for the past fifty years. A particularly ruthless swoop in search of arms into the Catholic Lower Falls district of Belfast at the beginning of July 1970 seems to have marked a turning-point in relations between the army and the Catholics. As the chief-of-staff of the Provisional I.R.A. subsequently commented, the incident 'was to provide endless water for the Republican guerrilla fish to swim in'.[1]

It also gave a boost to their recruitment so that by the beginning of 1971 the Provisionals were ready to go over to the offensive. On 6 February the first British soldier was killed on active service in Ireland since the troubles of the early 1920s. Major Chichester-Clark, the Prime Minister of Northern Ireland, resigned in March when London refused to send him the additional troops he wanted. His successor, Mr Brian Faulkner, had the reputation of being a hard-liner and it was he who introduced the policy of internment without trial in an attempt to stem the rising tide of bombings and shootings in the province. Mr Maudling, who was the British Cabinet minister responsible for Northern Ireland, advised him to intern some Protestant extremists as well in order to preserve at least a pretence of impartiality, but all 342 persons arrested by the security forces on 9 August were Catholics. According to the Provisionals' chief-of-staff, moreover, fewer than 60 of them had any connection with his organization. This, coupled with the fact that many of the detainees were subjected to particularly unpleasant methods of interrogation by the army, only succeeded in hardening Catholic opinion still further, thereby adding yet more grist to the Provisionals' bloody mill. In the four months preceding internment, 8 people were killed in Northern Ireland; in the four months after it, the total reached 84.

1. Sean MacStiofain, *Memoirs of a Revolutionary* (1975), p. 157.

On 30 January 1972 paratroopers in Londonderry shot and killed 13 people in disturbances following a banned Catholic demonstration in the city. The soldiers said that they had been fired upon, but while a subsequent Government inquiry supported this assertion, it was unable to show that any of those killed had been involved in the shooting.[1] The events of 'Bloody Sunday', as it was called, led to much international criticism of the British role in Ulster, and in Dublin, where politicians and people had hitherto regarded events in the north with concern rather than hysteria, an angry mob burned down the British embassy. The Conservative Government had already been reconsidering its Northern Ireland policy, particularly the unsatisfactory way in which the province's government was responsible for security measures while the British army had increasingly to carry them out, and 'Bloody Sunday' simply hastened the process. On 22 March 1972 Mr Heath put a package of proposals to Mr Faulkner, including the transfer of all security powers to Westminster. The Northern Ireland Prime Minister and his colleagues would not accept this curtailment of their powers and resigned, whereupon the British Government introduced direct rule from London under a specially appointed Cabinet minister, Mr William Whitelaw.

Direct rule came as a tremendous shock to Ulster's Protestants, who had enjoyed their privileged system of devolved government for half a century. Their angry reaction was compounded when Mr Whitelaw agreed first to a truce and then to negotiations with the Provisional I.R.A. in June 1972, even though both truce and negotiations soon collapsed. Hitherto most of the violence had come from the Provisionals, but 1972 witnessed the emergence of what became known as the 'Protestant backlash'. Its most

1. The families of all the victims later received financial compensation from the British Government.

sinister feature was the formation of assassination squads which killed members of the Catholic community. All told there were 467 violent deaths in Ulster in 1972, victims of the army, the Provisionals and the Protestants. This figure is all the more terrible when the relatively small size of Northern Ireland's population is taken into account, for the proportional number on the mainland of Great Britain would have been 16,345.

It was never intended that direct rule should be permanent, but merely that it should provide a breathing-space during which a lasting solution to Northern Ireland's problems could be devised. In 1973 the Government passed legislation which provided, among other things, for a new Northern Ireland legislature – elected by proportional representation in order to give more seats to the Catholics – and a new executive authority which would have to be acceptable to the latter. Elections to the new assembly took place in June 1973 and revealed a widening split between those Unionists, led by a chastened Mr Faulkner, who were prepared to give the new arrangements a chance and the diehards, who saw them as a sell-out to the Catholics and the Provisional I.R.A. Under Mr Whitelaw's aegis, Mr Faulkner's group entered into negotiations with the predominantly Catholic Social Democratic and Labour Party (S.D.L.P.) and the small, non-sectarian Alliance Party with a view to the formation of a power-sharing Executive. Agreement was reached in November and the new Executive, comprising 7 pro-Faulkner Unionists, 6 S.D.L.P. and 2 members of the Alliance Party, was sworn in on New Year's Day 1974. The previous month another important meeting had taken place at Sunningdale between representatives of the British Government, the Irish Government and the parties which were to form the Executive in order to draw up what was described as 'the Irish dimension' to the new settlement. The most significant points of their agreement were the establishment of an advisory Council of Ireland, comprising representatives of the Irish Republic and the Northern Ireland Executive, and a declaration by the Irish Government that the status of Northern Ireland could not be changed without the consent of a majority of its inhabitants.[1]

The formation of the Executive, the Sunningdale Agreement and the fact that the number of violent deaths in Northern Ireland fell by almost half in 1973, all seemed to offer a genuine prospect of hope to the strife-torn province. In reality, however, it was a mirage. The men of violence on both sides of the sectarian barrier had not only played no part in the negotiation of the settlement, but were bitterly opposed to it. The Northern Ireland results in the general election of February 1974 were also a bad omen: of Ulster's 12 M.P.s, no less than 11 had fought their campaign on the basis of opposition to Sunningdale and power-sharing. Within a few months the new edifice so proudly constructed by the Conservatives in Northern Ireland turned out to be a house of cards.

THE LABOUR GOVERNMENT, 1974-9

Mr Harold Wilson's Government of February 1974 contained some familiar faces: Mr Callaghan as Foreign Secretary, Mr Healey as Chancellor of the Exchequer, and Mr Jenkins, his quarrel with his party over Europe notwithstanding, as Home Secretary. The most interesting appointment, however, was that of Mr Michael Foot as Secretary of State for Employment. An admirer and biographer of the late Aneurin Bevan, Mr Foot was one of the standard-bearers of the Left in the Labour Party and had refused an offer from Mr Wilson to serve in his previous

1. This was an important point, for clauses in the constitution of the Irish Republic claimed jurisdiction over the whole of Ireland.

administration. His acceptance now was widely interpreted as proof of the party's shift to the Left during 1970–74, as was the fact that he ran a very close second to Mr Callaghan for the party leadership, and therefore for the post of Prime Minister, after Mr Wilson retired in March 1976. But Mr Foot, together with another prominent left-winger, Mr Tony Benn, remained a loyal member of a Government which was to introduce right-wing policies of financial retrenchment on a scale unparalleled since the 1930s.

The Government's electoral base was, as we have seen,[1] not very strong. Even though a second general election on 10 October 1974 gave it an overall majority, it was an extremely exiguous one of only three seats which eventually disappeared after a series of by-election defeats. Nevertheless, it succeeded in remaining in power until May 1979, partly because of a formal arrangement with the Liberals (the so-called 'Lib-Lab Pact'), which lasted from March 1977 until the end of the 1978 parliamentary session, and partly because the Nationalists (Scottish and Welsh) had no wish to see the Government fall before it had enacted the devolution measures which it had promised.[2] At the same time, the Government could not afford gratuitously to offend the minor parties which could, at any moment, combine with the Conservatives to overthrow it. For two-and-a-half years, therefore, the Mother of Parliaments experienced an almost continental European style of coalition politics.

In 1974 the Labour Government pinned its hopes for a solution of the country's economic problems upon its 'Social Contract' with the trade unions. Determined to avoid another rift between the political and industrial wings of the Labour movement of the kind which had occurred in

1. See above, p. 321.
2. See below, p. 347.

1969,[1] the Labour Party and the T.U.C. decided in the autumn of 1971 to set up a Liaison Committee which worked out many of the policies which were to form the basis of the 'Social Contract'. Broadly speaking, the T.U.C. pledged its cooperation in promoting productivity and restraining wage demands in return for Government action to repeal the Conservatives' industrial relations legislation and to abolish the statutory control of wages while retaining and strengthening that of prices. In addition, the Labour Party and the T.U.C. agreed on the need for higher pensions, a redistribution of wealth and a number of other Socialist economic and social measures. The 'Social Contract' did indeed provide the inspiration for much of the Labour Party's action when it returned to power. Pensions were increased and there were changes in income tax to benefit the lower-paid and shift more of the burden on to the better-off. The Prices Act of July 1974 abolished the Conservative Government's Pay Board, but strengthened the powers of its Price Commission and provided for food subsidies. The Trade Union and Labour Relations Act of the same month repealed virtually all of the Industrial Relations Act of 1971. After securing an overall majority in October 1974, the Government went even further: the Employment Protection Act of 1975 and the Trade Union and Labour Relations (Amendment) Act of 1976 gave workers much greater protection against dismissal, together with higher redundancy payments, and their unions more legal immunities, new access to company information relevant to wage bargaining, and improved arbitration machinery in the shape of the Advisory, Conciliation and Arbitration Service (A.C.A.S.).

Whether this legislation tilted the balance of power in favour of the unions to the extent claimed by the Con-

1. See above, pp. 300-301.

servatives and much of the press is a moot point. It is perhaps significant in this connection that, at local level, a
stubborn employer like Mr George Ward of the Grunwick
film processing firm could successfully defy considerable
Government and union pressure simply to recognize a trade
union in his factory, while at national level the T.U.C. was
totally unable to bring the Government to accept its
economic strategy after the financial crisis of 1976. Whatever the truth of this particular contention, there is no
doubt that the 'Social Contract' failed to halt the country's
slide towards the economic abyss. This was not entirely the
fault of the Government and the T.U.C., for the whole of
the western world was now in the grip of the worst economic
depression since the slump of the 1930s. Moreover, Britain's
inflation rate in 1974 – 16·1 per cent – was due less to wage
increases than to the rise in commodity prices and the
Conservative Government's reckless expansion of the money
supply. Nevertheless, short of the complete socialization of
Britain's economy, wages would have to be brought under
control and public expenditure curbed if inflation was not
to get any worse. This was not only because of the direct
effect of wage increases and public spending upon price
levels, but also because the financial community at home
and abroad, seeing that wages were running ahead of both
prices and productivity and that Government borrowing
was expanding rapidly, took the view that the country
was 'living beyond its means', a view which was translated
into a fall in the value of the 'floating' pound, a corresponding increase in the cost of Britain's imports and a further
twist to the inflationary spiral. Despite the 'Social Contract',
the T.U.C. proved quite powerless to prevent individual
unions from demanding, and in many cases obtaining, very
large wage increases which not only compensated their
members for the rise in the cost of living since the last
increase, but anticipated further price rises in advance of the

next. In 1974 the general index of earnings rose by 17·8 per cent, and in 1975 by 26·5 per cent.

It was a trade union leader, Mr Jack Jones, the General Secretary of the powerful Transport and General Workers' Union, who eventually rescued the Government and the T.U.C. from the hook upon which they had impaled themselves by refusing to contemplate a statutory incomes policy. He suggested a voluntary agreement by the T.U.C. in favour of a flat-rate increase for all workers, and in July 1975 this emerged as a Government proposal for a maximum increase of £6 a week for those earning less than £8,500 a year and nothing for those above. This 'rough justice' commended itself to nearly everyone except the Labour Left, although the unions were able in the event to ensure that the £6 was a universal entitlement and not a maximum. This new agreement between the Government and the T.U.C. came none too soon, for the inflation rate in 1975 reached the record level of 24·2 per cent and prophets of doom were grimly recalling the fate of the Weimar Republic in Germany where inflation, albeit on a much greater scale, had eroded the foundations of democracy and paved the way for Hitler. The £6 limit, followed by the second phase of the voluntary incomes policy announced in June 1976 and which provided for a 4 per cent increase in wages in 1976–7, undoubtedly helped to bring the rate of inflation down to 16·5 per cent in 1976 and 15·8 per cent in 1977, but this was only achieved at the cost of a real cut in the average worker's standard of living and a reduction in the differentials paid to the skilled. Like the Conservatives in 1972, however, the Government had come round to the view that some form of incomes policy was essential if inflation were to be brought under control.

It had also decided that public expenditure must be reduced. Many of the Conservative cuts of December 1973 had not been implemented and the so-called Public Sector

Borrowing Requirement (P.S.B.R.) rose to £10½ billion in 1975, an increase of 75 per cent in real terms in two years. Some spending cuts were announced in April 1975 and July 1976, but these were not enough to satisfy the Government's critics at home and abroad. A massive assault on the pound during the first ten months of 1976, which sent its value plummeting from just over $2 in January to less than $1.60 in October, forced the Government to go to the International Monetary Fund for help, but this was only forthcoming at the cost of the most stringent economies any Government had had to make since the war. The pound steadied thereafter and even strengthened in the first half of 1979, but the near collapse of sterling in 1976 was the main reason why Britain's inflation rate in 1977 remained higher than that of any of her principal competitors apart from Italy. The expenditure cuts also helped to perpetuate and indeed aggravate the unemployment caused by the slump. Peaking at 1·6 million in the third quarter of 1977, the number of people out of work remained stubbornly at around 1·4 million into 1979. While this level of unemployment was not as bad as that which had prevailed at the nadir of the pre-war depression, there had been nothing remotely approaching it since 1945.

The continuing high level of inflation meant that the trade unions were unwilling to endorse a third year of pay restraint in 1977. Nevertheless, the Government fixed a target increase for wages of 10 per cent and by standing firm in the public sector – which involved breaking a long strike by firemen – and by imposing sanctions upon private firms which ignored the guidelines, it managed to ensure that most settlements were within or close to the prescribed limit. At 8·2 per cent, inflation in 1978 was below double figures for the first time since 1973. When it came to the 1978–9 pay round, however, the Government made a disastrous error of judgement in fixing the target rate of wage increases at only 5 per cent, which was below the forecast rate of inflation. The policy was rejected by both the T.U.C. and Labour Party conferences and the trade unions were determined to destroy it.

Car workers at Ford's were the first major group to breach the guideline in November 1978 after a long and costly strike. Following its previous policy, the Government moved to impose sanctions upon their employer, but the Conservatives, taking advantage of the more fluid parliamentary situation following the end of the 'Lib-Lab Pact', challenged the constitutionality of sanctions and the Government was defeated in the House of Commons on 13 December. There was a piquant irony in the reversal of roles since 1973-4: then it had been the Conservatives struggling to sustain an incomes policy and the Labour Party extolling the virtues of free collective bargaining. The removal of the sanctions weapon from the Government's hands effectively killed the 5 per cent policy. There followed what commentators called a 'winter of discontent' as lorry drivers, sewage workers, grave-diggers, ambulance men and hospital workers among others engaged in various forms of industrial action to press home their pay claims, causing widespread dislocation and inconvenience.

When the general election took place on 3 May 1979,[1] therefore, the Labour Government not only had to answer the charge that it had presided over a doubling of prices and a tripling of unemployment, but also that its much-vaunted 'special relationship' with the trade unions, which was supposed to prevent the kind of industrial unrest which had occurred under the Heath Government, was a hollow sham. In the circumstances, it was hardly surprising that Labour lost, and even though the opinion polls consistently showed that the country preferred the reassuring and non-

1. For the circumstances in which the election came about, see below, pp. 349-50.

ideological figure of Mr Callaghan to the somewhat intimidating and dogmatic Mrs Margaret Thatcher, who had ousted Mr Heath from the Conservative leadership in February 1975, it was Mrs Thatcher who went to No. 10 Downing Street as Britain's, and indeed western Europe's, first woman Prime Minister. Thanks largely to the continued buoyancy of the Liberal vote, the Conservatives did not win as large a share of the poll as they had done in 1970, but they had a much larger majority in terms of seats (43), thus bringing the period of parliamentary uncertainty to an end. The Labour Party fared even worse than it had done in February 1974.[1]

The election campaign, however, was more reminiscent of 1970 than 1974. Once again the Labour Party presented itself as the 'responsible' party of government which had not been afraid to take tough, unpopular measures to put the economy to rights, although unkind critics would point out that, far from fulfilling its 1974 pledge 'to bring about a fundamental and irreversible shift in the balance of power and wealth in favour of working people and their families', its policies had actually resulted in a move in the opposite direction. Once again, too, the Conservatives attacked the Government's record on inflation, called for public expenditure cuts and advocated reductions in direct taxation in order to provide incentives. After a long period of reticence following the debacle of the Industrial Relations Act, moreover, they were beginning to argue again for legal curbs on trade-union power. The wheel, it seemed, had turned full circle. It only remained to be seen whether the Conservatives would prove any more successful in 1979–81 than they had been in 1970–72, or whether the wheel would continue to spin and the policies change once more. The omens were not particularly encouraging: inflation was rising again and

1. It received 36·9 per cent of the vote in May 1979 compared with 37·2 per cent in February 1974.

the new Government's virtual doubling of V.A.T. to help
pay for cuts in income tax would only make matters worse.
So, too, would another huge increase in the price of oil
which followed the revolution in Iran.

On the two key issues of foreign policy, the Labour
Government's performance was not much more effective
than it had been at home. In the first place, it failed dis-
mally to resolve the question of Britain's ambivalent
relationship to the European Community. Mr Wilson's own
long-term strategy became clear when, after Mr Callaghan
had succeeded in negotiating a few minor changes in the
terms which the Conservatives had obtained for British
entry, he announced, on 18 March 1975, the Government's
decision to recommend that Britain should remain a member
of the Community. But his Cabinet was divided, and in an
unprecedented departure from the principle of collective
ministerial responsibility, the Prime Minister allowed the
seven dissenters to campaign for a 'No' vote in the referendum which was to be held to fulfil the pledge to submit the
results of the re-negotiation to the British people. This
decision was followed by a two-to-one vote at a specially
convened Labour Party conference on 26 April in opposition
to the Government's policy and in favour of withdrawal
from the Community. By a curious coincidence, this was
precisely the proportion of those voting in the referendum
on 5 June who were in favour of staying in. It was a convincing victory,[1] and Mr Wilson could triumphantly claim,
'The debate is now over.' Everyone knew, however, that
with one-third of his Cabinet and two-thirds of his party
exceedingly unhappy about the result, the issue was still
not settled.

Opposition within the Labour Party and the trade union

1. Only Shetland and the Western Isles of Scotland voted against
continued membership of the Community, although the majority in
favour in Northern Ireland was a narrow one.

movement to British membership of the European Community no doubt accounted for much of what can only be described as a dog-in-the-manger attitude towards Europe by the Government over the next four years. It refused to agree to joint Community representation at a world energy conference in 1975 on the grounds that Britain was a significant oil producer.[1] From 1976 to 1979, its Minister of Agriculture, Mr John Silkin, who had been one of the seven Cabinet ministers who opposed continued membership of the Community, acquired an unenviable reputation among his European counterparts by the way in which he not only blocked many of their proposals, but openly proclaimed his unrepentant Little-Englandism. It blithely ignored Community regulations which might upset powerful supporters, the most notorious example being the refusal to introduce the tachograph, a device for monitoring the speed of and distance travelled by lorries, because of opposition from the Transport and General Workers' Union.[2] It delayed legislation providing for direct elections to the European Parliament, and at the beginning of 1979, it refused to join the proposed European Monetary System (E.M.S.), which was designed to prevent excessive fluctuations in the international value of the Community's currencies.

There were, of course, legitimate British grievances. Few outside the ranks of continental farmers and their spokesmen were prepared to defend the Community's wasteful farm support programme which resulted in 'lakes' and 'mountains' of excess produce. This accounted for more than 70 per cent of the Community's annual expenditure and the British Government was horrified to discover in 1978 that, although Britain was one of the poorest members of the

1. See below, p. 359.

2. 'The spy in the cab' was the name given to the tachograph by the union. It was strange that continental lorry drivers, not noted for their servility, did not see it in this light.

Community, it was by far the largest net contributor to the budget. The position would become even worse by 1980, when the transitional arrangements designed to ease the strain of Community entry upon the country's economy came to an end. Mr Callaghan, who publicly raised the issue on 13 November 1978, might have paused to reflect, however, that Britain's budgetary contribution and the Common Agricultural Policy were precisely two of the points upon which he was supposed to have won major concessions during the 1974–5 re-negotiation and to wonder whether his Government's persistent foot-dragging in Europe was the best way of encouraging the other members of the Community to regard Britain's plight with sympathy.

The Government's negative attitude undoubtedly had some effect upon public opinion. There was evidence of growing indifference and even hostility towards the Community, and when the direct elections to the European Parliament finally took place in June 1979, only 33 per cent of the electorate bothered to vote, the lowest proportion in any Community country. But this was also symptomatic of a deeper malaise. 'We've gotta get in to get on', had been one of the slogans of supporters of Britain's entry to the Community in 1971–2, but seven years later there seemed little sign that much had been gained. Even the net benefit from trade in 1978 was put by the Treasury at a trifling £120 million, or about one-fifth of one per cent of Britain's total trade turnover. It was typical of Britain in the 1970s, however, that something like Community membership should first be extolled as an answer to the country's ills and then be treated as a scapegoat when it failed to cure them. The British people, in fact, still has to make up its mind whether it is 'European' or whether General de Gaulle was right after all.

In the case of Rhodesia, which was the second key issue in foreign policy faced by the Labour Government, control of events had of course long since slipped out of British hands. What developments between 1974 and 1979 showed, however, was that even British influence was minimal. Labour's return to power in Britain coincided with the overthrow of the dictatorial regime which had ruled Portugal for more than forty years. Colonial wars in Angola and Mozambique had been the catalyst which led to the Portuguese revolution and the new government hastened to accord its African territories independence. This alarmed the South African Government, which saw the *cordon sanitaire* of friendly states to the north visibly crumbling, and it urged Mr Ian Smith in Rhodesia to come to some sort of arrangement with his own black nationalists which would avert the worst consequences for South Africa.

Portugal and South Africa were Mr Smith's life-line and he had little alternative but to make the attempt. However, the negotiations which took place in 1975-6 with the nationalists, some of whom had been released from detention for the purpose, got nowhere, thanks largely to Mr Smith's intransigence. In the second half of 1976, anxious to avoid a repetition of events in Angola, where a Soviet-backed regime had come to power with the aid of Cuban troops, the United States Government took a hand in the shape of its peripatetic Secretary of State, Dr Henry Kissinger. Between them, Dr Kissinger and the South African Government induced Mr Smith to agree in September 1976 to a two-year transition to majority rule in Rhodesia when he had proclaimed only the previous March that it would not happen in a thousand years.

Britain's role in all this had been, to say the least, somewhat limited, but since the British Government still had nominal responsibility for Rhodesia in international law, it convened a conference of all the interested parties in Geneva in October 1976 to discuss the Kissinger–Smith deal. Since the latter gave the Rhodesian whites effective control of the government during the transition period, however, it proved unacceptable to the black nationalists, who were in any case split into four different factions. Not surprisingly, the conference failed, and the more militant nationalists, headed by Mr Joshua Nkomo and Mr Robert Mugabe, retired to Zambia and Mozambique respectively to devote themselves to the organization of the guerrilla war which had already begun against Mr Smith's regime.

It was this guerrilla war and its effects upon the Rhodesian economy, together with further pressure from South Africa, which led Mr Smith to make more concessions. He did not like the proposed settlement drawn up in September 1977 by Mr Andrew Young, the U.S. Ambassador to the United Nations, and Dr David Owen, Mr Callaghan's youthful Foreign Secretary, because it seemed to give too much power to the guerrillas of Mr Nkomo's and Mr Mugabe's Patriotic Front, so he decided to negotiate with more moderate African leaders, such as Bishop Abel Muzorewa and the Reverend Ndabaningi Sithole, to produce an 'internal settlement' which was announced in March 1978. Although this conceded majority rule, it gave an entrenched position in the proposed new parliament to the whites and also ensured that they would remain in control of the civil service and the security forces. Elections were held in April 1979 and Bishop Muzorewa became the first black Prime Minister of Zimbabwe-Rhodesia, as the country was now known, with Mr Smith stepping down to become minister without portfolio. To the dismay of both the whites and the African supporters of the 'internal settlement', however, neither the British nor the American Governments would recognize the new regime or lift sanctions unless the Patriotic Front were involved. But the latter regarded Bishop Muzorewa and his black colleagues as stooges and announced its determination to prosecute the guerrilla war until complete victory had been attained.

The new Zimbabwe-Rhodesian Government seems to have believed that the Conservative Government of Mrs Thatcher would take a more sympathetic line than its Labour predecessor, but whatever her initial inclination might have been, the new British Prime Minister agreed, at a Commonwealth conference in Lusaka in August 1979, to a fresh attempt at a negotiated settlement. An all-party conference convened in London in September and, much to the surprise of some observers, succeeded after three months of hard negotiation in reaching an agreement. Fresh elections were held resulting in an overall majority for Mr Mugabe's wing of the Patriotic Front, and it was this allegedly Marxist bogey man of the Rhodesian whites who led Zimbabwe into internationally recognized independence in April 1980. Although tribute was rightly paid to the skill of the Foreign Secretary, Lord Carrington, and of Lord Soames, the man he sent to Salisbury to oversee the implementation of the London agreement, it is nevertheless arguable that the moderating influence of outsiders, and particularly of President Samora Machel of Mozambique, upon Mr Mugabe was the crucial factor in producing and maintaining the settlement. Whatever the cause, Britain was fortunate in escaping at long last from a situation in which its position was the reverse of that of the proverbial harlot: i.e. having the responsibility, but very little of the power.

It was not so successful in extricating itself from a similar dilemma in Northern Ireland. The limitations of British power were vividly brought home by the Protestant workers' strike of May 1974. On 14 May a body known as the Ulster Workers' Council (U.W.C.), which had strong links with Protestant para-military organizations, began a strike against Mr Brian Faulkner's power-sharing Executive. Intimidation was widespread, but the British army did little or nothing to stop it, apparently because its com-

manders felt unable to wage a two-front struggle against
both the Protestants and the Provisional I.R.A. The outcome has been succinctly described by Mr Faulkner:

... the strike supporters were delighted and surprised to find
themselves almost unopposed and ordinary citizens felt abandoned
by authority and defenceless against the bullying of the new rulers
of the streets of Ulster. What point was there in risking their necks
trying to go about their business when all over the Province they
could see evidence of the security forces standing by and watching
lawlessness flourish? During those first crucial days the Government lost its authority and the junta at Hawthornden Road, the
U.W.C. headquarters, established theirs.[1]

By 28 May, the 'Doomsday' situation which had been
predicted for the mainland at the time of the miners'
strikes in 1972 and 1973-4 had almost come about in
Ulster. Mr Faulkner told his colleagues on the Executive:

The Belfast gas plant was out of operation. The power stations
were dangerously near total shutdown, and even if the Army had
the technical capacity to restore partial functioning there would be
a total blackout for several days at least. The water supply and
sewerage services were at grave risk and the flooding of large parts
of Belfast with raw sewage was a real possibility. Basic food
distribution was in jeopardy. Supplies of feedstuffs to farms had
stopped.[2]

Mr Faulkner felt, albeit reluctantly, that the only solution
was to negotiate with the U.W.C. His Catholic S.D.L.P.
colleagues disagreed, and the power-sharing Executive
collapsed after only five months in office.

In the opinion of Mr Wilson's Press Secretary, the
Protestant workers' strike 'put a permanent recognizable
limit on the power of the British Government . . . We could
only do such things in Ireland as the organized Protestant

1. Brian Faulkner, *Memoirs of a Statesman* (1978), p. 264.
2. Ibid., p. 4.

population were prepared to agree with, acquiesce in, or tolerate with reluctance and grumbles.'[1]

True though this assertion is, it tells only half the story, for the Provisional I.R.A. also has an effective veto on any political settlement. Short of employing methods which would be unacceptable to both British and international opinion, the security forces in Northern Ireland are quite unable to destroy the Provisionals. Indeed, the resilience of the latter after almost ten years of police and army anti-terrorist campaigning was demonstrated on 28 August 1979, when 18 soldiers were killed in an ambush and Earl Mountbatten, one of Britain's most distinguished citizens and a member of the royal family, was assassinated with three other persons while on holiday in the Irish Republic.[2]

This joint veto of the Protestant extremists and the Provisional I.R.A. explains why the Labour Government was able to do little more during the five years which followed the collapse of the Executive than maintain the *status quo*, despite the fact that the vast majority of Ulster's population, both Protestant and Catholic, clearly want nothing more than to live in peace. In the circumstances, it is hard to see an early end to the violence and to the drain upon Britain's resources, the cost of security alone amounting to more than £1 million a day. One possible solution for Britain, if not for Northern Ireland, is withdrawal. If the Provisional I.R.A. had managed to sustain the terrorist campaign which they launched on the mainland in late 1974, public opinion might have become so embittered as to demand it, but aided by the Prevention of Terrorism Act which was rushed through Parliament in November, the

1. Joe Haines, *The Politics of Power* (1977), p. 133.
2. In April, another Republican organization, the Irish National Liberation Army, had assassinated the Conservative spokesman on Northern Ireland, Mr Airey Neave, by placing a bomb in his car in London.

authorities succeeded in rounding up most of those involved.
Elements in the Labour and Liberal Parties have called for
withdrawal, but have so far failed to convince the majority
of their colleagues. The general consensus among all major
parties seems to be that withdrawal would only precipitate
a blood-bath. It would also, of course, be a tremendous blow
to the prestige of any British Government thereby to admit
that its writ did not run in a part of the United Kingdom.

Such a concession would have been particularly damag-
ing at a time when the Government was experiencing
difficulties in its relations with two other nations within the
United Kingdom. Although *Plaid Cymru* and the Scottish
National Party (S.N.P.) had both been founded in the inter-
war years, it was not until the late 1960s that their performance in by-elections showed that nationalism had
become a powerful political force in Wales and Scotland.[1]
It is not easy to explain why, although it is worth pointing
out that tension between centralizing governments and
regions with different cultural and historical traditions was
occurring in other industrialized societies at the same time.[2]
There seemed to be a pervasive feeling that, as government
intervened increasingly in the lives of its citizens, it was
simultaneously becoming more remote and insensitive.
Government reactions to this feeling and its manifestations
varied from repression to concession; in Britain in 1968 Mr
Wilson's Labour Government resorted to the time-honoured
expedient of setting up a Royal Commission.

The Royal Commission on the Constitution (as it was
called) did not report until October 1973. As one authority
on the subject has written, it 'was unanimous only in

1. The key results were the *Plaid Cymru* victory at Carmarthen in July
1966 and that of the S.N.P. at Glasgow (Hamilton) in November 1967.
2. One thinks, for example, of the relations between the Canadian
Government and Quebec Province and the French Government and
Breton, Corsican and 'Occitan' nationalists.

rejecting separatism and federalism, in supporting a directly elected assembly for Scotland, and in recommending the single transferable vote system of proportional representation for elections to any devolved assembly'.[1] This left a whole series of questions, such as the establishment of a Welsh Assembly or whether power should be devolved to the major English regions, unanswered. In any case, the Government and the country, preoccupied with the threat of the miners' strike, were in no mood to consider abstruse constitutional matters. What re-focussed everyone's attention upon the problem was the spectacular success of the nationalists in the February 1974 election, particularly in Scotland, where the S.N.P. won seven seats and a fifth of the vote. In September Mr Wilson's minority Government issued a White Paper promising directly elected assemblies for both Scotland and Wales, although only the former would enjoy legislative powers.

In the October 1974 general election, *Plaid Cymru* gained one seat and the S.N.P. four. With over 30 per cent of the vote, the latter was now the second largest party in Scotland. The strength of the nationalists in a precariously balanced Parliament encouraged the Labour Government to implement proposals for Scottish and Welsh devolution, especially as the Liberals were also strongly in favour. After much preparatory discussion, the second reading of the Scotland and Wales Bill was carried on 16 December 1976, but it became bogged down in committee over such vexed questions as the reserve powers of the central government and the method of finance. Not the least of the Government's difficulties stemmed from the implacable hostility of a group of its own back-benchers who, in the tradition of centralizing socialism, opposed any measure of devolution

1. Vernon Bogdanor, *Devolution* (1979), p. 151.

whatever.[1] In an effort to break the deadlock, the Government introduced a guillotine motion to curtail debate, but this was defeated on 22 February 1977. Twenty-two Labour M.P.s voted with the Opposition and a further twenty-one abstained.

Thanks, on the one hand, to the 'Lib-Lab Pact', and on the other, to the realization by most Labour rebels that the issue of devolution could bring the Government down, new and separate Scotland and Wales Bills were successfully piloted through Parliament in 1977-8. They provided for directly elected assemblies in both Scotland and Wales. The Scottish Assembly would be able to pass laws on a variety of social questions, but its Welsh counterpart would merely have greater discretion in the implementation of legislation passed at Westminster. Even in the Scottish case, important areas, such as economic and industrial policy, were reserved for the United Kingdom Government, and there was endless scope in the complex provisions of the Act for deadlock and conflict between Edinburgh and London. This was especially true where finance was concerned. The Assembly would not be able to raise its own direct taxes; nor would it receive any direct revenue from the oil which had been discovered off the coast of Scotland[2] and which the S.N.P. regarded as Scottish rather than British. Instead, the bulk of the money to pay for the Assembly's measures would come from an annual block grant voted by the House of Commons. So little was given away by the Government's legislation, in fact, that one cannot help wondering why the nationalist parties were so keen to have it. The answer was that they regarded it as a useful first step, and in the case of the S.N.P. it was probably felt that continual

1. At the same time it should be noted that two left-wing Scottish Labour M.P.s who favoured self-government for Scotland had left the Party early in 1976 to form a new Scottish Labour Party.

2. See below, p. 359.

clashes between the Assembly and the British Government would so exasperate Scottish opinion that the party's long-term aim of complete independence would eventually gain the majority support it had hitherto lacked.

Before the devolution legislation could come into force, however, it had to be approved by referenda in Scotland and Wales, although not in England. This concession, granted by the Government to its own rebels during the discussion of the first Scotland and Wales Bill in 1977, was amended by these self-same rebels (with Conservative support) in 1978 to incorporate the additional proviso that more than 40 per cent of those qualified to vote would have to approve of the legislation. This was to have no significance as far as Wales was concerned, for the Welsh people rejected devolution by a huge majority of almost four to one when the referendum was held on 1 March 1979. Apart from the feeling that the reform was not worth having, the most plausible explanation of this result is that support for devolution, like support for *Plaid Cymru* itself, was strongest in the Welsh-speaking parts of Wales, and that English speakers, who form 80 per cent of Wales' total population, feared it as the thin end of a Welsh language wedge. In the case of Scotland, however, the 40 per cent provision was to prove crucial, for although there was a 51·6 per cent majority in favour of devolution, this represented barely a third of those entitled to vote. If the majority had been more decisive, the Government might have tried to press on with the legislation, but in the circumstances it merely proposed further consultations. The S.N.P., for whom a majority was a majority, was furious and tabled a motion of no confidence in the Government. The Conservatives gleefully followed it with one of their own, and when this was debated on 28 March 1979, the Government was defeated by 311 votes (including all the S.N.P.'s M.P.s) to 310. Mr Callaghan promptly called a general election, the first time a Prime

Minister had been forced to go to the country by an adverse vote in the House of Commons since Ramsay Macdonald in 1924.

The result of the Scottish referendum and the poor performance of the S.N.P. in the election, in which it lost 9 of its 11 seats and saw its share of the Scottish vote cut by almost half, led some observers to wonder whether nationalism, and with it the whole devolution debate, was past its peak. But whatever the fate of the S.N.P. – and it did succeed in winning the huge Highlands and Islands constituency in the election for the European Parliament in June 1979 – it may be premature to regard the issue of greater autonomy for Scotland, or indeed other parts of the British Isles, as closed. As long as London and the South-east remain, at one and the same time, the richest part of the country and the centre of decision, resentment is likely to exist in less favoured areas, resentment which could easily be translated into a demand for greater self-government.

THE CHANGING FACE OF BRITAIN

If the social changes of the 1950s and early 1960s had been rapid and often disturbing for the older generation, those of the late 1960s and the 1970s were no less so. Everywhere, it seemed, familiar landmarks were being swept away. The process could affect the name of the place where you lived. The Conservative Government's major reform of local government, which came into force in April 1974, abolished some of the old counties whose names had been household words for centuries and redivided others, so that people found themselves consigned to new, artificial entities, such as 'Humberside' or 'Gwent'.[1] It certainly affected the money in your pocket, for in February 1971 the currency

1. The reform was also unpopular because it was thought to have led to a huge increase in the size of the local government bureaucracy and a corresponding rise in the rates.

was decimalized on the basis of one hundred new pence to the pound. The familiar ten-shilling note and half-crown piece disappeared, while the shilling and florin were re-named. It was beginning to affect the shape and size of the things you bought in the shops as the traditional English weights and measures gave way to the continental kilogram and metre.

Education was another area in which there were import-ant changes. The grammar schools and the 'eleven-plus' examination which selected children for them came under increasing attack on the grounds that they were 'elitist' and 'socially divisive'. In January 1965 the Labour Govern-ment began a policy of actively encouraging comprehensive secondary schools, which catered for children of all abilities. Despite the changes of government, the number of these schools grew rapidly. While in 1965 less than 1 child in 10 in England and Wales attended them, by 1979 the pro-portion had risen to more than 4 in 5. Within comprehensive schools, traditional subjects such as Classics gave way to newcomers such as Liberal or Social Studies, while at all levels of education formal methods of teaching were being increasingly challenged by informal ones. Since the avowed intention of all these developments was to broaden the base of educational opportunity, it was ironic that the 1970s should end with renewed concern about basic standards of literacy and numeracy. Some blamed the comprehensives for 'levelling down', but it will be many years before the effects of the educational changes of the period can be properly assessed. In the meantime, the private sector, including the famous public schools, seem to be providing an increasingly popular alternative to the state system for those who can afford the fees, thus helping to perpetuate a form of 'elitism' and 'social divisiveness' from which so many Cabinet ministers, both Labour and Conservative, have benefited.

Changes in institutions were paralleled by changes in moral attitudes. The late 1960s saw the birth of what became known as the 'permissive society' in which some of the features of traditional Judaeo-Christian morality were successfully challenged. Following the Obscene Publications Act of 1959 and the abolition of the Lord Chamberlain's centuries-old role as theatre censor nine years later, books, magazines, plays and films were to become much more explicit where sex was concerned. Homosexual acts between consenting male adults were finally legalized in 1967, ten years after the Wolfenden Report. Later in the same year the Abortion Act made abortions much easier to obtain, and in 1969 the divorce law was liberalized to make divorce possible after two years' separation if both partners agreed and after five if only one did so. Not surprisingly, the number of abortions and divorces rose rapidly after the passage of this legislation. The rise in the divorce rate was particularly spectacular. Indeed, by 1979 it was calculated that for every three marriages in Britain there was one divorce.

It is, of course, far more difficult to measure changes in behaviour in areas where the law does not apply and where no statistics are kept. Nevertheless, it seemed that an increasing number of men and women were living together without going through the formality of a wedding ceremony and that the younger generation had less inhibitions than their parents about pre- and extra-marital sexual relations.[1] A survey of Britain's 15- to 24-year-olds carried out in 1979, for example, showed that not only did 53 per cent approve of 'sleeping with someone you are not married to', but also that no less than 36 per cent disapproved of marrying someone with whom they had not already slept.

1. This was undoubtedly connected with the development of a relatively cheap and effective form of female contraception which was also easy to use: the contraceptive pill.

One must not, however, exaggerate the scope of the 'permissive society'. Although their activities were no longer illegal, homosexuals were still the butt of jokes, while the leader of the Liberal Party, Mr Jeremy Thorpe, was forced to resign in 1976 because of allegations of a past homosexual relationship. There seemed little indication that Britain would follow the lead of some European countries and abolish censorship altogether. Indeed, the law was tightened up to prevent the exploitation of children. Outside the sexual area there was little support for proposals to legalize the use of even 'soft' drugs, such as marijuana, while public opinion polls invariably showed a huge majority in favour of capital punishment, although it had been suspended for five years in 1964 and finally abolished by a free vote in the House of Commons in 1969. Britain's schoolteachers, too, continued to claim and exercise an almost unique privilege in the civilized world: that of inflicting corporal punishment upon their pupils.

Similarly, it would be wrong to conclude, as some were tempted to do, that 'permissiveness' had spilled over into public life and produced a new willingness to challenge authority, to resort to strike action, and to engage in violent political demonstrations. In many respects, the fifteen to twenty years following the Second World War were abnormally quiet from the point of view of industrial and political militancy, so that while there undoubtedly were more strikes and demonstrations in the late 1960s and the 1970s, it can hardly be claimed that these years were more violent than those immediately before and after the First World War,[1] to say nothing of earlier periods in the country's history. Moreover, if one excludes Ireland, where there had long been an independent tradition of political violence, the United Kingdom remained a much more peaceful country than most others. Even where strikes were concerned,

1. See above, pp. 32–3; 66–7; 69.

Britain's record, although not good, was better than that of Australia, Canada and the United States, while the events of 1973-4 were a pale reflection of those of May 1968 in France.

If the liberal climate of the 1960s and 1970s induced the law to retreat from regulating some aspects of human behaviour, it compelled it to encroach upon others. Following a similar development in the United States, the period saw the emergence and growth in Britain of a vociferous feminist, or 'Women's Liberation' movement, which claimed, with considerable justification, that, despite the advances which had been won since the days of the suffragettes, women were still subject to widespread discrimination in all walks of life. An Equal Pay Act was among the last measures enacted by the Labour Government of 1964-70. It came into force at the end of 1975, a crucial piece of legislation in a country which had the highest proportion of working women in the European Community. In the same year, Mr Wilson's second Labour Government passed the Sex Discrimination Act, which made it unlawful to discriminate on grounds of sex in the areas of employment, education, housing, and goods and services. It also set up an Equal Opportunities Commission to investigate allegations of discrimination. While welcoming the Act, advocates of women's rights pointed out that important matters, such as taxation, pensions and social security, remained excluded from its provisions, and it was of course true that it was difficult to prove that, if discrimination had taken place, it was on grounds of sex. Nevertheless, women had taken at least some steps along the road towards full equality with men. Unfortunately, they were also catching up in some of the less desirable aspects of male behaviour. Thus, over the decade 1968-78 the average annual increase in the number of female criminal offenders per head of the population was double that among males.

The Race Relations Acts of 1965, 1968 and 1976,

introducing and extending the scope of measures against discrimination on grounds of race and colour, were another example of the way in which the law now intervened in areas hitherto left to the discretion of the individual. They were a result of what many would see as one of the most important social changes to affect Britain during the 1960s and 1970s: its transformation into a multi-racial society. Non-white immigration on a fairly large scale had begun in the 1950s,[1] but it did not reach its peak until a decade later. The majority of the early arrivals were blacks from the West Indies, but later on they were outnumbered by immigrants from the Indian subcontinent and by others of Asian descent who had been forced to leave the newly independent states of East Africa by racialist governments. It has been estimated that there were about 360,000 non-whites from the Commonwealth living in Britain in 1961. By 1976 the number had risen to 1·8 million, or a little over three per cent of the total population.

From a purely numerical point of view, it would be absurd to pretend that the country was unable to cope with immigration on this scale, especially as there was a net outflow of people from Britain in the late 1970s. The fact was, however, that the immigrants were visibly different from the indigenous population and in many cases brought with them quite different customs and life-styles. Prejudice could all too easily flourish in such circumstances, and a vicious circle tended to develop, in which coloured immigrants, for reasons of solidarity and lack of effective choice, congregated in inner-city areas already suffering from social deprivation and were thereupon accused of exacerbating or even causing it.

The political response to growing public concern over coloured immigration was, on the one hand, to condemn the prejudice it reflected by means of the race relations

1. See above, p. 279.

legislation referred to above, and, on the other, to pander
to it by progressively tightening controls upon immigration.
After bitterly opposing the Conservative Government's
Commonwealth Immigrants Act of 1962, the Labour Party
not only failed to repeal it when it came to power in 1964,
but introduced further restrictions. The Commonwealth
Immigrants Act of 1968, which was specifically designed to
regulate the anticipated flow of Asians from Kenya, was
the subject of particularly strong criticism by liberals, for,
unlike most of their fellow-immigrants, the Kenyan Asians
actually held British passports. There can be little doubt,
however, that the great majority of voters supported not
only this measure, but also the Conservative Government's
Immigration Act of 1971, which introduced even stricter
controls. Indeed, although it was in fact very difficult for
non-white immigrants to come to Britain in the late 1970s,
opinion polls consistently showed that the public still felt
not enough was being done to keep them out.

Popular fears and prejudices were skilfully articulated by
a former Conservative Cabinet minister, Mr Enoch Powell,
who, in a speech in Birmingham on 20 April 1968, predicted
racial conflict on a North American scale unless 'resolute
and urgent action' were taken. Although Mr Powell was
sacked from the Conservative Shadow Cabinet for his speech
and subsequently broke with the party altogether over the
Common Market issue,[1] periodic jeremiads kept his views
on the subject before the British people. The solution he
appears to envisage is repatriation, but apart from the
ethical considerations involved, this is hardly an option for
the growing proportion of Britain's coloured population
born in this country, which is already estimated at more than
40 per cent. Integration on the basis of full equality is the only
practical as well as moral solution in the long term, although

1. In October 1974 Mr Powell was elected to Parliament as an Ulster
Unionist member for a Northern Ireland constituency.

it will not be easy to achieve. Thus, a disturbing feature of the late 1970s was the growing friction between young blacks and the police, whom they regarded as prejudiced, and which erupted into street violence at Southall in west London in 1979 and St Paul's in Bristol in 1980.

In so far as they were related to the high unemployment rate among immigrants and the deterioration of the urban environment in which the latter lived, these disturbances were a reflection of the fact that the most important change which occurred in Britain in the 1960s and 1970s was not a shift in moral values or a minor alteration in the composition of its population, but a sharp decline in its economic position. This may seem a strange and unwarranted statement when one considers the evidence of a continuing improvement in the country's standard of living. By the end of the 1970s, for example, more people owned their own homes, had the regular use of a car, rented a telephone and possessed refrigerators, washing-machines and television sets than ever before.[1] It is only in relation to other countries that the decline becomes manifest. Its extent can be appreciated from the following table, which has been compiled from official European Community statistics:

INDEX NUMBERS OF GROSS DOMESTIC PRODUCT
PER HEAD IN PURCHASING POWER STANDARDS
(Europe of the Nine[2] = 100)

1964		1977	
Germany	115	Germany	117
U.K.	108	France	113
Netherlands	103	Belgium	108
France	102	Netherlands	107
Belgium	99	U.K.	93
Italy	72	Italy	74

1. See the valuable article by Jean Toland, 'Changes in living standards since the 1950s', in the official Government publication, *Social Trends 10* (1980), pp. 13–38.

2. i.e. the nine members of the European Community in 1977: Britain, France, Germany, Italy, Belgium, Netherlands, Luxembourg, Denmark and Ireland.

In other words, within the space of thirteen years, Britain had fallen from the postition of the second richest of the six most important industrialized nations of Western Europe to that of the second poorest.

Commenting on this state of affairs, the British Ambassador in Paris, Sir Nicholas Henderson, wrote to the Foreign Office on 31 March 1979:

... today we are not only no longer a world power, but we are not in the first rank even as a European one. Income per head in Britain is now, for the first time for over 300 years, below that in France. We are scarcely in the same economic league as the Germans or French. We talk of ourselves without shame as being one of the least prosperous countries of Europe. The prognosis for the foreseeable future is discouraging. If present trends continue we shall be overtaken in gdp per head by Italy and Spain well before the end of the century.

Sir Nicholas went on to draw attention to some of the consequences of Britain's relative poverty:

You have only to move about western Europe nowadays to realize how poor and unproud the British have become in relation to their neighbours. It shows in the look of our towns, in our airports, in our hospitals and in local amenities; it is painfully apparent in much of our railway system, which until a generation ago was superior to the continental one.[1]

In short, the standard of living which the British people had come to expect as a result of the technological and social advances of the twentieth century was under threat.

On one level, the reasons for Britain's plight are clear enough: poor productivity linked to a very low rate of investment.[2] But when one seeks to go beyond this, con-

1. *The Economist*, 2 June 1979, pp. 29-30.
2. It has been calculated that Britain had the lowest percentage of investment of the 18 most industrialized nations of the western world between 1953 and 1976. See the article by David Kern in the *National Westminster Bank Quarterly Review*, May 1978.

sensus rapidly disappears in an argument over whether
poor management, obstructive trade unions or a whole host
of other factors are to blame. There does seem to be a
measure of agreement, however, that Britain does possess a
unique opportunity to do something about the situation. In
1969 oil was discovered under the bed of the North Sea
off the coast of Scotland. By 1975 the first commercially
produced oil was coming ashore and the total deposits in
the North Sea had proved so large that the Department of
Energy estimates that Britain will have attained net self-
sufficiency in this vital source of energy by 1980/81. Apart
from the psychological boost, the enormous savings on the
balance of payments and the revenue accruing from
production royalties should provide a stimulus to the entire
economy. But the oil boom will not last indefinitely. Current
estimates forecast that net self-sufficiency will end after
about a decade, one which may well prove to be among the
most challenging Britain has ever had to face.

Envoi

HISTORIANS may well decide that the two pivotal dates of world history in the first half of the twentieth century were 1917 and 1941: for in these two years occurred decisive displacements of power which determined much that was to follow.

In April 1917 the United States entered the Great War, and six months later the Bolshevik Party came to power in Russia determined to take Russia out of the war. Thenceforth, in the logistics of power, Germany and her allies were sure to be beaten by the western allies, and Russia would become the first Communist State in the world. The two crucial decisions were taken in Washington and in Moscow: Britain's position in the world would be conditioned, for the foreseeable future, by her adjustments to the consequences of these two great decisions.

In June 1941 Hitler attacked the Soviet Union, and six months later the Japanese attacked Pearl Harbor. Thenceforth, in the logistics of power, Germany and her allies were sure to be beaten by the western allies in conjunction with Communist Russia; and China, relieved of Japanese pressure by Japan's eventual defeat, would undergo a Communist revolution. The two crucial decisions had been taken in Berlin and Tokyo: again Britain's position in the world was to be conditioned by her adjustments to the total eventual outcome of these two decisions.

Each of these moments of dramatic displacement had been prepared by a complex historical process of fracture and erosion in some areas, consolidation and strengthening in others. Thus the power of the United States and of Germany had been growing - whether demographic, economic, or political – long before 1914; whereas that of Britain and France had been retarded and strained, that of Russia deeply fractured, long before 1917. In the event, therefore, American power between the wars remained immense, though diminished by the economic crisis and muffled by her policy of neutrality and isolation: and German power remained great, though likewise checked by depression and masked for a time by formal defeat. Similarly, the power of France and Britain, which seemed so great after 1919, was in fact weakened by their losses in the war and by decline in their resolution to uphold the settlement and the organizations made in 1919. For Britain, as for France, the inter-war years were largely years of deception, not least of self-deception, about the realities of power-displacement which had taken place in the world. France paid the full penalty for her delusions by defeat in 1940. Britain escaped it, by a hairbreadth, for long enough to see the tide of events turn in her favour after 1941.

The more long-term consequences of the tide's turning were, however, a second major upheaval in world relationships. The acquisition by the Soviet Union of control over large areas of eastern Europe, and the emergence of a Communist China by 1949, constituted a new counterpoise to the greatly augmented wealth and military might of the United States and Canada. As soon as each side had possession of nuclear weapons and missiles capable of delivering nuclear warheads across the continents, the full repercussions of the new displacements of power began to be more apparent.

How successfully, and by what means, would Britain – and the completely reconstructed Commonwealth which it has been one of Britain's greatest post-war achievements to create – adjust herself to these new realities? The answer still lay hidden in the future in 1979. In common with other nations in the van of western civilization, the British people of the seventies was subject to frustrating economic problems, rapid social changes, cultural and intellectual dilemmas, and the implicit threat of great disaster and even total destruction should its qualities of intelligence and leadership fail to measure to the exacting demands of the time. Never had the penalty of failure been more terrible; but never had the opportunity for progress been more alluring.

MINISTRIES, 1910–79

Party	Date formed	Prime Minister	Chancellor of Exchequer	Secretary for Foreign Affairs
Liberal	December 1910	H. H. Asquith	D. Lloyd George	Sir E. Grey
Coalition	May 1915	H. H. Asquith	R. McKenna	Sir E. Grey
Coalition	December 1916	D. Lloyd George	A. Bonar Law	A. J. Balfour
Coalition	January 1919	D. Lloyd George	A. Chamberlain (from April 1921, Sir R. S. Horne)	A. J. Balfour (from October 1919, Lord Curzon)
Conservative	October 1922	A. Bonar Law	S. Baldwin	Lord Curzon
Conservative	May 1923	S. Baldwin	S. Baldwin (from August 1923, N. Chamberlain)	Lord Curzon
Labour	January 1924	J. R. MacDonald	P. Snowden	J. R. MacDonald
Conservative	November 1924	S. Baldwin	W. S. Churchill	A. Chamberlain
Labour	June 1929	J. R. MacDonald	P. Snowden	A. Henderson
National	August 1931	J. R. MacDonald	P. Snowden	Lord Reading

MINISTRIES, 1910–79—continued

Party	Date formed	Prime Minister	Chancellor of Exchequer	Secretary for Foreign Affairs
National	November 1931	J. R. MacDonald	N. Chamberlain	Sir J. Simon
National	June 1935	S. Baldwin	N. Chamberlain	Sir S. Hoare
National	November 1935	S. Baldwin	N. Chamberlain	Sir S. Hoare (from December 1935, A. Eden)
National	May 1937	N. Chamberlain	Sir J. Simon	A. Eden (from February 1938, Lord Halifax)
National	September 1939	N. Chamberlain	Sir J. Simon	Lord Halifax
Coalition	May 1940	W. S. Churchill	Sir K. Wood (from September 1943, Sir J. Anderson)	Lord Halifax (from December 1940, A. Eden)
Conservative	May 1945	W. S. Churchill	Sir J. Anderson	A. Eden
Labour	July 1945	C. R. Attlee	H. Dalton (from November 1947, Sir S. Cripps)	E. Bevin
Labour	March 1950	C. R. Attlee	Sir S. Cripps (from October 1950, H. Gaitskell)	E. Bevin (from March 1951, H. Morrison)

Party	Date formed	Prime Minister	Chancellor of Exchequer	Secretary for Foreign Affairs
Conservative	October 1951	W. S. Churchill	R. A. Butler	A. Eden
Conservative	April 1955	Sir A. Eden	R. A. Butler (from December 1955, H. Macmillan)	H. Macmillan (from December 1955, S. Lloyd)
Conservative	January 1957	H. Macmillan	P. Thorneycroft (from January 1958, D. Heathcoat Amory)	S. Lloyd
Conservative	October 1959	H. Macmillan	D. Heathcoat Amory (from July 1960, S. Lloyd; from July 1962, R. Maudling)	S. Lloyd (from July 1960, Lord Home)
Conservative	October 1963	Lord Home (Sir A. Douglas-Home)	R. Maudling	R. A. Butler
Labour	October 1964	H. Wilson	J. Callaghan	P. Gordon Walker (from January 1965, M. Stewart)
Labour	March 1966	H. Wilson	J. Callaghan (from November 1967, R. Jenkins)	M. Stewart (from August 1966, G. Brown; from March 1968, M. Stewart)

MINISTRIES, 1910–79 – continued

Party	Date formed	Prime Minister	Chancellor of Exchequer	Secretary for Foreign Affairs
Conservative	June 1970	E. Heath	I. Macleod (from July 1970, A. Barber)	Lord Home
Labour	February 1974	H. Wilson	D. Healey	J. Callaghan
Labour	October 1974	H. Wilson	D. Healey	J. Callaghan
Labour	April 1976	J. Callaghan	D. Healey	A. Crosland (from May 1977, D. Owen)
Conservative	May 1979	M. Thatcher	Sir G. Howe	Lord Carrington

A Note On Books

A T appropriate points in the text the main sources for the more controversial topics have been indicated in footnotes. The lists below do not necessarily repeat these, but indicate some books which the reader in search of further reading may find useful. They are, of course, highly selective.

A. GENERAL

W. N. Medlicott's *Contemporary England 1914–64* (1967) covers the same period, and there is a valuable survey of a part of it in C. L. Mowat, *Britain between the Wars, 1918–1940* (1955) and in briefer form in H. Pelling, *Modern Britain, 1885–1955* (1960). Robert Graves and Alan Hodge wrote a famous and amusing social history, *The Long Week-end: A Social History of Great Britain, 1918–1939* (1940; Four Square ed., 1961). In similar vein are John Montgomery, *The Twenties: An informal social history* (1957); Malcolm Muggeridge, *The Thirties (1930–1940) in Great Britain* (1940): and James Laver, *Between the Wars* (1961). A useful work of reference is D. E. Butler and J. Freeman, *British Political Facts, 1900–1967* (1963, rev. 2nd ed. 1968).

B. PARTICULAR ASPECTS

The economic history of the period has been ably summarized in S. Pollard, *The Development of the British Economy, 1914–1950* (1962), which can be supplemented by A. J. Youngson, *The British Economy, 1920–1957* (1960). More specialized studies include E. V. Morgan, *Studies in British Financial Policy, 1914–1925* (1952); A. C. Pigou, *Aspects of British Economic History, 1918–1925* (1947); W. K. Hancock and M. M. Gowing, *British War Economy* (1949); A. J. Brown, *The Great Inflation, 1939–1951* (1955); and A. A. Ragow, *The Labour Government and British Industry, 1945–1951* (1955).

The electoral and constitutional aspects have been interestingly studied by D. E. Butler, *The Electoral System in Britain, 1918-1962* (1963), and J. F. S. Ross, *Parliamentary Representation* (1943; rev. ed., 1948). There are two useful symposia, *British Government since 1918* (Sir Gilbert Campion and others, 1950) and *Parliament: A Survey* (1952).

The political life of the half-century as a whole is attractively covered in two royal biographies, Sir Harold Nicolson, *King George V: His Life and Reign* (1952), and Sir J. Wheeler-Bennett, *King George VI: His Life and Reign* (1958). See also the many memoirs, autobiographies, and biographies of the leading political figures (c and D below).

Special aspects of English society, its structure and life, can be studied in David C. Marsh, *The Changing Social Structure of England and Wales, 1871-1951* (1958); A. M. Carr-Saunders, D. Caradog Jones, and C. A. Moser, *A Survey of Social Conditions in England and Wales as illustrated by Statistics* (1958); B. Seebohm Rowntree and G. R. Lavers, *English Life and Leisure: A Social Study* (1951) and *Poverty and the Welfare State* (1951); R. Lewis and A. Maude, *The English Middle Classes* (1949; Pelican Book ed., 1953) and *Professional People* (1952); R. Hoggart, *The Uses of Literacy: Aspects of working-class life with special reference to publications and entertainments* (1957; Pelican Book ed., 1958); *Education 1900-1950* (Cmd. 8244, 1951, Report of Ministry of Education).

As usual, diplomatic history has been well surveyed: in W. N. Medlicott, *British Foreign Policy since Versailles, 1919-1939* (1940); Sir E. L. Woodward, *British Foreign Policy in the Second World War* (1962); F. S. Northedge, *British Foreign Policy: The Process of Adjustment, 1945-1961* (1962). For Commonwealth developments see the *Surveys of British Commonwealth Affairs*, by W. K. Hancock, 2 vols. (1937-42), and by N. Mansergh, 2 vols. (1952).

C. MEMOIRS AND AUTOBIOGRAPHIES

Public men have been prolific in their memoirs, and many have been quoted in the text. Pre-eminent among them are D. Lloyd George, *War Memoirs*, 6 vols. (1933-6) and *The Truth about the Peace Treaties*, 2 vols. (1938); and W. S. Churchill, *The World Crisis*, 5 vols. (1923-31) and *The Second World War*, 6 vols. (1948-54). Each writes with supreme authority, but neither, of course,

with impartiality. The issues and atmosphere of the period are well
captured in a handful of political diaries and memoirs: L. S.
Amery, *My Political Life*, 3 vols. (1953–5); Beatrice Webb's
Diaries, 1912–1924 (ed. M. I. Cole, 1952); Hugh Dalton, *Call Back
Yesterday, 1887–1932* (1953) and *The Fateful Years, 1931–1945*
(1957); Thomas Jones, *A Diary with Letters, 1931–1950* (1954);
Earl of Woolton, *Memoirs* (1959); Lord Beveridge, *Power and Influ-
ence* (1953) and Janet Beveridge, *Beveridge and his Plan* (1954); Sir
Anthony Eden, *Facing the Dictators* (1962) and *Full Circle* (1960).
Many memoirs are more anxious to conceal or to vindicate than to
reveal, and have little to offer.

Among memoirs and autobiographies of men and women not
immediately in politics the author's personal (and arbitrary) choice
among a host of others would be: Sir Ernest Barker, *Age and Youth*
(1953); Sir Harold Butler, *The Lost Peace* (1941); Wilson Harris,
Life so Far (1954); Sir Patrick Hastings, *Autobiography* (1948);
Albert Mansbridge, *Fellow Men: A Gallery of England, 1876–1946*
(1948); Violet Markham, *Return Passage: An Autobiography* (1953);
and one priceless biography, Millie Toole, *Our Old Man: A Bio-
graphical Study of Joseph Toole* (1948). One can learn more about
English life in the twentieth century from such works than from
many learned sociological studies.

D. BIOGRAPHIES

Biographies are often strongly partisan, though their bias is usually
abundantly evident. Those containing documentary sources tend
to be most valuable, and semi-political ones are often more reveal-
ing than the purely political. The following have merit: A. W.
Baldwin, *My Father: The True Story* (1955); Lord Beaverbrook,
The Decline and Fall of Lloyd George (1963); R. Blake, *The Unknown
Prime Minister: The Life and Times of Andrew Bonar Law, 1858–1923*
(1955); J. Bowle, *Viscount Samuel: A Biography* (1957); A. Bullock,
The Life and Times of Ernest Bevin, vol. I (1960); Sir H. Clay, *Lord
Norman* (1957); Lord Elton, *The Life of James Ramsay MacDonald,
1866–1919* (1939); Sir K. Feiling, *The Life of Neville Chamberlain*
(1946); Michael Foot, *Aneurin Bevan*, Vol. I, 1897–1945 (1962);
Sir R. F. Harrod, *The Life of John Maynard Keynes* (1951); F. A.
Iremonger, *William Temple, Archbishop of Canterbury, His Life and*

Letters (1948); Roy Jenkins, *Asquith* (1964); Thomas Jones, *Lloyd George* (1951); R. Postgate, *The Life of George Lansbury* (1951); R. Ellis Roberts, *H. R. L. Sheppard: Life and Letters* (1942); Sir J. Wheeler-Bennett, *Sir John Anderson, Viscount Waverley* (1962).

E. CONTEMPORARY WRITING AND THOUGHT

The novels of D. H. Lawrence, Virginia Woolf, George Orwell, J. B. Priestley, and Walter Allen are, in their very different ways, illustrative of contemporary life and thought. So are the plays of John Galsworthy, T. S. Eliot, Noël Coward, and Dylan Thomas. For some guidance through the rich diversity of the literature of the time see W. Y. Tindall, *Forces in Modern British Literature, 1885–1946* (1947); R. C. Churchill, *Disagreements: A Polemic on Culture in the English Democracy* (1950); Raymond Williams, *Culture and Society, 1780–1950* (1958; Pelican Book ed., 1961).

On scientific thought see A. E. Heath (ed.), *Scientific Thought in the Twentieth Century* (1952), and on religious thought, G. S. Spinks (ed.), *Religion in Britain since 1900* (1954).

Addendum

IN the same way that David Thomson's original text has been left largely as it stood, so his bibliography has not been revised. It was thought desirable, however, to add a few titles dealing with the period covered in the new Part IV of the book. Apart from the books and articles cited in the footnotes, of which the first-hand accounts by participants are the most valuable, the following studies may prove helpful: on the economy, W. Beckerman and others, *The Labour Government's Economic Record 1964–1970* (1972), and A. R. Prest, D. J. Coppock and others, *The UK Economy: A Manual of Applied Economics* (1966; seventh revised edition, 1978); on trade unions, Robert Taylor, *The Fifth Estate: Britain's Unions in the Modern World* (1978; revised Pan edition, 1980); on changes in central and local government, Frank Stacey, *British Government 1966–1975: Years of Reform* (1975); on Northern Ireland, Richard Rose, *Northern Ireland: A Time of Choice* (1976); on the Common

Market, Uwe Kitzinger, *Diplomacy and Persuasion: How Britain joined the Common Market* (1973), and L. J. Robins, *The Reluctant Party: Labour and the EEC 1961–75* (1979); and on Rhodesia, Elaine Windrich, *Britain and the Politics of Rhodesian Independence* (1978). Finally, one must include an indispensable work of reference, now in its fifth edition: D. Butler and A. Sloman, *British Political Facts 1900–79* (1980).

Index

READ MORE IN PENGUIN

In every corner of the world, on every subject under the sun, Penguin represents quality and variety – the very best in publishing today.

For complete information about books available from Penguin – including Puffins, Penguin Classics and Arkana – and how to order them, write to us at the appropriate address below. Please note that for copyright reasons the selection of books varies from country to country.

In the United Kingdom: Please write to *Dept. JC, Penguin Books Ltd, FREEPOST, West Drayton, Middlesex UB7 OBR*

If you have any difficulty in obtaining a title, please send your order with the correct money, plus ten per cent for postage and packaging, to *PO Box No. 11, West Drayton, Middlesex UB7 OBR*

In the United States: Please write to *Penguin USA Inc., 375 Hudson Street, New York, NY 10014*

In Canada: Please write to *Penguin Books Canada Ltd, 10 Alcorn Avenue, Suite 300, Toronto, Ontario M4V 3B2*

In Australia: Please write to *Penguin Books Australia Ltd, 487 Maroondah Highway, Ringwood, Victoria 3134*

In New Zealand: Please write to *Penguin Books (NZ) Ltd,182–190 Wairau Road, Private Bag, Takapuna, Auckland 9*

In India: Please write to *Penguin Books India Pvt Ltd, 706 Eros Apartments, 56 Nehru Place, New Delhi 110 019*

In the Netherlands: Please write to *Penguin Books Netherlands B.V., Keizersgracht 231 NL–1016 DV Amsterdam*

In Germany: Please write to *Penguin Books Deutschland GmbH, Friedrichstrasse 10–12, W–6000 Frankfurt/Main 1*

In Spain: Please write to *Penguin Books S. A., C. San Bernardo 117–6° E–28015 Madrid*

In Italy: Please write to *Penguin Italia s.r.l., Via Felice Casati 20, I–20124 Milano*

In France: Please write to *Penguin France S. A., 17 rue Lejeune, F–31000 Toulouse*

In Japan: Please write to *Penguin Books Japan, Ishikiribashi Building, 2–5–4, Suido, Tokyo 112*

In Greece: Please write to *Penguin Hellas Ltd, Dimocritou 3, GR–106 71 Athens*

In South Africa: Please write to *Longman Penguin Southern Africa (Pty) Ltd, Private Bag X08, Bertsham 2013*